JOHN W. R. TAYLOR
and GORDON SWANBOROUGH

Military
Aircraft
of the
World

Charles Scribner's Sons

New York

Printed in Great Britain
Library of Congress Catalog Card Number 73-1597

SBN 684-13367-9

Introduction

When first published in its present format in 1971, *Military Aircraft of the World* received an encouraging welcome and filled the need for a "quick-reference" guide to the equipment of the world's air forces. Despite the growing pressure for disarmament, and an inevitable slowing down of rearmament programmes as equipment costs soar, the pace of new military aircraft development and production world-wide continues at a high level, as a glance at the contents of this new and completely revised edition will show.

In the space of only two years, 30 types of aircraft have appeared or have been newly adopted for military use, and are therefore included in this title for the first time. Still others are under development, but to time scales that would make the inclusion of details and illustrations premature. Like old soldiers, the more elderly aircraft types seldom die, and they are very slow even to pass away. A few that have been excluded from this edition to make room for the new may still serve in odd corners of the world, although in such small numbers that their omission is not significant.

This edition is noteworthy not only for the inclusion of so many completely new aircraft types, but for the extensive revision of the entire text to reflect new orders, new variants and new information right up to press-time. The opportunity has been taken, also, to introduce new photographs all the way through the book, and to revise many of the silhouettes in order to show more recent variants.

As before, the book is divided into two parts—conveniently separated by eight pages of full-colour photographs. The first part contains photographs, silhouettes and descriptive information about first-line fighters, bombers, electronic and photographic reconnaissance aircraft, tactical support helicopters and strategic and tactical transports. In part two, photographs and descriptions are included, but not silhouettes, for second-line combat aircraft, obsolescent types, light transports, communications aircraft and trainers.

Many companies and individuals contributed photographs and data to help make *Military Aircraft of the World* complete and accurate; the authors are grateful to them all. The silhouettes, which are Pilot Press copyright, came from the skilled pen of Dennis Punnett.

GS/JWRT

Contents

First-line aircraft   4–144

Colour section   145–152

Second-line types   153-231

Photo credits   232

Index   233–241

Aeritalia G91 *Italy*

Data and photograph: G91Y. Silhouette: G91R/1B.

Single-seat light tactical strike-reconnaissance fighter, in production and service.

Powered by: Two 2,720lb (1,235kg) st General Electric J85-GE-13A turbojets.
Span: 29ft 6½in (9.01m).
Length: 38ft 3½in (11.67m).
Empty weight: 8,598lb (3,900kg).
Gross weight: 19,180lb (8,700kg).
Max. speed: 690mph (1,110km/h) at sea level.
Typical combat radius: 466 miles (750km) at sea level.
Armament: Two 30mm cannon in sides of front fuselage. Four underwing attachments for up to 4,000lb (1,816kg) of bombs, Nord AS.20 missiles, air-to-ground rockets or 0.50in machine-gun pods.

The original G91 was the winner of a design competition for a standardised strike fighter for NATO forces. Three prototypes and 27 pre-production G91s were ordered initially by NATO. The first prototype, with a 4,050lb (1,837kg) st Orpheus B.Or.1, flew on August 9, 1956. The second had a modified tail, B.Or.3, slightly raised cockpit, ventral fin and armament. It won the NATO evaluation contest in October 1957 and the G91 was ordered into production. The first pre-production model flew on February 20, 1958, and the Italian Air Force formed the first G91 development squadron in August 1958, equipped with the pre-production machines. These were the only pure fighter G91s, subsequent operational aircraft being G91Rs with three Vinten 70mm cameras in a less-pointed nose. Variants, all with 5,000lb (2,268kg) st Orpheus 803, are the G91R/1, R/1A and R/1B, of which 98 were built for the Italian Air Force, and the G91R/3 and R/4 of which 100 were built by Fiat for the German Air Force, with 282 more licence-built in Germany. The R/4s have been passed on to the Portuguese Air Force. Italian G91Rs have four 0.50in guns instead of the cannon fitted to the German versions. Tandem two-seat training versions with a larger wing and longer fuselage are the G91T/1 (76 for Italy) and G91T/3 (an initial batch of 44 for Germany, followed by a repeat order for 22). The G91Y, described above, was evolved from the G91T for the Italian Air Force, with the same enlarged wing and two J85s replacing the single Orpheus engine. The first of two prototypes flew on December 27, 1966. An initial batch of 20 has been delivered and work was in hand on a second batch of 55 during 1972, together with a few more G91Ts for the Italian Air Force.

Aeritalia G222

Italy

Medium-range tactical transport, in production.

Powered by: Two 3,400shp General Electric T64-P-4D turboprops.
Span: 94ft 6in (28.80m).
Length: 74ft 5½in (22.70m).
Empty weight: 32,408lb (14,700kg).
Gross weight: 57,320lb (26,000kg).
Max speed: 329mph at 15,000ft (530km/h at 4,575m).
Range: 2,020 miles (3,250km).
Accommodation: Crew of three and 44 troops, 32 paratroops, or up to 36 stretchers and eight attendants or seated casualties.

Design studies began in 1963, under Italian Air Force contracts, with a view to developing a V/STOL tactical transport. Using a conventional high-wing layout, with two turboprop engines, Fiat proposed to obtain STOL performance by installing four direct-lift engines in each nacelle. This project had the capability of taking off in 230ft (70m) and carrying its design payload a distance of 310miles (500km), but an alternative was also schemed in which the lift-engines were deleted and the weight saved was taken up by extra fuel, giving a greatly increased range at the expense of take-off performance. Two flying prototypes (and a static test specimen) of this conventional version were eventually ordered, with the stipulation that the work be shared throughout the Italian industry under Fiat direction. First flights of the two prototypes were made on July 18, 1970 and July 22, 1971 respectively, and following evaluation in the early months of 1972 the Italian Air Force placed a production order for 44 G222s. The work is again being shared within the industry, with the final assembly line to be established in a new factory set up by Aeritalia (which now incorporates the Fiat Aviation Division) near Naples.

5

Aermacchi MB326, AT-26 Xavante and Impala

Italy

Two-seat basic trainer and light attack aircraft, in production and service.
Data: MB326K. Photograph: Xavante.

Powered by: One 4,000lb (1,814kg) st Rolls-Royce Bristol Viper 632-43 turbojet.
Span: 35ft 7in (10.85m).
Length: 34ft 11in (10.64m).
Gross weight: 12,000lb (5,443kg).
Max. speed: Mach 0.82 (576mph; 927km/h).
Armament: Two 30mm Aden or DEFA cannon in front fuselage. Four underwing pylons for stores weighing up to 1,000lb (454kg) each, and two outer pylons for 750lb (340kg) each.

The first of two prototypes of this widely-used tandem two-seat basic trainer flew on December 10, 1957 powered by a 1,750lb (794kg) st Rolls-Royce Bristol Viper 8 turbojet. Production models had the 2,500lb (1,134kg) st Viper 11 and the first of 100 for the Italian Air Force flew on October 5, 1960. Delivery of this batch was completed in 1966 but a further small batch was ordered subsequently. Eight MB326B and seven MB326F, delivered to the Tunisian and Ghana Air Forces respectively, are similar but have six underwing strong points for such stores as machine-gun pods, 260lb bombs, rockets, camera pods or fuel tanks. In the spring of 1967, Aermacchi flew the prototype MB326G, an armed version with a 3,410lb (1,547kg) st Viper 540 engine. Production versions are known as the MB326GB and orders include 17 for the Congolese Air Force, eight for the Argentine Navy, 12 for the Zambian Air Force and 112 for the Brazilian Air Force (the majority of which are being made under licence by Embraer in Brazil as the AT-26 Xavante. MB326H is the version for the Royal Australian Air Force and Navy, with Viper 11 engine; 12 were supplied by Aermacchi, with the balance of orders totalling 87 for the RAAF and 10 for the RAN built by CAC in Australia. In South Africa, Atlas Aircraft is building some 200 MB326M Impalas, similar to the MB326G with armed capability. On August 22, 1970, the single-seat MB326K made its first flight; this prototype had a Viper 540, but the second prototype has the characteristics given above and production models will be similar.

Aérospatiale SA316/319 Alouette III   *France*

General-purpose, armed reconnaissance and anti-tank helicopter, in production and service.

Powered by: One 870shp (derated to 570shp) Turboméca Artouste IIIB turboshaft.
Rotor diameter: 36ft 1¾in (11.02m).
Length: 32ft 10¾in (10.03m).
Empty weight: 2,474lb (1,122kg).
Gross weight: 4,850lb (2,200kg).
Max. speed: 130mph (210km/h) at sea level.
Max. range: 335 miles (540km).
Accommodation: Pilot and up to six passengers, two litters and two other patients, or equivalent freight.
Armament (optional): Various installations of machine-guns, 20mm guns, AS.11 or AS.12 missiles and rockets.

The Alouette III, a larger and more powerful development of the Alouette II (see page 156), is available for military use as a tactical troop transport or assault helicopter, and can carry a variety of armament. The basic version is powered by an Artouste engine, as described above. It first flew on February 28, 1959, and serves as the SA316A and the SA316B with strengthened transmission and increased weights.

By the beginning of 1973 orders totalled 1,070, including 124 for French military and civil operators and others for 97 operators in 60 countries. Sixty are being built in Switzerland and 50 in Romania. India is using a special anti-submarine variant carrying Mk.44 torpedoes. A variant is the SA319 which is in production for the French Services with a 600shp Astazou XIV engine. Gross weight of the SA319 is 4,960lb (2,250kg), max. speed 137mph (220km/h), and max. range 375 miles (600km). The earlier Alouette II variants and the more recent Lama, which have open-framework fuselages, are described separately in Part Two of this volume.

Aérospatiale SA321 Super Frelon   *France*

Heavy assault and anti-submarine helicopter, in production and service.
Photograph: SA321G

Powered by: Three 1,550shp Turboméca Turmo IIIC6 turboshafts.
Rotor diameter: 62ft 0in (18.90 m).
Fuselage length: 65ft 10¾in (20.08m).
Empty weight (Naval version): 14,600lb (6,625kg).
Gross weight: 28,660lb (13,000kg).
Max. speed: 171mph (275km/h) at sea level.
Endurance: 4hrs.
Accommodation: Crew of two, 30 troops, 15 litters or equivalent freight.
Armament: Anti-submarine attack weapons in naval version, including up to four homing torpedoes, in pairs on each side of the cabin.

Largest helicopter yet built in France, the Super Frelon (Hornet) was developed from the lower-powered Frelon, of which two prototypes were flown. A technical collaboration agreement with Sikorsky led to the introduction of some typical Sikorsky design features, including a boat-type hull to permit amphibious operations, with stabilising floats on the main undercarriage legs. The rotor systems are also of Sikorsky design.

The first of two prototypes of the Super Frelon flew on December 7, 1962, with 1,320 hp Turmo engines, and subsequently set a helicopter speed record of 217.77mph (350.47km/h) over a 15/25-km course which stood until 1971.

The second prototype was representative of the naval anti-submarine version, with crew of four, sonar, search radar in the stabilising floats and provision for other special equipment and weapons. Four pre-production Super Frelons followed the prototypes, with 1,500hp engines; the first of these flew on January 31, 1964 and the last on January 9, 1965. Orders to date include 18 SA321G anti-submarine versions for the French Navy, 16 transports for the South African Air Force, 12 transports for the Israel Defence Force and nine transports for Libya.

In French naval operations, one Super Frelon carrying detection and tracking equipment is usually accompanied by two or three others armed with attack weapons. The first unit was commissioned in May, 1970.

Aérospatiale/Westland SA330 Puma

France/Great Britain

Assault helicopter, in production and service.

Powered by: Two 1,320shp Turboméca Turmo IIIC4 turboshafts.
Rotor diameter: 49ft 2½in (15.00m).
Fuselage length: 46ft 1½in (14.06m).
Empty weight: 7,403lb (3,358kg).
Gross weight: 14,110lb (6,400kg).
Max. speed: 174mph (281km/h) at sea level.
Max. range: 390 miles (620km) with standard fuel.
Accommodation: Crew of 2 plus 16–20 troops, six litters and four seated patients, or freight.
Armament: None.

Aérospatiale (then Sud-Aviation) developed the SA330 to meet a French Army requirement for a "helicoptère de manoeuvre"—an aircraft of medium size able to operate in all weathers and climates in the tactical assault and transport roles. The SA330 was the first entirely new helicopter to bear an "SA" designation, its predecessors having been either "SE" or "SO" types to indicate their connection with the original Sud-Est and Sud-Ouest state factories. Development of the SA330 was authorised in June 1963 with a contract for two prototypes and six pre-production aircraft. The first of these flew on April 15, 1965. The SA330 is one of three helicopters in a joint Anglo-French programme agreed early in 1968, aircraft for the RAF being assembled by Westland using British and French components. The eighth French SA330 was imported to Britain in 1968 to serve as a pattern aircraft (serial No. XW241) and the first British production Puma HC Mk.1 (XW198) flew on 25 November 1970. Deliveries began in 1969 and the first French army unit became operational in June 1970; while the first RAF unit, No.33 Squadron, formed on the type a year later. French Army orders total 130, and the RAF ordered 40; other military users of the type include the French Air Force, Algeria, Portugal, South Africa, Rhodesia and Abu Dhabi.

Agusta A106

Italy

Light anti-submarine helicopter, in production.

Powered by: One 330hp Turboméca-Agusta TAA 230 turboshaft.
Rotor diameter: 31ft 2in (9.50m).
Overall length: 36ft 0in (10.97m).
Empty weight: 1,520lb (690kg).
Gross weight: 3,086lb (1,400kg).
Max speed: 110mph (177km/h).
Range: 155 miles (249km).
Accommodation: Pilot only.
Armament: Two Mk.44 homing torpedoes beneath the fuselage.

Since it acquired a licence to build the Bell 47 in 1952, the Agusta company has been engaged almost exclusively in the production of Bell designs, and has also added Sikorsky and Boeing-Vertol licences to its activities. One of the few helicopters of original Agusta design was the A103, flown in 1959. From that prototype the company evolved the A106, first flown in November 1965 and intended to meet an Italian Navy requirement for a light anti-submarine aircraft. In this role the A106 can carry two Mk.44 torpedoes and equipment for contact identification. Two prototypes have undergone prolonged evaluation by the Italian Navy and production of a small initial batch for service use began in 1972.

Antonov An-12 (NATO code-name: Cub)

U.S.S.R.

Medium/long-range transport, in production and service.

Powered by: Four 4,000ehp Ivchenko AI-20K turboprops.
Span: 124ft 8in (38.0m).
Length: 108ft 3in (33.0m).
Gross weight: 134,480lb (61,000kg).
Max. cruising speed: 373mph (600km/h).
Range: 2,110 miles (3,400km) at 342mph (550km/h) with 22,050lb (10,000kg) payload.
Accommodation: Crew of five and troops, vehicles or freight.
Armament: 20mm cannon in tail turret.

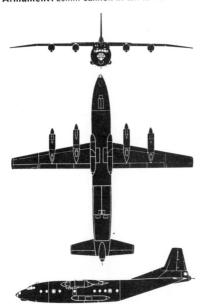

Developed from the An-10 commercial airliner, this turboprop transport is standard equipment in the Soviet Air Force for paratroop-dropping, air supply and heavy transport duties. Its undercarriage has four-wheel bogie main units, retracting into fairings on each side of the cabin, and is fitted with low-pressure tyres, enabling the An-12 to operate from unprepared airfields. Take-off and landing runs are under 950 yards (870m). A loading ramp for vehicles and freight forms the undersurface of the upswept rear fuselage and can be opened in flight for air-dropping of troops and supplies. Size of the main cabin is 44ft 3½in (13.50m) long, by 9ft 10in (3.0m) wide and 7ft 10½in (2.40m) high.

Current Soviet Air Force An-12s have an enlarged under-nose radome, as shown in the photograph.

Foreign air forces which have been supplied with An-12s include those of Algeria, Egypt, India, Indonesia, Iraq and Poland. A civil version, without the tail gun turret, is operated on pure freight services by Aeroflot and has been supplied to several other nations in the Soviet bloc. At least one Aeroflot An-12 has been operated on skis during service in the Arctic and is one of the largest aeroplanes ever equipped in this way.

Antonov An-22 (NATO code-name: Cock)

U.S.S.R.

Long-range heavy strategic transport, in production and service.

Powered by: Four 15,000shp Kuznetsov NK-12MA turboprops.
Span: 211ft 4in (64.40m).
Length: 189ft 7in (57.80m).
Max. payload: 176,350lb (80,000kg).
Gross weight: 551,160lb (250,000kg).
Max. speed: 460mph (740km/h).
Range: 6,800 miles (10,950km) with max. fuel and 99,200lb (45,000kg) payload; 3,100 miles (5,000km) with max. payload.
Accommodation: Crew of five or six: 28–29 passengers plus freight.

First flown on February 27, 1965, the Antonov An-22 was the World's largest transport aircraft until the appearance of the Lockheed C-5A (see page 80). A natural progression from the An-10/12 series, the An-22 was in service with Aeroflot and the Soviet Air Force by mid-1967, at which time two prototypes in civil markings were operating an experimental freight service and three others in military markings took part in the display at Domodedovo. The latter disgorged, after landing, batteries of *Frog-3* and *Ganef* missiles on tracked launchers. The An-22 has a normal payload of 176,350lb (80,000kg) but in a series of record flights in October 1967, a max. load of 221,443lb (100,445kg) was lifted. A feature of the An-22 design is that four gantries are installed on overhead rails running the entire length of the cabin to facilitate freight handling through the rear door and ramp. By 1969, An-22s were in service with several Soviet Air Force units, and in 1970 one was lost in the Atlantic during relief flights after the Peruvian earthquake. There have been no reports of An-22s being supplied to Soviet allies.

Avro Shackleton

Great Britain

Long - range maritime - reconnaissance and AEW aircraft, in service.
Data: Shackleton MR.Mk.3. Silhouette & photo: Shackleton AEW. Mk.2.

Powered by: Four 2,455hp Rolls-Royce Griffon 57A piston-engines.
Crew: 10.
Span: 119ft 10in (36.52m).
Length: 92ft 6in (28.19m).
Gross weight: 100,000lb (45,360kg).
Max. speed: 302mph (486km/h).
Typical range: 3,660 miles (5,890km) at 200mph (320km/h) at 1,500ft (460m).
Armament: Two 20mm cannon in nose; bombs, mines, depth charges, torpedoes, etc. in bomb bay.

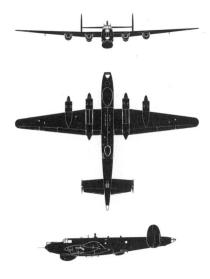

The Shackleton MR. (originally GR.) Mk.1 was developed as the Avro Type 696, a variant of the Lincoln bomber, for maritime reconnaissance duties. The first Shackleton MR.Mk.1 (77 built) entered service with No. 120 Squadron of RAF Coastal Command late in 1951. The Mk.1 aircraft could be distinguished from later versions by their shorter, more rounded nose with fixed under-nose radome, and blunt rear fuselage. The MR.Mk.2 (prototype WB833) was developed in 1952 with a longer, more streamlined nose, pointed tail-cone and retractable ventral radar. With equipment brought up to Mk.3 standard, the Mk.2C continued in RAF service until 1972.

The Shackleton MR. Mk.3 has wingtip tanks, nose-wheel undercarriage in place of the former tail-wheel type and other refinements. The first production model (WR970) flew on September 2, 1955 and production deliveries began early in 1958. A total of 69 Mk.2 and 42 Mk.3 aircraft were built. To increase the capabilities of the RAF's Mk.3 Shackletons, they underwent extensive modification to Phase 3 standard, including structural strengthening, increase in fuel capacity and the addition of two Rolls-Royce Bristol Viper auxiliary turbojets, mounted in the rear of the outboard engine nacelles, to improve take-off performance. A squadron of eight Mk.3 Shackletons, without Viper boost engines, serves with the South African Air Force. Conversion of 12 Shackleton 2s for use in the airborne early warning role by No. 8 Squadron began during 1971 and the first of these, with the designation AEW. Mk.2, flew on September 30, 1971. They are now the only Shackletons in RAF service.

13

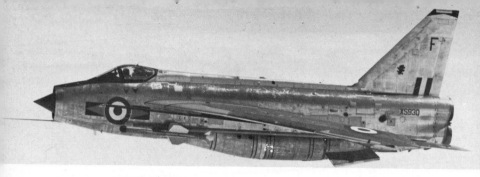

BAC Lightning

Great Britain

Data, photograph and silhouette:
Lightning F.Mk.6.
Single-seat supersonic fighter, in service.

Powered by: Two 16,360lb (7,420kg) st Rolls-Royce Avon 301 turbojets with afterburning.
Span: 34ft 10in (10.61m).
Length: 55ft 3in (16.84m).
Gross weight: approx. 50,000lb (22,680kg).
Max speed.: Mach 2 (1,320mph; 2,124km/h).
Armament: Two Red Top or Firestreak air-to-air missiles, or two packs of 24 air-to-air rockets plus, optionally, two 30mm guns in ventral pack.

The Lightning F.Mk.1, evolved from the P.1A research aircraft, first flew on April 4, 1957. This version (20 built) and the F.Mk.1A (28 built), with provision for flight refuelling,

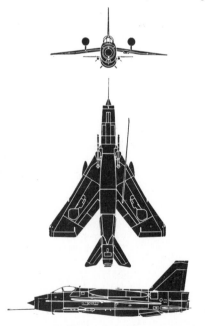

equipped three RAF squadrons but only a few now remain in service as high-speed targets for squadrons flying later Marks. The F.Mk.2, first flown on July 11, 1961, introduced many improvements and could carry Red Top as well as Firestreak. This version remains operational, 30 examples having been modified to F.Mk.2A with some features of the F.Mk.6 for service in Germany. First flown on June 16, 1962, the F.Mk.3 has Series 300 Avons, a larger square-tip tail fin and much improved equipment, although the two 30mm Aden cannon fitted to earlier Marks are deleted. From it was evolved the fully-developed F.Mk.6 (prototype flown on April 17, 1964), in which the outer portion of the wing leading-edge has slightly less sweep and incorporates conical camber, and the capacity of the ventral fuel tank has been more than doubled. This version can carry two overwing fuel tanks for long-range ferrying. Seven RAF squadrons, at home and overseas, fly Mk.3 and Mk.6 Lightnings. Also in service are the Lightning T.Mk.4 (prototype first flown May 6, 1959; 20 built) and T.Mk.5 (prototype first flown March 29, 1962; 22 built), which are side-by-side dual-control fully-operational counterparts of the F.Mk.1 and F.Mk.3 respectively. Saudi Arabia received 35 Lightning F.Mk.53 multi-role interceptor/ground-attack fighters, with underwing and overwing pylons for rockets or bombs, 44 rockets in retractable fuselage packs and two 30mm cannon in the forward portion of the ventral pack. Pending delivery of the first of these aircraft, seven ex-RAF Mk.2 and Mk. 4 Lightnings were supplied, the former as F.Mk.52s. Kuwait took delivery of a smaller number of Lightning fighters and both countries also received small numbers of the T.Mk.55 export version of the T.Mk.5. Production of the Lightning ended in 1972.

BAC 167 Strikemaster (and Jet Provost)

Great Britain

Two-seat counter-insurgency strike aircraft and trainer, in production and service.
Data, photograph and silhouette: Strikemaster.

Powered by: One 3,410lb (1,360kg) st Rolls-Royce Bristol Viper 535 turbojet.
Span: 36ft 11in (11.25m).
Length: 33ft 8½in (10.27m).
Gross weight: 11,500lb (5,215kg).
Max. range: 1,382 miles (2,224km).
Max. speed: 472mph (760km/h) at 20,000ft (6,100m).
Armament: Two 7.62mm FN machine-guns in fuselage. Eight wing strong points for maximum underwing load of 3,000lb (1,360kg).

The BAC 167 Strikemaster was developed from the basic armed Jet Provost to meet the needs of small air forces for a relatively cheap armed counter-insurgency aircraft and trainer. It differs from the RAF's Jet Provost T.Mk.5 trainer primarily in having an uprated engine, permanently-attached tip-tanks and increased armament capability. Common to both the Strikemaster and the Jet Provost 5 is a pressurized cockpit. The first Strikemaster flew on October 26, 1967, and over 100 have been ordered, for the Saudi Arabian Air Force (Mk.80), the South Yemen People's Republic (Mk.81), the Sultan of Oman's Air Force (Mk.82), the Kuwait Air Force (Mk.83), the Singapore Air Defence Command (Mk.84), the Kenya Air Force (Mk.87), the Royal New Zealand Air Force (Mk.88) and the Ecuadorian Air Force (Mk. 89).

A total of 110 Jet Provost T.Mk.5s were built for the RAF, with 2,500lb (1,134kg) st Viper 202, pressure cabin and optional wing-tip tanks. They replaced the Jet Provost T.Mk.4, which was unpressurized, and the T.Mk.3 which had a 1,750lb (794kg) st Viper 102 engine. Export models of the Jet Provost, with provision for two 0.303in machine-guns in the air intakes and limited underwing stores capability, were the T.Mk.51 (Viper 102) for Ceylon, the Sudan and Kuwait and T.Mk.52 (Viper 202) for Venezuela, Sudan, Iraq and the South Yemen. An armed version of the Jet Provost T.Mk.5 has been sold to the Sudan to supplement its Mk.51s and 52s, and is designated Jet Provost 55 (BAC 145).

BAC VC10

Great Britain

Long-range troop and freight transport, in service.

Powered by: Four 21,800lb (9,888kg) st Rolls-Royce Conway R.Co.43 turbojets.
Span: 146ft 2in (44.55m).
Length (without refuelling probe): 133ft 8in (40.74m).
Gross weight: 323,000lb (146,510kg).
Max. cruising speed: 581mph (935km/h).
Typical range: 3,900 miles (6,275km) with 57,400lb (26,030kg) payload at 425mph (683km/h) at 30,000ft (9,145m).
Accommodation: 150 passengers in rearward-facing seats, or freight.

Fourteen VC10 C.Mk.1 (Model 1106) jet transports were delivered to No. 10 Squadron of RAF Air Support Command. Although similar in overall dimensions to the BOAC version, the Model 1106 has the more powerful Conway 43 engines and fin fuel tank of the Super VC10. Other changes include the installation of a large cargo door at the front of the cabin on the port side, an optional nose-probe for flight refuelling and a Bristol Siddeley Artouste auxiliary power unit in the tail-cone for engine starting and electric power on the ground. The primary duty of the RAF's VC10s is to carry troops or personnel at high speed to any part of the world, while their equipment and supplies are carried out in Short Belfast transports. The first RAF VC10 C.Mk.1 made its first flight on November 26, 1965. Deliveries began on July 7, 1966, and were completed in 1968. The aircraft are named individually after holders of the Victoria Cross.

During 1969, one of the RAF VC10s was loaned to Rolls-Royce Ltd. for conversion to a test-bed for the RB.211 engine. The remainder serve with No. 10 Squadron, now part of No. 46 Group, Strike Command.

Bell AH-1 HueyCobra/SeaCobra *U.S.A.*

Armed helicopter, in production and service.
Data and photograph: AH-1J. Silhouette: AH-1G.

Powered by: One 1,800shp Pratt & Whitney T400-CP-400 coupled turboshaft.
Rotor diameter: 44ft 0in (13.41m).
Fuselage length: 44ft 7in (13.59m).
Gross weight: 10,000lb (4,535kg).
Max. speed: 207mph (333km/h).
Max. range: 359 miles (577km).
Armament: Turret-mounted XM-197 three-barrel 20mm cannon in nose, plus four external attachment points for Minigun pods or rockets, etc.

Bell developed the HueyCobra from the UH-1 "Hueycopter", initially as a private venture, against US Army requirements for an interim armed helicopter, pending production of the now-cancelled Lockheed AH-56A Cheyenne. The requirement was specifically for operations in Vietnam, experience there having shown the value of armed helicopters in suppressing ground fire during airborne assault and casevac operations by unarmed helicopters. The prototype Bell 209 HueyCobra flew on September 7, 1965 and retained the UH-1 engine/rotor system with a new low-profile fuselage seating a gunner and pilot in tandem. After Army evaluation, two pre-production aircraft and an initial production batch were ordered in April 1966, with the designation AH-1G. Operational service in Vietnam began in mid-1967 and a total of 1,078 have been ordered to date. Early Army AH-1Gs had a TAT-102A nose turret with a six-barrel 7.62mm Minigun. Later aircraft have the XM-28 armament system with two Miniguns or two XM-129 40mm grenade launchers, or one of each. In May 1968, the US Marine Corps ordered an initial batch of 49 AH-1J SeaCobras (data above), with a T400 power plant and revised armament. Pending delivery of these, the Marines acquired 38 AH-1Gs. Iran ordered 202 AH-1Js in early 1973. Spain has a few AH-1Gs.

Bell UH-1 Iroquois (and Agusta-Bell 204B/205)

U.S.A.

Utility helicopter, in production and service.
Data and silhouette: UH-1H. Photo: Agusta-Bell 204 ASW.

Powered by: One 1,400shp Lycoming T53-L-13 turboshaft.
Rotor diameter: 48ft 0in (14.63m).
Fuselage length: 41ft 10¾in (12.77 m).
Empty weight: 4,667lb (2,116kg).
Gross weight: 9,500lb (4,309kg).
Max. speed: 127mph (204km/h).
Range: 318 miles (511km) at 127mph (204km/h).

Deliveries of the HU-1A (Model 204) Iroquois, with T53-L-1A engine, began on June 30, 1959, for utility transport and casualty evacuation, with six seats or two stretchers. First flown in 1960, the HU-1B (now UH-1B) had a larger cabin for eight passengers or three stretchers, and 960shp T53-L-5 engine. Large numbers were built for the US Army, and for the Australian, Austrian, Italian, Netherlands, Norwegian, Saudi-Arabian, Spanish, Swedish, and Turkish Services, and by Fuji in Japan. In Vietnam, many UH-1Bs were used in the armed support role, with machine-guns or rocket packs carried on each side of the fuselage. The UH-1C, with 1,100shp T53-L-11 engine and wide-chord rotor, was also used in Vietnam. The UH-1D (Model 205) has a larger cabin, for 12–14 troops or six stretchers, and a T53-L-11 driving a larger-diameter rotor. In addition to large US Army orders, this model serves in New Zealand, Australia, Brazil and Chile, and was built by Dornier for the German Services. For the US Army and New Zealand, the UH-1H superseded the D, with 1,400shp T53-L-13 engine. More than 600 of this version had been transferred to the South Vietnam Air Force by early 1973; the UH-1H is also in production in Taiwan for the Chinese Nationalist Army. A version of the UH-1B won a US Marines design contest for an assault support helicopter in 1962 and is in service as the UH-1E. In 1963 the USAF adopted the UH-1F, with 1,100shp T58-GE-3 engine, for support duties. A few TH-1Fs were also supplied, and some UH-1Fs modified for psychological warfare missions in Vietnam were re-designated UH-1P. In production to succeed the UH-1F is the UH-1N (Model 212) which has a Canadian Pratt & Whitney PT6T-3 Twin Pac engine and has been ordered by the US Navy, Marine Corps and Air Force, and foreign military users. The HH-1K is a Navy air-sea rescue version of the UH-1E; the TH-1L and UH-1L are Navy training and utility versions. Army UH-1Ms have equipment for night sighting of their armament. Canada has ordered CUH-1H and CUH-1N variants, and in Italy Agusta produces

Beriev Be-12 (NATO code-name: Mail)
U.S.S.R.

Maritime reconnaissance amphibian, in production and service. Data are estimated.

Powered by: Two 4,000shp Ivchenko AI-20D turboprops.
Span: 97ft 6in (29.70m).
Length: 99ft 0in (30.20m).
Gross weight: 65,035lb (29,500kg).
Max. speed: 379mph (610km/h).
Range: 2,485 miles (4,000km).
Armament: Attack weapons on six underwing pylons and in bomb-bay in rear of hull.

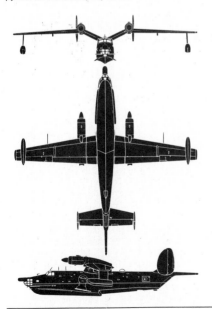

Existence of this turboprop-engined amphibian became known in 1961, when a single example appeared during the Soviet Aviation Day fly-past over Moscow. This fleeting appearance revealed the type to be a close relative of the piston-engined Be-6 which was then standard equipment in flying-boat squadrons of the *Morskaya Aviatsiya*. The prototype is believed to have flown for the first time during 1960.

Little more was heard of the new type until October 1964 when a series of altitude records was established by the Be-12, named Tchaika (Seagull) and designated M-12 by the Soviet forces. These records showed that the Be-12 was capable of lifting a payload of 22,266lb (10,100kg) and of reaching nearly 40,000ft (12,185m) with no payload.

Several examples of the Be-12 participated in the display at Domodedovo in July 1967, showing that it had entered service, presumably as a replacement for the Be-6. Although resembling the latter type in all general respects other than the engines and undercarriage, in detail it shows many design refinements. A speed record of 351 mph (565km/h) around a 500km circuit was set up by a Be-12 in April 1968, in the flying-boat, rather than amphibian, category.

Be-12s are operational with units of the Soviet Northern and Black Sea fleets, and there have been reports of some being based in Egypt for patrol duties over the Mediterranean.

equivalent versions of the Bell Model 204 and 205 for the Italian Army, Navy and Air Force and for export, in particular to the Iranian Imperial Air Force. Iran is also procuring 287 Bell Model 214A Huey Plus utility helicopters direct from the USA.

Boeing B-52 Stratofortress   *U.S.A.*

**Strategic heavy jet bomber, in service.
Data, photograph and silhouette: B-52H.**

Powered by: Eight 17,000lb (7,718kg) st Pratt &
Whitney TF33-P-3 turbofans.
Span: 185ft 0in (56.42m).
Length: 156ft 0in (47.55m).
Gross weight: 488,000lb (221,350kg).
Max. speed: About 650mph (1,040km/h) at
50,000ft (15,240m).
Range: 12,500 miles (20,120km).
Armament: One 20mm multi-barrel cannon in
remote-control rear turret. Primary armament
comprises eight SRAM internally and six under
each wing, as alternative to conventional HE
bombs internally. Provision for ALE-25 diver-
sionary rocket pods under wings.
Accommodation: Crew of six.

Development of the B-52 began in mid-1945,
before the first flight of the smaller B-47, and
production totalled 744 between 1954 and
1962. First operational version was the
B-52B, in service from June 1955 onwards.
Continual refinement and introduction of
new equipment and more powerful engines
resulted in the B-52C, B-52D, B-52E and
B-52F, each of which was built at both
Boeing factories, in Seattle and Wichita.
Most-produced variant was the Wichita-
built B-52G, distinguished by a "wet" wing
with integral fuel tanks for greater capacity
and hence range, and provision for a
Hound Dog air-launched nuclear stand-off
bomb under each wing. A remotely-
controlled rear turret was introduced on this
version, which first flew on October 26,
1958. Production totalled 193. Final variant
was the B-52H, with turbofan engines, instead of the former P. & W. J57 turbojets,
and improved defensive armament including
a Vulcan multi-barrel gun in the tail turret.
The B-52H first flew on March 6, 1961, and
102 were built at Wichita, the last being
delivered to SAC in October 1962.
Stratofortresses have been operational
against targets in Vietnam from bases in
Thailand, carrying large numbers of non-
nuclear bombs under their wings and internally. In a major modification programme
started in 1971, several hundred B-52s of
various models are being adapted to carry 20
Short Range Attack Missiles (SRAM) for
continued service with SAC.

Boeing KC-97 Stratofreighter   *U.S.A.*

Transport and flight refuelling tanker, in service.
Data and silhouette: KC-97G. Photo: KC-97L.

Powered by: Four 3,500hp Pratt & Whitney R-4360-59 piston-engines.
Span: 141ft 3in (43.1m).
Length: 110ft 4in (33.64m).
Empty weight: 82,500lb (37,450kg).
Gross weight: 175,000lb (79,450kg).
Max. speed: 375mph (603km/h) at 25,000ft (7,620m).
Max. range: 4,300 miles (6,880km) at 297mph (478km/h).
Accommodation: Crew of 5; up to 96 troops or 69 litters.

The first of three prototypes of the Boeing XC-97 flew on November 15, 1944, the design having originated as a transport version of the B-29 Superfortress. It had the same wing, power plant and tail unit, with a new fuselage of double-bubble section. Production began in 1945 and Boeing built a series of different transport versions for the USAF designated YC-97, YC-97A, YC-97B, C-97A, VC-97A, C-97C and VC-97D. After trials with three modified C-97As, fitted with the Boeing-developed Flying-Boom refuelling gear, the KC-97E tanker went into production in 1951. It was followed by the KC-97F and KC-97G models. Production ended in July 1956 with 888 C-97s built, 811 of these being tankers. The 592 KC-97Gs delivered to the USAF were replaced in due course by KC-135As. Many were then assigned to Air National Guard Units. Those used by the Guard as tankers were converted (by Hayes) to KC-97L with the addition of two J47 jet pods, one beneath each wing, to operate with TAC fighters. In another programme, 135 were converted (by AiResearch) to plain C-97Gs in cargo configuration, and another 26 went to SAC for mission support duties in passenger configuration as C-97Ks. Fairchild Stratos converted 28 to HC-97G for search and rescue. In 1972, three KC-97Ls were supplied to the Spanish Air Force to support its F-4C Squadrons. The Israeli Air Force has about a dozen KC-97s and ex-civil Stratocruisers in service as two-point flight refuelling tankers, troop and freight transports and on ECM duties.

Boeing KC-135 Stratotanker and C-135 Stratolifter

U.S.A.

Refuelling tanker and strategic transport, in service.
Data: KC-135A. Photograph: RC-135U.
Silhouette: C-135B.

Powered by: Four 13,750lb (6,237kg) st Pratt & Whitney J57-P-59W turbojets.
Span: 130ft 10in (39.88m).
Length: 136ft 3in (41.53m).
Empty weight: 98,466lb (44,663kg).
Gross weight: 297,000lb (134,715kg).
Max. speed: 600mph (966km/h) at 36,000ft (10,972m).
Range: 1,150 miles (1,850km) with full load of transfer fuel.
Accommodation: Crew of six and up to 80 passengers.

The KC-135A jet tanker-transport first flew on August 31, 1956 and deliveries of 732 began in June 1957. They are standard flight refuelling tankers for Strategic Air Command bombers, with a total fuel capacity of 31,200 US gallons (118,100 litres), and can also be used as cargo or personnel transports.

For use by MATS as interim jet transports, the C-135A and C-135B were ordered in 1961, with tanker gear deleted and space for 87,100lb (39,510kg) of cargo or 126 troops. The first of 15 C-135As flew on May 19, 1961; the 30 C-135Bs differed in having TF33-P-5 turbofans; the first flew on February 12, 1962. Three KC-135As were also converted to C-135A standard and eleven C-135Bs became VC-135Bs when fitted with VIP interiors. France purchased 12 C-135F tankers similar to the KC-135A, to refuel Mirage IVs. Other aircraft in the KC-135A series were modified during production for special duties, bringing the total quantity built (all as Boeing Model 717 or 739) to 820. These special variants were 17 KC-135B (later EC-135C) SAC Airborne Command Posts; 4 RC-135A for photo-reconnaissance and mapping; and ten RC-135B for electronic reconnaissance. Other designations were applied to various aircraft which changed their role after initial delivery; these included ten WC-135Bs for weather reconnaissance, RC-135C, D, E, M, S and U electronic reconnaissance versions and EC-135G, H, J, K, L and P command posts. Eight EC-135Ns served as airborne radio and telemetry relay stations for the Apollo programme. The KC-135Q variant was specially adapted to refuel Lockheed SR-71s, and other "specials" were the KC-135R and KC-135T.

Boeing Vertol CH-46 Sea Knight and UH-46

U.S.A.

Transport and utility helicopter, in production and service.
**Data: KV-107/II-2. Photograph: HKP-4.
Silhouette: CH-46D.**

Powered by: Two 1,400shp General Electric T58-GE-10 turboshafts.
Rotor diameter (each): 50ft 0in (15.24m).
Fuselage length: 44ft 7in (13.59m).
Empty weight: 10,732lb (4,868kg).
Gross weight: 19,000lb (8,618kg).
Max. speed: 166mph (270km/h).
Range: 109 miles (175km) with 6,600lb (3,000kg) payload.
Accommodation: 25 equipped troops plus crew of two.

The Sea Knight is a derivative of the Boeing Vertol 107-II tandem-rotor helicopter. Three examples of the design were purchased for US Army evaluation, powered by YT58-GE-6 engines, and the first of these flew on August 27, 1959. The original designation of YHC-1A was later changed to CH-46C. Produced for the US Marine Corps as a medium assault transport helicopter, the CH-46A Sea Knight was the winner of a design competition in February 1961. Among its special features are a rear-loading ramp, water landing and take-off capability, and a powered rotor-blade folding system. The first CH-46A, with 1,250shp T58-GE-8B engines, flew on October 16, 1962, and over 600 of the CH-46 series were ordered. The original CH-46A was followed in August 1966 by the CH-46D with 1,400shp T58-GE-10 engines; and the CH-46F, introduced in July 1968, had added avionics. A US Navy model for vertical replenishment of ships at sea appeared in 1964 as the UH-46A. After 24 had been delivered, a switch was made to -10 engines, producing the UH-46D.

A variant known as Model 107-II-9 was produced for Canada; six operated as CH-113 Labradors with the RCAF and 12 as CH-113A Voyageurs with the Army. With British-built Bristol Siddeley Gnome H1200 engines, the 107-II-15 was delivered to the Royal Swedish Air Force (ten) and Navy (four) with the designation HKP-4; the first of these flew on April 19, 1963. In Japan, Kawasaki builds versions of the Model 107-II for commercial and military use, and substantial orders for the type are being worked on for the Japanese Navy (six KV-107/II-3 for minesweeping duties), Army (42 KV-107/II-4 transports) and Air Force (17 KV-107/II-5 for search and rescue). Sweden placed a further order for seven Model 107/II-5s with Kawasaki in 1972.

Boeing Vertol CH-47 Chinook   *U.S.A.*

Medium transport helicopter, in production and service.
Photograph: Agusta/Meridionali CH-47C. Data: CH-47C. Silhouette: CH-47B.

Powered by: Two 3,750shp Lycoming T55-L-11 turboshafts.
Rotor diameter (each): 60ft 0in (18.29m).
Fuselage length: 51ft 0in (15.54m).
Empty weight: 20,547lb (9,320kg).
Max. gross weight: 46,000lb (20,865kg).
Max. speed: 190mph (306km/h) at sea level.
Mission radius: 115 miles (185km) at 160mph (257km/h) with 13,450lb (6,080kg) payload.
Accommodation: 33–44 equipped troops or 27 paratroops or 24 stretchers, plus crew of two.

The Vertol Model 114 tandem-rotor helicopter was selected in March 1959 as the winner of a US Army design competition for a "battlefield mobility" helicopter, capable of carrying a two-ton load internally or eight tons on an external sling. The design was based on that of the Model 107 (see page 23) but was considerably larger with a number of new features. Five prototypes of the larger helicopter were ordered with the designation YHC-1B, and initial production aircraft became HC-1B; the basic designation was changed to H-47 in July 1962, with prototypes and first production versions becoming YCH-47A and CH-47A respectively, the latter having 2,200shp T55-L-5 or, later, 2,650shp T55-L-7 engines. Developed as weapon support system SS471L, the Chinook first flew on September 21, 1961, by which time the Vertol company had become a Division of Boeing. Delivery of aircraft to the Army began in December 1962, and the CH-47 is now a standard US Army transport helicopter, a total of 681 having been delivered by early 1972. In early October 1966, the first CH-47B made its first flight, with 2,850shp T55-L-7C engines, and production of this version began in 1967. On October 14, 1967, Boeing Vertol flew the first CH-47C with 3,750shp T55-L-11 engines and the first production aircraft of this type reached Vietnam in September 1968. The US Army transferred 49 Chinooks to the South Vietnamese Air Force in 1970-72 and a small number to Turkey in 1972. The RAAF has ordered 12 Chinooks, the Spanish Army has six, and in Italy Agusta/Meridionali has contracts for 26 for the Italian Army, 14 for the Iranian Imperial Army, and 2 for the IIAF.

Breguet Br.1050 Alize

France

Three-seat carrier-borne anti-submarine aircraft, in service.

Powered by: One 2,100eshp Rolls-Royce Dart R.Da.21 turboprop.
Span: 51ft 2in (15.6m).
Length: 45ft 6in (13.86m).
Empty weight: 12,565lb (5,700kg).
Gross weight: 18,100lb (8,200kg).
Max. speed: 292mph (470km/h) at 10,000ft (3,050m).
Endurance: 5hr 10min at 144mph (230km/h) at 1,500ft (460m).
Armament: Internal weapon bay for three 160kg depth charges or one torpedo. Racks under inner wings for two 160kg or 175kg depth charges. Racks under outer wings for six 5in rockets or two Nord AS.12 air-to-surface missiles. Sonobuoys in front of wheel housings.

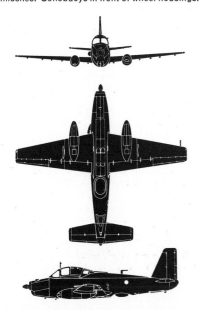

Development of the Alizé began in 1948 when Breguet designed the two-seat Br.960 Vultur strike aircraft to meet a French Navy requirement. The first of two prototype Vulturs flew on August 3, 1951, with a 980shp Armstrong Siddeley Mamba turboprop in the nose and a 4,850lb (2,200kg) st Hispano-Suiza Nene turbojet in the rear fuselage. When the French Navy abandoned the concept of a turboprop strike aircraft in 1954, Breguet was given a contract to adapt the Vultur design into a three-seat single-engined anti-submarine aircraft, and this became the Br.1050 Alizé. The first stage was to modify the second prototype Vultur into an aerodynamic prototype of the new design. A 1,650shp Mamba was installed; the Nene was removed to make way for a large retractable "dustbin" radome in the rear fuselage and dummy undercarriage/sonobuoy nacelles were fitted to the wings. This aircraft flew for the first time on March 26, 1955. Meanwhile, two genuine prototypes and three pre-production Alizés had been ordered, with Dart turboprop in place of the Mamba. The first of these flew on October 6, 1956, and the first of 75 production Alizés for the French Navy, with detail changes, was delivered on March 26, 1959. These aircraft equip two French Navy squadrons for service on board the carriers *Foch* and *Clémenceau*. Fourteen Alizés were supplied to the Indian Navy and equip No. 310 Squadron serving on board the carrier INS *Vikrant*, from which they were in operational use during the 1971 Indo-Pakistan War.

Breguet Br.1150 Atlantic   *France*

Long-range maritime reconnaissance aircraft, in production and service.

Powered by: Two 6,105eshp SNECMA/Rolls-Royce Tyne R.Ty.20 Mk.21 turboprops.
Span: 119ft 1in (36.30m).
Length: 104ft 2in (31.75m).
Gross weight: 95,900lb (43,500kg).
Max. speed: 409mph (658km/h).
Max. range: 5,590 miles (9,000km) at 195mph (320km/h).
Crew: 12.
Armament: Internal weapon bay accommodates all standard NATO bombs, 385lb depth charges and homing torpedoes. Underwing pylons for air-to-surface rockets, air-to-surface missiles, etc.

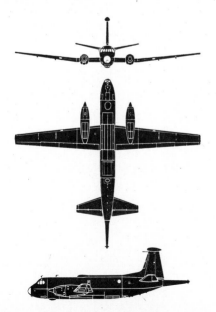

Two prototypes of the Atlantic were ordered in December 1959, following a NATO design competition for a Neptune replacement which had attracted a total of 25 entries from manufacturers in several countries. The governments of France, Federal Germany, Belgium, the Netherlands and U.S.A. assumed joint responsibility for the programme, and design and manufacture of the aircraft was undertaken by a consortium of companies in several countries, under the overall leadership of Breguet.

Operational equipment includes a retractable radar "dustbin" under the front fuselage, MAD (magnetic anomaly detection) tail-sting and an electronic countermeasures pod at the top of the tail fin. The first of two prototype Atlantics flew on October 21, 1961. Two pre-production aircraft (first flown on February 25, 1963) introduced a 3ft (1m) longer front fuselage, giving more room in the operations control centre. Breguet then delivered 40 production machines for the French Navy and 20 for the German Navy. The first delivery of an operational Atlantic was made to the French Navy on December 10, 1965. During 1968, additional orders were placed by the Netherlands for nine aircraft, and by Italy for 18. The first of the Netherlands aircraft flew on January 30, 1971 but, by special arrangement, five French Atlantics were transferred to the Dutch Navy ahead of production deliveries, new aircraft being supplied to France in their place. The first Atlantic for service with Italy's No. 41 anti-submarine squadron was handed over on June 27, 1972.

Bristol 175 Britannia

Great Britain

Long-range troop and freight transport, in service. Data apply to Britannia C.Mk.1.

Powered by: Four 4,310ehp Bristol Siddeley Proteus 255 turboprops.
Span: 142ft 3½in (43.83m).
Length: 124ft 3in (37.89m).
Gross weight: 185,000lb (83,915kg).
Cruising speed: 357mph (575km/h).
Range: 4,310 miles (6,936km) at 357mph (575km/h) with maximum payload
Accommodation: Up to 139 troops, 53 stretchers and 6 attendants, or 37,400lb (16,964kg) freight.

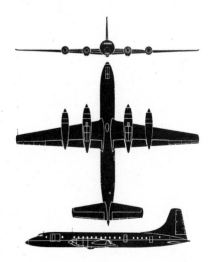

The Britannia for the RAF has the maker's designation of Britannia 253 and is outwardly similar to the Britannia 310 which was widely used by commercial airlines during the 'sixties. Orders totalled 20, of which Short Bros. and Harland built 15, ending late in 1960. The first Britannia C.Mk.1 (XL635) made its first flight at Belfast on December 29, 1958, and deliveries to the RAF began in mid-1959. No. 99 Squadron was the first equipped, followed by No. 511, both based at Lyneham. In addition, Air Support Command received three Britannia C.Mk.2s of similar standard, built originally for Ministry of Supply trooping as Britannia 252s. Now serving in No. 46 Group, Strike Command, the RAF Britannias all carry individual names, as follows: Denebola, Aldebaran, Procyon, Atria, Antares, Accrux, Altair, Canopus, Rigel, Adhara, Polaris, Alphard, Regulus, Schedar, Hadar, Avior, Spica, Capella, Argo, Vecia, Sirius and Arcturus. One aircraft has been written-off while in RAF service.

Of similar appearance to the Britannia, but with greater fuselage length, was the Canadair CC-106 Yukon, powered by Rolls-Royce Tyne 515 engines. Twelve were purchased by the RCAF in 1960 and were operated by No. 437 Squadron until 1971, when the Yukons began to be phased out.

Canadair CL-41 (including CT-114 Tutor)

Canada

Two-seat basic trainer and light attack aircraft, in service.
Data, photograph and silhouette: CL-41G.

Powered by: One 2,950lb (1,340kg) st General Electric J85-J4 turbojet.
Span: 36ft 6in (11.13m).
Length: 32ft 0in (9.75m).
Empty weight: 5,296lb (2,400kg).
Gross weight: 11,288lb (5,131kg).
Max. speed: 480mph (774km/h) at 28,500ft (8,700m).
Max. range: 1,340 miles (2,156km) with six underwing tanks.
Armament: Up to 4,000lb (1,815kg) of missiles, bombs, rockets and gun pods on six attachments under wings and centre-section.

The first of two prototypes of the Canadair CL-41 two-seat basic trainer flew on January 13, 1960, powered by a 2,400lb (1,090kg) st Pratt & Whitney JT12A-5 turbojet. It was developed to meet the anticipated needs of the RCAF for a basic jet trainer and, after evaluation of the prototypes, the RCAF ordered 190 CL-41A production models, powered by a 2,633lb (1,194kg) st General Electric J85-Can-40, under the designation CT-114 Tutor. The first of these was delivered on October 29, 1963, and all were in service by 1966. In June 1964, Canadair flew a Tutor converted to CL-41G configuration as a light counter-insurgency aircraft and armament trainer. This prototype had four underwing points for bombs, rockets or Minigun pods, but production CL-41Gs had two additional strong points under the centre-section. Twenty CL-41Gs were supplied to the Royal Malaysian Air Force in 1967/68 and currently equip two squadrons—No. 6 for light strike duties and No. 9 for training, both based at Kuantan. The RMAF name for the CL-41G is *Tebuan* (Wasp).

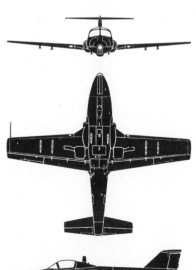

Canadair CP-107 (CL-28) Argus   *Canada*

Maritime reconnaissance aircraft, in service. Photograph and silhouette: Argus Mk.2.

Powered by: Four 3,700hp Wright R-3350-EA-1 Turbo-Compound piston-engines.
Span: 142ft 3½in (43.38m).
Length: 128ft 9½in (39.09m).
Empty weight: 81,000lb (36,740kg).
Gross weight: 148,000lb (67,130kg).
Max. speed: 315mph (507km/h) at 20,000ft (6,100m).
Max. Range: 5,900 miles (9,495km) at 223mph (359km/h).
Crew: 15.
Armament: Approx. 8,000lb (3,630kg) of weapons internally, plus 3,800lb (1,725kg) under each wing if required.

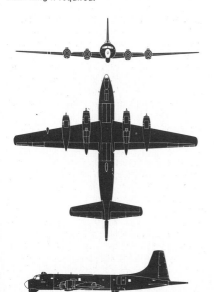

Development of the Argus began in 1953 when the RCAF drew up a specification for a new long-range overwater reconnaissance aeroplane to replace the Avro Lancasters then in service. To meet this requirement, Canadair projected an aeroplane based on the Bristol Britannia, and having secured an RCAF contract to go ahead, obtained a licence for Britannia development on March 16, 1954. In the CL-28 design, a completely new fuselage was introduced, and Wright R-3350 Turbo-Compound engines were adopted to obtain the necessary long duration at sea level. The basic Britannia wing design was retained, together with the tail unit, undercarriage and some other components. Equipment for the search role includes a large nose radome, MAD in the tail and a 70-million candle-power searchlight on one wing. The CL-28 first flew on March 28, 1957 and the first squadrons, Nos. 404 and 405, were equipped at Greenwood, Nova Scotia, on May 17, 1958. After production of 13 Mk.1s, including the prototype, Canadair built 20 Mk.2s with new equipment identifiable by a smaller chin radome, production being completed in July 1960. Two further squadrons, Nos. 407 and 415, have been equipped, and all four squadrons, with six aircraft each, are scheduled to continue flying the Argus at least until 1973. Its Canadian Armed Forces designation is CP-107.

Cessna A-37 and T-37   *U.S.A.*

Light attack aircraft and basic jet trainer, in production and service.
Photograph and data: A-37B. Silhouette: A-37A.

Powered by: Two 2,850lb (1,293kg) st General Electric J85-GE-17A turbojets.
Span: 35ft 10½in (10.93m).
Length: 29ft 3½in (8.93m).
Gross weight: 14,000lb (6,350kg).
Max. speed: 507mph (816km/h) at 16,000ft (4,875m).
Ferry range: 1,010 miles (1,628 km).
Armament: One 7.62mm multi-barrel Minigun; eight underwing strong points for more than 5,000lb (2,270kg) of ordnance.

Cessna's first design for a jet aeroplane won a competition in 1954 for a primary jet trainer for the USAF. The first of two XT-37 prototypes flew on October 12, 1954, and the first of an evaluation batch of 11

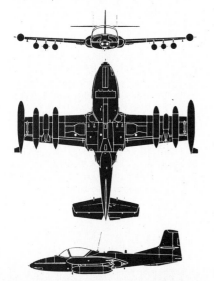

T-37s flew a year later. A total of 416 T-37As were built, with two Continental J69-T-9 turbojets, before being superseded in production by the T-37B with 1,025lb (465kg) st J69-T-25 engines. All T-37As were converted to 'B' standard, and production of the T-37B continued into 1972, side-by-side with the export T-37C. The latter has provision for underwing armament, including machine-gun pods, rockets and bombs. Through MAP and by direct purchase, T-37Bs and Cs have been delivered to Greece, Thailand, Peru, Turkey, Cambodia, Chile, Pakistan, Colombia, Brazil, Portugal, Burma and Vietnam, while Germany purchased 47 T-37Bs for use in its training programmes based in the USA. T-37 production totalled 1,204 by mid-1972.
The A-37 was evolved from the T-37 for service in Vietnam, following evaluation by the USAF of two YAT-37D prototypes (first flown on October 22, 1963). In August 1966 the USAF ordered Cessna to complete 39 T-37Bs then in production as A-37As and the first of these was delivered in May 1967. These aircraft had eight underwing hardpoints, J85-GE-17A engines each de-rated to 2,400lb (1,090kg) st, and other minor changes. A-37As have equipped a squadron of the South Vietnamese Air Force since April 1969. Deliveries began in May 1968 of the A-37B, of which 300 had been built by mid-1972. These have fully-rated engines, in-flight refuelling provision, 6g airframe stressing, provision for increased fuel capacity and other operational improvements. During 1970, the USAF began to transfer A-37Bs to the ANG and to overseas units, including a wing in the Panama Canal Zone. Production continues for supply to foreign nations, primarily South Vietnam, which had received 164 by the beginning of 1973.

Convair F-102 Delta Dagger   *U.S.A.*

All-weather interceptor fighter, in service. Photograph and silhouette: F-102A.

Powered by: One 17,200lb (7,808kg) st Pratt & Whitney J57-P-23 or -25 afterburning turbojet.
Span: 38ft 1½in (11.62m).
Length: 68ft 4¼in (20.81m).
Gross weight: Approx. 32,000lb (14,515kg).
Max. speed: Mach 1.25 (825mph; 1,328km/h) at 36,000ft (11,000m).
Range: Approx. 1,100 miles (1,770 km).
Accommodation: Pilot only (pupil and instructor in TF-102A).
Armament: Internal missile bay accommodates, typically, one Hughes AIM-26A and three AIM-4C Falcons.

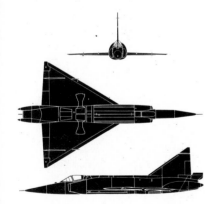

The Delta Dagger or Convair Model 8 design was begun in 1950, continuing Convair work on delta wings which had begun with the proposed F-92 (Convair Model 7) designed in collaboration with Dr. Alexander Lippisch. As part of the F-92 programme, Convair built and flew the XF-92A in 1948; and the Convair Model 8, which won a USAF design competition in 1950, was basically the XF-92A scaled up in size. The two prototype YF-102s flew, respectively, on October 24, 1953 and January 11, 1954. After initial trials showed deficiencies in high-speed performance, the YF-102A was developed and flew on December 20, 1954. This introduced an area-ruled fuselage, cambered leading-edge and "wash-in" on the wingtips. The production model F-102A was similar, and 875 were built for service with Air Defense Command, starting in mid-1956. For use as combat trainers, the USAF also purchased 63 TF-102As with a wider front fuselage and two seats side-by-side: the first flew on November 8, 1955. The F-102B became the F-106—see page 32. F-102As have been up-dated since delivery to have in-flight refuelling and external drop tanks but were virtually out of A.D.C. service by 1972, although 13 Air National Guard squadrons are equipped with this type. Many F-102As formerly used by the USAF in Europe were transferred during 1969–70 to the Greek and Turkish Air Forces. For use as targets in connection with the F-15A Eagle flight programme, the USAF initiated two target conversion schemes of the Delta Dagger in 1972, producing the QF-102A manned drone and PQM-102A unmanned drone.

Convair F-106 Delta Dart

U.S.A.

Interceptor fighter, in service. Photograph and silhouette: F-106A.

Powered by: One 24,500lb (11,123kg) st Pratt & Whitney J75-P-17 afterburning turbojet.
Span: 38ft 3½in (11.67m).
Length: 70ft 8¾in (21.56m).
Empty weight: 23,646lb (10,726kg).
Gross weight: About 35,000lb (15,875kg).
Max. speed: Mach 2.3 (1,525mph; 2,450km/h) at 36,000ft (11,000m).
Range: 1,150 miles (1,850km).
Accommodation: Pilot only (pilot and observer in F-106B).
Armament: One Douglas AIR-2A Genie or AIR-2B Super Genie rocket and four Hughes AIM-4F or AIM-4G Super Falcon air-to-air missiles in internal weapons bay.

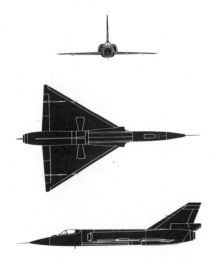

Development of the F-102 to accommodate the more powerful J75 engine began in 1955. The designation was initially F-102B but this was later changed to F-106. While the wing remained substantially unchanged, the fuselage was extensively redesigned with the air intakes moved farther aft and the cockpit moved relatively farther forward. The shape of the fin and rudder was changed, the undercarriage was improved and provision was made for later weapons in the bomb-bay. A Hughes MA-1 guidance and control system was introduced to permit the F-106 to operate with the SAGE defence system. The first F-106A flew on December 26, 1956. Production of 277 was completed by the end of 1960, deliveries to Air Defense Command having begun in mid-1959. On April 9, 1958, the first of 63 F-106Bs flew; this variant is a combat trainer with two seats in tandem and full operational capability. The F-106A and F-106B serve with Aerospace Defense Command, still equipping eleven squadrons in 1971. This represented the largest single force of manned interceptors in service with the USAF. New drop tanks suitable for supersonic operation and capable of being refuelled in flight were added to the F-106s some years ago, and various schemes have been proposed to prolong the useful life of the F-106s, including installation of a multi-barrel gun in the so-called "Six Shooter".

Dassault Etendard IV

France

Photograph, data and silhouette: Etendard IV-M.

Single-seat carrier-based interceptor and fighter-bomber, in service.

Powered by: One 9,700lb (4,400kg) st SNECMA Atar 8B turbojet.
Span: 31ft 6in (9.60m).
Length: 47ft 3in (14.40m).
Empty weight: approx. 13,000lb (5,900kg).
Gross weight: 22,650lb (10,275kg).
Max. speed: Mach 1.02 (675mph; 1,086km/h) at 36,000ft (11,000m).
Range: 1,750 miles (2,816km) with external tanks, at 510mph (820km/h).
Armament: One or two 30mm cannon. Four underwing attachments for up to 3,000lb (1,360kg) of rockets, bombs, Sidewinder air-to-air or Nord AS.30 air-to-surface missiles, or drop tanks.

The Etendard began life as a low-level land-based strike fighter to meet French Air Force and NATO requirements. First version to fly was the Etendard II with two 2,425lb (1,100kg) st Turboméca Gabizo turbojets, on July 23, 1956. It was followed on July 24, 1956, by the private-venture Etendard IV, with a single 8,155lb (3,700kg) st Atar 101.E4 turbojet, and on March 13, 1957, by the NATO-specification Etendard VI with a 4,850lb (2,200kg) st Orpheus B.Or.3. None of these models progressed beyond the prototype stage, but the French Navy decided to adapt the Etendard IV for service from its two attack carriers, the *Clémenceau* and *Foch*, and the prototype of the navalised Etendard IV-M flew on May 21, 1958. It was followed by five pre-production and 69 production IV-Ms. Compared with the land-based version, these have a long-stroke undercarriage, deck hook, catapult fittings, folding wingtips, modified nose containing AIDA all-weather fire-control radar, and a high-lift system combining leading-edge and trailing-edge flaps, plus two under-fuselage air-brakes. Some of the IV-Ms were delivered with nose refuelling probes and "buddy" refuelling packs. Also in service is the Etendard IV-P, of which 21 were delivered (plus one prototype) as dual-purpose reconnaissance/tankers, with nose and ventral camera positions, self-contained navigation system and flight refuelling nose-probe.

Dassault Mirage III

France

Data and silhouette: Mirage III-E.
Photograph: Mirage III-EE.
Single-seat long-range fighter-bomber, in production and service.

Powered by: One 13,670lb (6,200kg) st SNECMA Atar 09C afterburning turbojet and, optionally, one 3,307lb (1,500kg) SEP 844 rocket-engine.
Span: 27ft 0in (8.22m).
Length: 49ft 3½in (15.03m).
Empty weight: 15,540lb (7,050kg).
Max. gross weight: 29,760lb (13,500kg).
Max. speed: Mach 2.2 (1,460mph; 2,350km/h) at 40,000ft (12,000m).
Tactical radius: 745 miles (1,200km) in ground attack configuration.
Armament: Two 30mm cannon in fuselage and one AS.30 air-to-surface missile or Matra R.530 air-to-air missile under fuselage, and two rocket pods or 1,000lb bombs under wings. Two Sidewinders can also be carried.

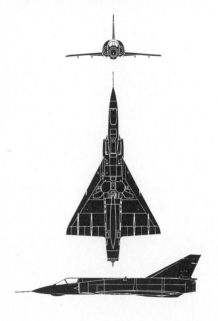

The Mirage III was designed as an all-weather fighter capable of operating from short unprepared airstrips. The prototype flew on November 17, 1956, with a 9,900lb (4,500kg) st Atar 101G turbojet, with which it reached a speed of Mach 1.5. Later, with a rocket supplementing its turbojet, it attained Mach 1.9. It was followed by the Mach 2 Mirage III-A with 13,225lb (6,000kg) st Atar 9B turbojet, of which ten were built, and the generally-similar Mirage III-C (first flown October 9, 1960) of which 95 were built for all-weather interception and day ground attack duties with the French Air Force, with optional rocket-engine, and one for the Swiss Air Force. Others were delivered to Israel (III-CJ) and to South Africa (III-CZ). Alongside the Mirage III-C, Dassault developed and produced the III-B, a tandem two-seat trainer which is 2ft (60cm) longer and retains the same strike capability as the III-C. This version first flew on October 20, 1959, and has been produced for the French Air Force, Israel (III-BJ), Lebanon (III-BL), Switzerland (III-BS), South Africa (III-BZ and III-DZ), Australia (III-D), Pakistan (III-DP), Brazil (III-DBR), Spain (III-DE) and the Argentine (III-DA).

Following the Mirage III-C was the III-E, first flown on April 5, 1961. This is a long-range fighter-bomber version with Atar 09C engine, fuselage lengthened by 1ft (30cm) and new nav/attack equipment. French orders for 180 are supplemented by export orders from the Argentine (III-EA), Brazil (III-EBR), Pakistan (III-EP), South Africa (III-EZ), Spain (III-EE), Lebanon (III-EL), Australia (III-O, licence-built), and Switzerland (III-S, licence-built). A reconnaissance version of the III-E is designated Mirage III-R and was first flown in prototype form in November 1961. It carries five cameras in the nose and has been built for the French Air Force (III-R and III-RD, the latter with improved equipment), Pakistan (III-RP), Switzerland (III-RS), South Africa (III-RZ and III-RDZ) and Libya.

Dassault Mirage IV-A

France

Two-seat supersonic strategic bomber, in service.

Powered by: Two 15,400lb (6,985kg) st SNECMA Atar 09K afterburning turbojets.
Span: 38ft 10½in (11.85m).
Length: 77ft 1in (23.50m).
Empty weight: 31,965lb (14,500kg).
Max. gross weight: 73,800lb (33,475kg).
Max. speed: Mach 2.2 (1,460mph; 2,350km/h) at 36,000ft (11,000m).
Tactical radius: 770 miles (1,240km).
Armament: One nuclear weapon recessed into bottom of fuselage, or sixteen 1,000lb bombs or four Martel air-to-surface missiles under fuselage and wings.

To meet French Air Force requirements for a supersonic bomber to deliver France's atomic bomb, Dassault scaled up the highly-successful Mirage III fighter design and the result was the prototype Mirage IV, which flew for the first time on June 17, 1959. Powered by two 13,225lb (6,000kg) st Atar 09 turbojets with afterburning, this aircraft exceeded Mach 2 during its 33rd test flight. It was followed by three pre-production Mirage IVs, of which the first flew on October 12, 1961. The first two had 14,110lb (6,400kg) st Atar 09Cs and introduced a circular under-fuselage radome and dummy missiles, some containing test equipment. The third pre-production machine, first flown on January 23, 1963, was to operational standard, with Atar 09Ks, flight-refuelling nose-probe and armament. A total of 62 production Mirage IV-As were ordered for the French Air Force. The first of these flew on December 7, 1963, and all had been delivered to the French Air Force by 1967. During the time that they represented the primary French nuclear strike force (*Force de Frappe*), the aircraft were kept in protective shelters, and could take off straight out of the shelters with their engines running at full power. The nuclear bomb was designed for free-fall delivery, carried semi-recessed in the underside of the fuselage. As land-based and submarine-launched nuclear missiles have taken over the primary strike role, the Mirage IV-A force has been re-assigned to a low-level tactical strike role. Six aircraft had been lost by mid-1972.

Dassault Mirage 5 and Milan   *France*

Single-seat fighter-bomber, in production and service.
Data, photograph and silhouette: Mirage 5-COA.

Powered by: One 13,670lb (6,200kg) st SNECMA Atar 09C afterburning turbojet.
Span: 27ft 0in (8.22m).
Length: 51ft 0½in (15.55m).
Empty weight: 14,550lb (6,600kg).
Gross weight: 29,760lb (13,500kg).
Max. speed: Mach 2.2 (1,460mph; 2,350km/h) at 40,000ft (12,000m).
Combat radius: 400–805 miles (650–1,300km) with 2,000lb (907kg) bomb-load.
Armament: Two 30mm cannon in fuselage. Typical external weapon load comprises two 1,000lb bombs, ten 500lb bombs and two 250lb bombs, plus two external fuel tanks. Other weapons can include one AS.30 or R.530 missile, rocket pods and Sidewinder missiles.

By simplifying the electronics and other systems of the basic Mirage III-E airframe, Dassault produced a day fighter-bomber with increased internal fuel capacity, considerably greater weapon-carrying capability and reduced maintenance requirements. The Mirage 5, as this version is known, is of particular appeal to countries that do not need, or cannot afford, the all-weather, rocket-boosted Mirage III-E. The prototype flew on May 19, 1967. Subsequently, 50 Mirage 5-J were ordered by Israel, but delivery of these was blocked by the French government and in 1972 they were in process of being absorbed by the French Air Force as Mirage 5-Ms. Belgium ordered a total of 106 in three versions: the 5-BA for ground attack, the 5-BR reconnaissance model and the 5-BD two-seater. The first of three Belgian Mirage 5s completed by Dassault flew on March 6, 1970; the remainder are being assembled in Belgium by SABCA. Other customers include Peru (14 5-P and two 5-PD two-seaters); Libya (58 5-D, 32 5-DE, 10 5-DR and 10 two-seat 5-DD); Colombia 14 5-COA, plus two camera-equipped 5-COR and two two-seat 5-COD); the Abu Dhabi Air Force (14) and Venezuela (5-V and two-seat 5-DV). Dassault has also developed a derivative of the Mirage III/5 family known as the Milan (Kite), with retractable 'moustache' foreplanes which improve the low-speed handling. After trials on a Mirage III-R, a prototype Milan S-01 with Atar 09K-50 flew on May 29, 1970. This aircraft was converted from a French Air Force Mirage III-E and is similar to the production variant offered to Switzerland as the Milan S.

Dassault Mirage F1

France

Single-seat all-weather multi-purpose fighter, in production and service.

Powered by: One 15,798lb (7,166kg) st SNECMA Atar 09K-50 afterburning turbojet.
Span: 27ft 6¾in (8.40m).
Length: 49ft 2½in (15.00m).
Empty weight: 16,314lb (7,400kg).
Gross weight: 32,850lb (14,900kg).
Max. speed: Mach 2.2 (1,460mph; 2,350km/h) at 40,000ft (12,000m). Mach 1.2 at low altitude
Endurance: 3hr 45min.
Armament: Two 30mm DEFA cannon in forward fuselage. One underfuselage strong point, and two under each wing, for max. external load of 8,820lb (4,000kg). Provision for Sidewinder missile attached at each wingtip.

This multi-purpose fighter is a development of the Mirage III-E, with a basically similar fuselage and the same weapon systems. Its primary role is all-weather interception at all altitudes, but it also offers a formidable ground attack capability. The major innovation compared with the rest of the Mirage family is its use of a sweptback wing and conventional all-moving horizontal tail surfaces instead of the delta configuration of its predecessors. The wing is fitted with a drooping saw-tooth leading-edge and large double-slotted flaps, enabling the Mirage F1 to take off and land in under 700 yards (640m) and to use unprepared runways. The prototype flew for the first time on December 23, 1966, but was destroyed on May 18, 1967. Three replacements were ordered by the French Air Force, and the first of these, the F1-02, flew on March 20, 1969, followed by F1-03 on September 18, 1969 and F1-04 on June 17, 1970. For its first 62 flights, F1-02 was powered by an Atar 09K-31, but the definitive 09K-50 was then fitted, and powers the subsequent pre-production aircraft. The French Air Force has ordered 85 Mirage F1s and plans procurement of another 20 powered by the 18,650lb (8,460kg) st M53 afterburning turbofan. Spain has ordered 15 Mirage F1s and South Africa is reported to have acquired a licence for production of the type.

Dassault MD-452 Mystere IVA   *France*

Single-seat interceptor, in service.

Powered by: One 7,716lb (3,500kg) st Hispano-Suiza Verdon 350 turbojet.
Span: 36ft 5½in (11.12m).
Length: 42ft 1½in (12.85m).
Empty weight: 12,950lb (5,870kg).
Gross weight: 18,700lb (8,482kg).
Max. speed: Mach 0.91 (695mph; 1,120km/h) at sea level.
Endurance: 1hr 10min without external tanks.
Armament: Two 30mm cannon and pack of 55 rockets in fuselage. Underwing racks for two 1,000lb bombs, napalm containers, packs of six air-to-ground rockets or packs of 19 air-to-air rockets.

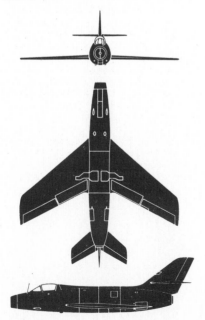

Developed from the Mystère IIC, which served briefly with the French Air Force, the Mystère IVA (first flown September 28, 1952) introduced a thinner (7.5 per cent thickness/chord ratio) wing, increased sweepback (41°), larger fuselage and more powerful turbojet. An "offshore" procurement order for 225 production models was placed by the USAF in April 1953, followed by a French Government order for 100, and the first Mystère IVAs entered service in 1955. The first 50 aircraft had 6,280lb (2,850kg) st Hispano-Suiza Tay 250 turbojets, after which a switch was made to the more powerful Verdon.

Altogether 421 Mystère IVAs were built, of which 110 were exported to the Indian Air Force and 60 to the Israel Air Force, which used them in combat against Egyptian MiG-15s and 17s during the Sinai campaign in 1956 and again in June 1967. The French Air Force has replaced its Mystères with Mirages; a few remain in service in India and one squadron was still operational in Israel in 1972.

Variants of the Mystère IV were three prototypes and 16 pre-production IVBs (first flown December 16, 1953) with Avon RA7R engine and F-86-type lipped air intake, and the IVN prototype (flown July 19, 1954), an Avon-powered tandem two-seat all-weather interceptor with a nose radome similar to that of the F-86D and L Sabres.

Dassault Super Mystère B-2   *France*

Single-seat interceptor and tactical strike fighter, in service.

Powered by: One 9,700lb (4,400kg) st SNECMA Atar 101G afterburning turbojet.
Span: 34ft 5⅜in (10.52m).
Length: 46ft 1in (14.04m).
Gross weight: 22,046lb (10,00Ckg).
Max. speed: Mach 1.13 (743mph; 1,200km/h) at 36,000ft (11,000m).
Range: 600 miles (966km).
Armament: Two 30mm cannon and pack of 55 air-to-air rockets in fuselage. Underwing racks for two 19-rocket packs, two 500kg bombs, napalm tanks, air-to-air missiles or 12 air-to-surface rockets.

The Super Mystère is a development of the Mystère IVB, with thinner, more sharply swept wing, better visibility for the pilot and an improved, elliptical air intake. The prototype Super Mystère B-1 (flown March 2, 1955) had an Avon RA7R engine with afterburning, and exceeded Mach 1 on its fourth test flight. A switch was made to the Atar 101 for the five pre-production and 180 production (first flown February 26, 1957) Super Mystère B-2s, the last of which was delivered in 1959. Three squadrons of B-2s are still operational with French air defence elements, which are expected to keep these elderly aircraft until re-equipped with the Mirage F1. The Super Mystère B-2 also remains in front-line service as a fighter-bomber in Israel, which purchased a total of 24, and had one squadron operational on the type in 1972.

One airframe was re-engined as a flying test-bed for the SNECMA Atar 9 turbojet (13,250lb; 6,000kg st with afterburning) and was designated Super Mystère B-4. It flew for the first time on February 9, 1958, and had a rate of climb of almost 30,000ft (9,150m)/min at sea level.

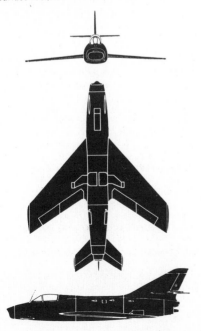

De Havilland (Canada) DHC-4 Caribou

Canada

Light tactical transport, in service.

Powered by: Two 1,450hp Pratt & Whitney R-2000-7M2 piston-engines.
Span: 95ft 7½in (29.15m).
Length: 72ft 7in (22.13m).
Empty weight: 18,260lb (8,283kg).
Normal gross weight: 28,500lb (12,928kg).
Max. speed: 216mph (347km/h) at 6,500ft (1,980m).
Range: 242 miles (390km) with max. payload.
Accommodation: Crew of 3 plus 32 combat troops or 26 paratroops or 22 litters and 8 other persons.

De Havilland Canada began design of this STOL tactical transport in 1955. The project gained US Army support in 1957 with a contract for five prototypes designated YAC-1; the Canadian Government ordered two, of which one was for RCAF evaluation as the CC-108.

The first Caribou flew on July 30, 1958 and the first YAC-1 in March 1959. Deliveries to the US Army began in October 1959 and the first of a continuing series of production orders was placed in 1960. The US Army AC-1s (later redesignated CV-2As) were delivered with a gross weight of 26,000lb (11,790kg); later aircraft (CV-2Bs) were to DHC-4A standard with a weight of 28,500lb.

A total of 159 Caribou were acquired by the US Army; 134 still in service in January 1967 were taken over by the USAF and redesignated C-7A. Four Caribou Mk.1A (DHC-4) ordered by the RCAF in August 1960 were allocated to UN forces in the Congo and four Mk.1B (DHC-4A) were purchased later, all with the CC-108 designation. Two CV-2As were transferred to the Indian Air Force in 1963 for evaluation, and 20 Caribou were subsequently purchased by India. Other air forces which have bought Caribou include those of Ghana (8), Australia (30), Kuwait (2), Kenya (4), Zambia (4), Malaysia (13), Tanzania (4), Spain (16), Oman (3), and the Abu Dhabi Air Force (4).

De Havilland (Canada) DHC-5 Buffalo

Canada

Assault transport, in production and service.
Data apply to CC-115.

Powered by: Two 3,055eshp General Electric CT64-820-1 turboprops.
Span: 96ft 0in (29.26m).
Length: 79ft 0in (24.08m).
Empty weight: 24,500lb (11,113kg).
Gross weight: 41,000lb (18,597kg).
Max. speed: 282mph (454km/h) at 10,000ft (3,050m).
Range: 507 miles (814km) with max. payload.
Accommodation: Crew of 3; up to 41 troops or 35 paratroops or 24 litters and 6 other people.

As the Caribou II, this design originated in a US Army requirement which was put out to industry in May 1962. De Havilland Aircraft of Canada, one of 25 companies invited to submit designs, had already sold three earlier types to the US Army in quantity—the Beaver, Otter and Caribou. The new requirement was for an aeroplane of rather higher performance than the Caribou, and able to carry considerably greater loads; the cargo capability had to be compatible with that of the CH-47A Chinook helicopter. The DHC-5, which was selected as winner of the design competition, was based on the Caribou wing and had the same general configuration, with a new, more capacious fuselage, a T-tail and T64 turboprop engines. The US Army ordered four DHC-5s for evaluation and development, originally with the designation YAC-2, this being changed later to YCV-7A and then to C-8A when the USAF took over US Army transports in January 1967. The first of these aircraft flew on April 9, 1964 and was delivered a year later. Late in 1964, the Canadian Armed Forces ordered 15 Buffaloes, of which six were equipped for search and rescue duties. These were designated CC-115 and have a 20in (50cm) increase in overall length due to the nose radome, and more powerful engines. Twenty-four similar aircraft were ordered for the Brazilian Air Force and 16 by Peru, deliveries taking place in 1971/72.

De Havilland Venom

Great Britain

Single-seat fighter-bomber, in service. Data, photograph and silhouette: Venom FB Mk.4.

Powered by: One 4,850lb (2,200kg) st de Havilland Ghost 103 turbojet.
Span: 41ft 8in (12.70m).
Length: 31ft 10in (9.70m).
Gross weight: 15,400lb (6,985 kg).
Max. speed: 640mph (1,030km/h).
Range: over 1,000 miles (1,610km) with external fuel.
Armament: Four 20mm cannon in nose and up to 2,000lb (907kg) of bombs or rockets under wings.

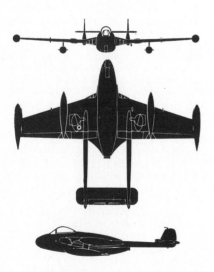

The D.H.112 Venom prototype first flew on September 2, 1949, as a direct modification of the Vampire with thinner, slightly swept-back wings, tip-tanks and Ghost turbojet. Production deliveries of the Venom FB. Mk.1 to the RAF began in 1951 and the type was used to equip squadrons of the 2nd TAF in Germany and others in the Middle and Far East.

Re-equipment of these squadrons with the Venom FB. Mk.4, with powered ailerons, redesigned tail unit and other changes, began in the mid-fifties; and the two-seat, radar-equipped Venom NF. Mk.2 and 3 night fighters were also supplied to several squadrons. All Venoms had been phased out of operational service with the RAF by 1962; but the FB. 50 version of the Mk.1 remains operational in Switzerland, where 150 were built under licence, followed by 100 Venoms similar to the FB. Mk.4. The latter variant also continued in service in Venezuela in 1972.

Development of a naval version of the two-seat Venom began in the early 'fifties to give the Royal Navy its first radar-equipped all-weather fighter, and eight front-line Fleet Air Arm squadrons operated Sea Venoms between 1954 and 1961. The type was also built in France as the Sud Aquilon, a few examples of which may still survive.

Douglas A-1 Skyraider   *U.S.A.*

Single- and two-seat counter-insurgency attack bomber and armed escort, in service.
Data and silhouette: A-1J.
Photograph: A-1E.

Powered by: One 3,050hp Wright R-3350-26WB piston-engine.
Span: 50ft 9in (15.49m).
Length: 38ft 10in (11.84m).
Empty weight: 12,550lb (5,700kg).
Gross weight: 25,000lb (11,340kg).
Max. speed: 318mph (512km/h) at 18,000ft (5,500m).
Range: up to 3,000 miles (4,830km) with external tanks.
Armament: Fixed armament comprises four 20mm cannon in wings; up to 8,000lb (3,630kg) of assorted stores under wings.

One of the most versatile light attack bombers ever produced, the Skyraider originated from a US Navy requirement in 1944 and 3,160 had been built when production ended in 1957. Although too late for service in World War II, the Skyraider, under its earlier AD designation, was one of the USN's most potent weapons in the Korean War, and is still operational in South Vietnam. Versions designated from AD-1 to AD-7 were redesignated from A-1A to A-1J in 1962. Until 1967, the USN was using several versions in Vietnam, including the A-1H low-altitude model, A-1J with strengthened airframe and EA-1E and EA-1F electronic countermeasures versions. These had been withdrawn from service by the end of 1967, leaving the USAF and Vietnamese Air Force the principal users of the Skyraider, primarily with the A-1E two-seater, known universally in Vietnam as the "Spad". Among foreign users of the A-1, Britain received a batch of 51 under MDAP for airborne early warning duties with the Royal Navy (no longer in service), and a quantity went to the French Air Force, which continues to use them primarily in support of its forces based in former French territories in North Africa.

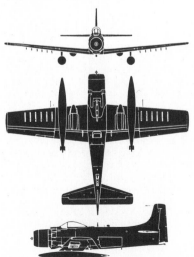

Douglas A-3 Skywarrior   *U.S.A.*

Carrier-based electronic reconnaissance aircraft, in service.
Data and silhouette: A-3B. Photograph: EKA-3Q.

Powered by: Two 10,500lb (4,763kg) st Pratt & Whitney J57-P-10 turbojets.
Span: 72ft 6in (22.07m).
Length: 76ft 4in (23.27m).
Empty weight: 38,298lb (17,372kg).
Gross weight: 73,000lb (33,112kg).
Max. speed: 610mph (982km/h) at 10,000ft (3,050m).
Range: over 2,900 miles (4,667km).
Armament: Two 20mm cannon in radar-controlled tail mounting (not always fitted). Assorted weapons in bomb-bay.

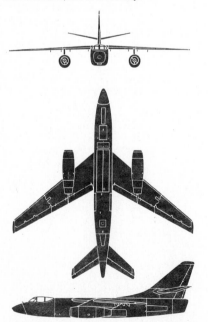

Development of the Skywarrior began soon after the end of the War, when the US Navy drew up plans for super-carriers such as the USS *Forrestal*. It was the largest aircraft produced for carrier operations when the prototype first flew on October 28, 1952, designated XA3D-1. This and the second prototype were powered by Westinghouse XJ40-WE-3 engines but production aircraft switched to J57-P-6s. All Skywarriors were built with A3D designations, changed to A-3 in 1962. The first production A-3A flew on September 16, 1953 and deliveries to the Navy began in March 1956. Subsequent modifications to five of the 50 A-3As built produced the EA-3A for electronic countermeasures and the single YRA-3A for reconnaissance. The A-3B, which began to reach the fleet in 1957, has more powerful engines and provision for flight refuelling; 164 were built. The first of 30 RA-3Bs was flown on July 22, 1958 and carries cameras in the weapon bay. The EA-3B for electronic countermeasures has a crew compartment in the bomb-bay, seating four, and first flew on December 10, 1958; 24 were built. Final version, first flown on August 29, 1959, was the TA-3B, a trainer for radar operators serving on EA-3Bs. It carried an instructor and six pupils in the fuselage; 12 were built and one was modified to VA-3B as an executive transport. Primary operational deployment of the Skywarrior in 1972 was for electronic reconnaissance in support of US operations over Vietnam. Others, converted to KA-3 and EKA-3 tankers, were scheduled to be replaced by KA-6Ds.

Douglas B-66 Destroyer   *U.S.A.*

Electronic reconnaissance aircraft, in service.
Data and silhouette: B-66C. Photograph: EB-66C.

Powered by: Two 10,000lb (4,540kg) st Allison J71-A-13 turbojets.
Span: 72ft 6in (22.11m).
Length: 75ft 2in (22.90m).
Empty weight: 42,369lb (19,200kg).
Gross weight: 83,000lb (37,648kg).
Max. speed: 620mph (998km/h) at 10,000ft (3,050m).
Range: Over 1,500 miles (2,400km).
Armament: Two 20mm cannon in radar-controlled tail turret; internal stowage for up to 15,000lb (6,800kg) of bombs.

Successful development of the A3D Skywarrior for the US Navy led to adoption of the same basic design by the USAF, which ordered five RB-66As for development trials in 1952. These differed in many details from the Skywarrior and were powered by Allison J71 engines. First flight was on June 28, 1954. Like the RB-66A, the RB-66B was designed for day and night photographic reconnaissance with cameras and flash bombs in the fuselage. Deliveries began during 1954 and 145 were built. For service as a tactical bomber, the B-66B differed only in bomb-bay details; 72 of this model were built, the first flying on January 4, 1955. For electronic reconnaissance, the RB-66C carried a specially-equipped four-crew pod in place of the bomb-bay. The first flight was on October 29, 1955 and 36 were built. Final production variant was the WB-66D for weather reconnaissance, with a crew of two in the equipment pod. Production totalled 36. The last B-66 was delivered in 1958. Primary operational deployment of the Destroyer is now in the electronic counter-measures and reconnaissance roles over Vietnam, and with the USAF in Europe. For operation in these specialised roles, the rear turret is removed and much new equipment installed, the modified aircraft being designated EB-66B (converted from B-66B), EB-66C (from RB-66C) or EB-66E (from RB-66B).

Douglas C-124 Globemaster II   *U.S.A.*

Long-range strategic transport, in service.

Photograph, data and silhouette: C-124C.

Powered by: Four 3,800hp Pratt & Whitney R-4360-63A piston-engines.
Span: 174ft 2in (53.08m).
Length: 130ft 5in (39.75m).
Empty weight: 101,165lb (45,890kg).
Gross weight: 194,500lb (88,223kg).
Max. speed: 304mph (490km/h) at 20,000ft (6,100m).
Range: 4,030 miles (6,485km) with 26,375lb (11,963kg) payload.
Accommodation: Crew of eight and 200 troops or 127 stretchers or 68,500lb (31,070kg) cargo.

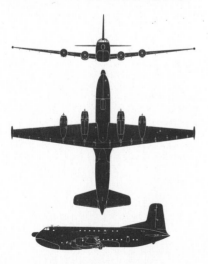

Douglas began work during World War II on a long-range heavy transport developed from the C-54 with accommodation for 125 passengers. Fifteen of these new transports, called C-74 Globemasters, were delivered between October 1945 and April 1947. Using the same wing, power plant and tail unit, the C-124 Globemaster II had a new deep-section fuselage with nose-loading doors in place of the rear-fuselage freight-lift of the C-74. The YC-124 flew on November 27, 1949 and later became YC-124B with new engines. The USAF took delivery of 204 C-124As, with 3,500hp R-4360-20WA engines, starting in May 1950, and these were followed by 243 C-124Cs with more powerful engines, nose radome for APS-42 weather radar and wingtip pods for combustion heaters. Delivery of the C-124Cs ended in May 1955. The type has served with most operational USAF Commands, with MATS (now MAC) and with the Air Force Reserve. From the beginning of 1968, the 160 Globemaster IIs still serving with MAC were gradually transferred to the AF Reserve and Air National Guard, and the type eventually equipped 14 Reserve and 10 ANG units.

Douglas C-133 Cargomaster   *U.S.A.*

Long-range strategic transport, in service.
Data, photograph and silhouette: C-133B.

Powered by: Four 7,500shp Pratt & Whitney T34-P-9WA turboprops.
Span: 179ft 8in (54.75m).
Length: 157ft 6in (48.0m).
Empty weight: 120,260lb (54,595kg).
Gross weight: 286,000lb (129,730kg).
Max. speed: 359mph (578km/h) at 8,500ft (2,590m).
Range: 4,030 miles (6,485km) with 51,850lb (23,550kg) payload.
Accommodation: Crew of ten and 200 troops or more than 110,000lb (49,895kg) of cargo.

The Cargomaster was born of an operational requirement for an aeroplane to carry outsize cargo, including missiles and special Army vehicles. Douglas won a design competition with their Model DTS-1333 design for this Support System SS402L and a USAF contract for 35 was placed in 1954. The first C-133A flew on April 23, 1956 and deliveries to MATS began 16 months later at Dover AFB. Flight trials led to a change of shape in the rear fuselage cone after the first seven aircraft had been built, and a change of power plant, from P-3 to 6,500shp P-7W or -7WA versions of the T34, was made during the production run. A second production contract covered 15 C-133Bs, which had new clam-shell rear-loading doors to permit carriage of the Titan missile, and P-9W engines. The first C-133B flew on October 31, 1959. All Cargomasters are used by Military Airlift Command at Dover AFB or Travis AFB. A reduction from three to two squadrons took effect in 1971 as the C-5A force built up.

English Electric Canberra
Great Britain

Data and silhouette: Canberra B.Mk.6.
Photograph: Canberra B. (I) Mk. 12.
Three-seat tactical light bomber, in service.

Powered by: Two 7,400lb (3,357kg) st Rolls-Royce Avon 109 turbojets.
Span: 63ft 11½in (19.51m).
Length: 65ft 6in (19.96m).
Max. speed: 580mph (933km/h) at 30,000ft (9,145m).
Gross weight: 55,000lb (24,950kg).
Range: 3,790 miles (6,100km).
Armament: As bomber carries 6,000lb (2,720kg) of weapons internally. Later aircraft modified to carry up to 1,000lb (455kg) of bombs, rocket pods or guided weapons under each wing.

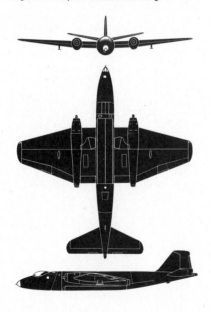

Over 100 Canberras remain in RAF service, and work is continuing on a rebuilding programme to supply ex-RAF aircraft to customers overseas. Canberra B.2s remain in service in Rhodesia; Ethiopia has four similar B.52s; Peru has B.72s and Venezuela uses B.82s. B.6s serve in Ecuador and similar B.(I) 56s in Peru, with B.(I) 78s in Peru and B.(I) 88s in Venezuela. The B.(I) 12 is a version of the Mk.8 sold to New Zealand and South Africa; the B. (I) Mk.58 for the Indian Air Force is similar and B.(I) 12s have also been acquired by India from New Zealand. Latest deliveries have included B.Mk.62s for Argentina and B.Mk. 66s for India.

Photographic reconnaissance versions for the RAF were the Canberra PR.Mk.7, with Avon 109s, and the PR.Mk.9, now the RAF's only variant in front-line service, with 11,000lb (4,990kg) st Avon 206 engines, offset canopy, increased span (67ft 10in; 20.67m) and additional tailplane area for higher operating altitudes. India acquired ten PR.Mk. 57s, similar to the PR.7s, and Venezuela has some PR.83s. Canberra trainers include the RAF's T.Mk.4 based on the B.Mk.2 with full dual control, also sold to India, Venezuela (T.84), Rhodesia, South Africa and Peru (T.74); the similar T.Mk.13 for the RNZAF and the RAF's T.Mk.17 ECM trainer. Other trainer variants are the T.Mk.64 for Argentina and T.Mk.67 for India. The TT.Mk.18 (16 converted) is an RAF target tug and the T.Mk.19 is a "silent target" based on the T.Mk.11. The RAF also uses the E.Mk.15 for special radar and radio calibration duties, and delivery of seven T.Mk.22s began in 1973, for a special RN training rôle as a radar target.

Australia built 49 Canberra B.Mk.20 and seven T.Mk.21. More than 400 derivatives of the Canberra were also built in the USA (see page 92) bringing total production to 1,385.

Fairchild C-119 Flying Boxcar U.S.A.

Tactical transport and gunship, in service. Data apply to C-119K.
Photograph: C-119G.

Powered by: Two 3,700hp Wright R-3350-999 piston-engines, plus two 2,850lb (1,293kg) st General Electric J85-GE-17 turbojets.
Span: 109ft 3in (33.30m).
Length: 86ft 6in (26.36m).
Empty weight: 44,747lb (20,300kg).
Gross weight: 77,000lb (34,925kg).
Max. speed: 243mph (391km/h) at 10,000ft (3,050m).
Range: 990 miles (1,595km) with max. payload.
Accommodation: Crew of four and 62 troops or 20,000lb (9,070kg) of cargo.

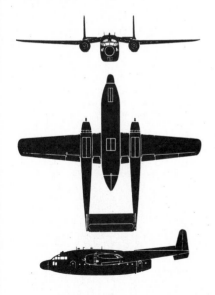

A total of 1,112 Flying Boxcars were built for the USAF and for countries associated with the Mutual Aid Programme. The type originated in 1947 as an outgrowth of the similar C-82 Packet and was then designated XC-82B. Modifications included a change of power plant from Pratt & Whitney R-2800s to R-4360s, and a new nose design with the flight deck further forward and lower than before. Production versions for the USAF comprised the C-119B and C, with R-4360 engines, and the C-119F and G, which switched to R-3350s. The US Navy had 39 C-119Bs as R4Q-1 (now out of service) and 58 C-119Fs as R4Q-2, now redesignated C-119F. Other users of the C-119 include the air forces of India, Morocco, South Vietnam, Italy and Nationalist China. During 1963–64, 26 of the Indian Air Force machines were modified to Steward-Davis Jet Packet standard by having a Westinghouse J34-WE-36 auxiliary turbojet mounted above the fuselage. More powerful Orpheus turbojets have since replaced the J34s.

In February 1967, Fairchild flew a YC-119K prototype, with J85 jet pods under the wings. This was followed by USAF contracts for the conversion of 26 C-119Gs to AC-119G "Shadow" armed configuration and 26 to AC-119Ks, both armed and jet-podded. The "Shadows" each carry four side-firing 7.62mm Miniguns and target illuminating devices, plus two 20mm cannon on the "Ks". Eight C-119Gs were converted into unarmed C-119Ks and supplied through MAP to the Ethiopian Air Force. The Air Force Reserve had two C-119 transport units in 1972, equipped with C-119J conversions of C-119Fs with "beaver-tail" rear doors.

Fairchild C-123 Provider   *U.S.A.*

Tactical transport, in service.
Data and silhouette: C-123K.

Powered by: Two 2,300hp Pratt & Whitney
R-2800-99W piston-engines and two 2,850lb
(1,293kg) st General Electric J85-GE-17 turbojets.
Span: 110ft 0in (33.53m).
Length: 76ft 3in (23.92m).
Empty weight: 35,366lb (16,042kg).
Gross weight: 60,000lb (27,215kg).
Max. speed: 228mph (367km/h) at 10,000ft
(3,050m).
Normal range: 1,035 miles (1,666km) with
15,000lb (6,800kg) payload.
Accommodation: Crew of two and 61 troops,
50 stretchers or 24,000lb (10,886kg) of freight.

This tactical assault transport was derived
from a cargo glider designed in 1949 by
Chase Aircraft. After building two XG-20
prototypes, Chase modified one into a
powered transport called the XC-123 Avi-
truc, first flown on October 14, 1949. Five
pre-production C-123Bs were built for
Chase at Willow Run by the Kaiser-Frazer
Corporation in 1953, after which the production contract was transferred to Fairchild.
As the C-123B Provider, Fairchild flew the
first of 300 on September 1, 1954. Six of
these were diverted to Saudi Arabia, 18 to
Venezuela and about four to Thailand.
Stroukoff Aviation, formed by the original
designer of the XG-20, produced two C-123
prototypes, the YC-123D with suction slots
for BLC, and the YC-123E with a Pantobase
undercarriage. In 1962, Fairchild added a
General Electric CJ-610 podded turbojet
under each wing of the single YC-123H,
which had been built to test a wide-track
undercarriage. First flown on July 30, 1962,
it was tested subsequently in South Vietnam
in the counter-insurgency role. A modification programme was put in hand for the
conversion of 183 aircraft to similar standard
with J85 engines in the pods, and the first
of these, designated C-123K, flew on May
27, 1966. This conversion programme was
completed in September 1969, and most of
the aircraft were deployed to Vietnam. Ten
C-123Js had Fairchild J44 jets in wingtip
pods for operation by the USAF (later ANG)
in Alaska. Other Providers adapted for
special duties in Vietnam, including
spraying defoliating liquids, were designated UC-123B and UC-123K. By early
1972, all but one squadron of C-123s in
Vietnam had been taken over by the RVNAF.

Fairey (Westland) Gannet   *Great Britain*

Data, photograph and silhouette: Gannet AEW. Mk.3.
Three-seat airborne early-warning monoplane, in service.

Powered by: One 3,875ehp Bristol Siddeley Double Mamba 102 turboprop.
Span: 54ft 6in (16.56m).
Length: 44ft 0in (13.41m).
Gross weight (estimated): 24,000lb (10,886kg).
Max. speed (estimated): 250mph (402km/h) at 5,000ft (1,525m).
Range (estimated): 800 miles (1,287km).
Armament: None.

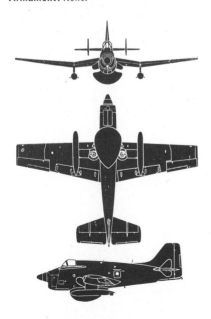

The Gannet AEW.Mk.3 was developed from the anti-submarine versions of the Gannet to provide the Royal Navy with a replacement for its Douglas Skyraiders in the specialised role of providing early warning of an impending attack by enemy aircraft on the Fleet at sea. Extensive changes were necessary in the fuselage, to permit installation of the electronic equipment and two operators in a midships cabin. The jet-pipe system of the anti-submarine Gannet, passing through the centre-fuselage and exhausting aft of the wing on each side, had to be exchanged for shorter pipes passing under the wing leading-edges, above the large ventral radome. The vertical tail surfaces were enlarged, and pylons were added for two underwing fuel tanks. The prototype of the resulting Gannet AEW.3 flew for the first time on August 20, 1958, and the first of 43 production models followed on December 2, 1958. Deliveries were completed by Westland after they took over Fairey's aircraft factories in 1960. The first few Gannet 3s went to No. 700G Flight in August 1959 for intensive flying trials, and this unit was reconstituted as "A" Flight of No. 849 Squadron in February 1960, with headquarters at Brawdy. No. 849 provided detached flights on board each Royal Navy carrier during its periods at sea. About a dozen aircraft remain in commission to serve from HMS *Ark Royal*. The AEW radars from other Gannet 3s have been transferred to the RAF for use in Shackleton AEW.Mk.2s.

FMA I.A.58 Pucara

Argentina

Counter-insurgency attack aircraft, in production.

Powered by: Two 1,022shp Turboméca Astazou XVIG turboprops.
Span: 47ft 6¾in (14.50m).
Length: 46ft 3in (14.10m).
Max. speed: 323mph (520km/h).
Range: 1,890 miles (3,042km).
Accommodation: Two seats in tandem.
Armament: Two 20mm Hispano cannon and four 7.62mm FN machine-guns in fuselage. Three strong points under fuselage and wings.

The Pucara is the latest product of the Argentinian Military Aircraft Factory (the Fábrica Militar de Aviones) at Cordoba. It is a counter-insurgency and light tactical aircraft designed to meet the requirements of the Argentine Air Force, which is reported to have planned to acquire 50 production examples. Flight testing of the design (originally named the Delfin) began with a full-scale unpowered prototype, with dummy engines and fixed undercarriage, which was first flown on December 26, 1967. This was followed by a powered prototype with 904shp Garrett-AiResearch TPE 331-U-303 engines, first flown on August 20, 1969, and a second prototype with 1,022shp Turboméca Astazou XVIG engines, first flown on September 6, 1970. A pre-production batch of five was under construction in 1972.

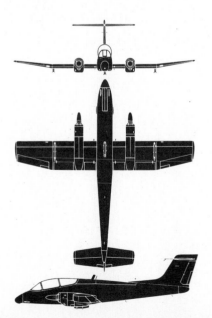

Fokker-VFW F.27M Troopship   *Netherlands*

Short/medium-range military transport aircraft, in production and service. Data for Mk.400M.

Powered by: Two 2,210shp Rolls-Royce Dart R.Da.7 Mk.532-7 turboprops.
Span: 95ft 2in (29.00m).
Length: 77ft 3½in (23.56m).
Empty weight: 23,430lb (10,628kg).
Gross weight: 45,000lb (20,410kg).
Normal cruising speed: 302mph (486km/h) at 20,000ft (6,100m).
Range: 1,285 miles (2,000km) with max. payload.
Accommodation: Crew of two or three and up to 45 troops, or freight.

Although it is best-known as a 40/56-seat airliner, the F.27 Friendship—built by Fokker-VFW in Holland and Fairchild in America—is also in service as a military transport. The Royal Netherlands Air Force has three more-or-less standard Friendship airliners and the Philippine Air Force has one. In addition, the RNAF has nine F.27M Troopships with accommodation for 45 paratroops, 13,800lb (6,260kg) of freight or 24 litter patients and 7 attendants in an air ambulance role. The Troopship has a large cargo door at the front on the port side and an enlarged rear cabin door, for parachuting, on each side. Four were supplied to the Sudanese Air Force in 1965 and the Argentine Air Force ordered ten in 1968, primarily for use by LADE, an Air Force organisation which provides regular air transport services in underdeveloped areas of Argentina. The Uruguayan Air Force has acquired two F.27s, together with two Fairchild FH-227Bs, and the Imperial Iranian Air Force has taken delivery of 14 F.27s. Late in 1971, Nigeria ordered six F.27s from Fokker. Others are used in military markings as VIP transports, in places such as the Ivory Coast.

Friendships are available with either 1,720shp Dart 514 turboprops or more powerful Dart 532s, as described above. In the Series 500 Friendship, the fuselage has been "stretched", to give an overall length of 82ft 2½in (25.06m).

53

GAF Nomad 22

Australia

STOL utility transport, in production.

Powered by: Two 400shp Allison 250-B17 turboprops.
Span: 54ft 0in (16.46m).
Length: 41ft 2¼in (12.56m).
Empty weight: 4,330lb (1,964kg).
Gross weight: 8,000lb (3,628kg).
Max. cruising speed: 199mph (320km/h).
Range: 731 miles (1,175km)
Accommodation: Two pilots and up to 13 persons in cabin.

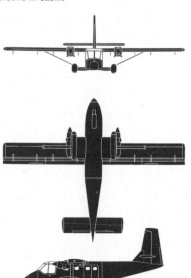

Design of a small utility transport with both military and civil applications began at the Government Aircraft Factories at Fishermen's Bend in 1965, this being the first full-scale design project of the GAF. Previously the Factories had built a number of European aircraft under licence, including the Canberra and Mirage, and had developed and produced the Jindivik target and the Ikara anti-submarine weapon. The transport design was designated Project N and evolved as a conventional high-wing aircraft with single fin and rudder, retractable undercarriage, and emphasis upon simple construction and ease of operation. Two prototypes were built, making their first flights respectively on July 23 and December 5, 1971, and these subsequently became known as Nomad 22s. During 1972, an initial production batch of 20 was ordered by the Australian government, of which 11 are earmarked for service with the Australian Army Aviation Corps. With deliveries due to begin early in 1974, the military Nomad 22 has ejection seats for the two pilots and armour protection around the flight deck. During 1972 one N22 prototype was under conversion to Nomad N24 standard with fuselage lengthened by 5ft (1.52m).

General Dynamics F-111 *U.S.A.*

Two-seat tactical fighter, in production and service.
Data: F-111E. Photograph: F-111F.

Powered by: Two 21,000lb (9,525kg) st Pratt & Whitney TF30-P-3 afterburning turbofans.
Span: 63ft 0in (19.20m) spread; 31ft 11½in (9.74m) swept.
Length: 73ft 6in (22.40m).
Empty weight: 47,500lb (21,545kg).
Max. gross weight: 91,500lb (41,500kg).
Max. speed: Mach 2.5 (1,650mph; 2,655km/h) at 36,000ft (11,000m).
Tactical radius: About 1,600 miles (2,575km) with 16,000lb (7,257kg) combat load.
Armament: No fixed armament; up to eight bombs or missiles under wings, plus fuselage weapon bay which can carry bombs or a 20mm M-61A1 multi-barrel cannon.

Two-and-a-half years after the joint USAF/USN TFX requirement was formulated, General Dynamics' Fort Worth Division was named the winner of a final competitive evaluation of its design and one by the Boeing company. Initial contracts were for 18 F-111A (USAF) and 5 F-111B (USN) for development flying; these were followed by production of several variants for the USAF. The Navy's F-111B was abandoned after production of seven aircraft, including the five development models. The first F-111A flew on December 21, 1964, and the variable-sweep wing was operated on the second flight, on January 6, 1965. The first F-111A (a trials aircraft) delivered for service went to a training unit, the 4,480th TF Wing, in July 1967. The first operational unit was the 474th TFW, which received its first aircraft (the 31st F-111A) in October. Production of the F-111A totalled 141, followed by 94 F-111Es which have revised intake geometry. The first of these swing-wing aircraft deployed to Europe were F-111Es assigned to the 20th TFW at Upper Heyford in September 1970. These were followed by 96 F-111Ds, with uprated avionics, and 82 F-111Fs, with 25,000lb (11,340kg) st TF30-P-100 turbofans to equip two more TAF Wings, the 27th and 374th respectively. Two F-111Ks, intended for but not delivered to the RAF, went to USAF as YF-111As; one development aircraft was flown as RF-111A, and the RAAF has ordered 24 F-111C strike aircraft, of which delivery was to begin in 1973. (See page 56 for FB-111).

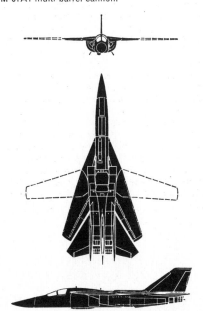

General Dynamics FB-111A

U.S.A.

Two-seat strategic bomber, in service.

Powered by: Two 20,350lb (9,230kg) st Pratt & Whitney TF30-P-7 afterburning turbofans.
Span: 70ft 0in (21.34m) spread; 33ft 11in (10.34m) swept.
Length: 73ft 6in (22.40m).
Gross weight (estimated): 100,000lb (45,360kg).
Max. speed: Mach 2.5 (1,650mph; 2,655km/h) at 36,000ft (11,000m).
Armament: External points for up to six 2,200lb (1,000kg) Boeing AGM-69A SRAM short-range attack missiles, or up to 37,500lb (17,000kg) of conventional weapons. Typical load comprises two 750lb bombs in internal weapon-bay and 48 in twin clusters of three on eight underwing attachments with wings at 26° sweep. (Only 20 such bombs can be carried at full wing-sweep.)

The FB-111A was derived from the original swing-wing F-111 (page 55) to provide Strategic Air Command of the USAF with an advanced supersonic bomber to supplement its B-52 force. Procurement of as many as 253 FB-111As was planned originally, but development hold-ups, cost escalation and changes in the US strategic posture led to successive reductions to a total production run of 76, completed in 1971, to equip only two wings. The FB-111A airframe is a hybrid, using the larger wing, with six pylons, developed originally for the Navy's F-111B, with the fuselage and intakes of the F-111E. It also has a new avionics fit, higher gross weight, beefed-up structure and landing gear, and uprated engines. The FB-111A prototype was a conversion of the last F-111A development airframe (No. 18), first flown on July 30, 1967. Two other modified F-111As were used in the development programme before the first flight of the first production FB-111A on July 13, 1968 (fitted temporarily with TF30-P-3 engines). The first SAC unit to equip with the new bomber was the 340th Bomb Group at Carswell AFB, on October 8, 1969; this unit provides combat crew training for the two two-squadron wings which are equipped with the FB-111A—the 50th Bomb Wing at Pease AFB, NH, and the 380th Strategic Aerospace Wing at Plattsburgh, NY.

Grumman A-6 Intruder   *U.S.A.*

Two-seat carrier-based strike and reconnaissance aircraft, in production and service.
Data, photograph and silhouette: A-6A.

Powered by: Two 9,300lb (4,218kg) st Pratt & Whitney J52-P-8A turbojets.
Span: 53ft 0in (16.15m).
Length: 54ft 7in (16.64m).
Empty weight: 25,684lb (11,650kg).
Max. gross weight: 60,626lb (27,500kg).
Max. speed: Mach 0.9 (685mph; 1,102km/h) at sea level.
Armament: Up to 15,000lb (6,805kg) of assorted stores on four underwing attachments and in a semi-recessed fuselage bay.

US Navy and Marine Corps experience in Korea led to a new requirement for a long-range, all-weather low-altitude attack aircraft, able to carry a heavy load of conventional or nuclear weapons. A design competition was held in May 1957 and Grumman was named the winner at the end of that year. Features of the Grumman design, originally called A2F-1, included tilting tailpipes on the engines, to help shorten take-off distances, but this was regarded as an unacceptable complication for carrier operation and production aircraft have a fixed downward tilt on the jet pipes. The Intruder has a digital integrated attack navigation system (DIANE), which can fly the aircraft and deliver its weapons automatically. Apart from weapons, the A-6 can carry four 300 US gallon (1,135 litre) external fuel tanks under the wings and a buddy refuelling pack under the fuselage. The US Navy ordered eight Intruders for trials and the first flew on April 19, 1960. By early 1970, about 450 Intruders had been delivered, almost all being A-6As for US Navy and Marine Corps squadrons. Other variants are the A-6B, modified to carry weapons such as the AGM-78A Standard ARM anti-radar missile; the A-6C with special electro-optical sensors in an under-fuselage pack; the KA-6D shipboard flight-refuelling tanker; and the A-6E which has uprated avionics. The first A-6E flew on February 27, 1970 and deliveries began early in 1971. Three A-6A prototypes were used as flight refuelling tankers in the F-14A flight test programme and were designated NA-6As. The EA-6A and -6B are described separately (page 60).

Grumman C-2A Greyhound *U.S.A.*

Naval transport, in service.

Powered by: Two 4,050eshp Allison T56-A-8A turboprops.
Span: 80ft 7in (24.56m).
Length: 56ft 8in (17.27m).
Empty weight: 31,154lb (14,131kg).
Gross weight: 54,830lb (24,870kg).
Max. speed: 352mph (567km/h).
Range: 1,650 miles (2,660km) at 297mph (478 km/h) at 27,300ft (8,320m).
Accommodation: Up to 39 troops, 20 litters and four attendants or 10,000lb (4,535kg) of cargo.
Armament: None.

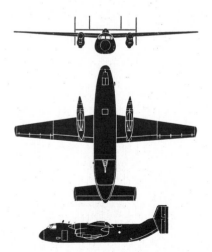

Grumman developed the C-2A under US Navy contract as a carrier on-board delivery (COD) aircraft, taking the E-2A Hawkeye (see p. 59) as the basis for the design. The wing, main landing gear, flight deck and tail unit are basically the same as the equivalent components of the E-2A, the fuselage being the obvious new feature. This has been designed to seat up to 39 passengers in a high-density layout, and can also accommodate a wide variety of typical stores and supplies used on an aircraft carrier, including spare jet engines, small vehicles and standard US freight pallets. Loading doors and a ramp are incorporated in the rear fuselage. The initial US Navy order was for three C-2A airframes, including one for static testing. The first prototype flew on November 18, 1964, and the Navy began accepting production C-2As in 1966. Production of an initial batch of 17 ended in 1968; procurement of a further eight C-2As was included in the FY 1970 budget, bringing total production to 25.

Grumman E-2 Hawkeye   *U.S.A.*

Five-seat carrier-borne airborne early warning and fighter control aircraft, in service.
Data and Photograph: E-2C. Silhouette: E-2B.

Powered by: Two 4,050eshp Allison T56-A-8A turboprops.
Span: 80ft 7in (24.56m).
Length: 57ft 7in (17.55m).
Empty weight: 37,616lb (17,062kg).
Gross weight: 51,490lb (23,355kg).
Max. speed: Over 363mph (584km/h).
Ferry range: 1,722 miles (2,771km) with full internal fuel.
Armament: None.

Like the E-1 which it was designed to succeed, the E-2 carries a large saucer-shaped radome above the fuselage, and a mass of electronic devices to process the information provided by the radar. The complete installation is called Airborne Tactical Data System—ATDS—and the information provided by it is transmitted to a Naval Tactical Data System. Taking information from a team of E-2s disposed around a Naval task force, the NTDS can assess and act upon the threat of attack from any direction.

An aerodynamic prototype of the E-2 flew on October 21, 1960, followed by the first with full electronic equipment on April 19, 1961. Deliveries began on January 19, 1964, and the first Hawkeye unit, VAW-11, became operational in 1966, followed by VAW-12, both squadrons providing detached flights on board operational aircraft carriers. Production of the E-2A ended in 1967 with a total of 59 built. Between 1969 and 1971, the entire Hawkeye force was modified to E-2B standard by installation of an updated general-purpose computer of increased capacity. A further development is the E-2C, which has a completely revised electronic system. A prototype flew on January 20, 1971 and a second followed later in the year. An initial production contract for 11 E-2Cs has been placed and follow-on orders are planned; the first production E-2C flew on September 23, 1972.

Grumman EA-6B Prowler   *U.S.A.*

Four-seat carrier-based electronic countermeasures aircraft, in production and service.

Powered by: Two 9,300lb (4,218kg) st Pratt & Whitney J52-P-8A turbojets.
Span: 53ft 0in (16.15m).
Length: 59ft 5in (18.11m).
Empty weight: 34,581lb (15,686kg).
Max. gross weight: 58,500lb (26,535kg).
Max. speed: approx. 600mph (966km/h).
Armament: Normally unarmed; external weapons attachment points retained as on A-6A.
Accommodation: Pilot, navigator and two radar operators.

A version of the Intruder (see page 57) intended specifically for electronic countermeasures duties was developed soon after the basic A-6A had entered service in 1963. Designated EA-6A, this was selected for operation by the US Marine Corps and differed in having an extensive array of special electronic detection and jamming devices, carried internally, in pods on the fuselage and underwing strongpoints and in a new radome atop the fin. A prototype, converted from an A-6A, flew in 1963 and 27 production EA-6As were built. To further enhance the ECM capability of the aircraft, the EA-6B was then developed, having a new front fuselage section incorporating two additional seats for radar/ECM operators. The avionic equipment was also revised and updated. First flight of a prototype was made on May 25, 1968 and nearly 50 EA-6Bs had been ordered up to mid-1972. After entering service, this variant was named Prowler to avoid confusion with the Intruder attack versions of the A-6.

Grumman F-14 Tomcat   *U.S.A.*

Two-seat carrier-borne air superiority and general-purpose fighter, in production and service. Data: F-14A.

Powered by: Two 20,600lb (9.344kg) st Pratt & Whitney TF30-P-412 afterburning turbofans.
Span: 64ft 1½in (19.54m) spread; 38ft 2in (10.12m) swept.
Length: 61ft 10½in (18.86m).
Empty weight: 37,500lb (17,010kg).
Max. gross weight: 66,200lb (30,028kg).
Max. speed: Over Mach 2.
Armament: One General Electric M61-A1 multi-barrel gun in port side of front fuselage. Four missile bays semi-recessed under fuselage for Sparrow or, later, Phoenix air-to-air missiles. Two underwing pick-ups for a combination of a fuel tank and two Sidewinder air-to-air missiles on each pylon.

The US Navy issued a Request for Proposals for a new carrier-based air superiority fighter to five US aerospace companies on June 21, 1968. The requirement, identified originally as the VFX, was triggered by failure of the GD/Grumman F-111B to meet Navy requirements. From the initial proposals, the Navy selected Grumman and McDonnell Douglas, on December 17, 1968, for final competition, as a result of which the Grumman design was selected on January 15, 1969. Since that date, the company has received two contracts, each for six development aircraft, and production contracts for 74 aircraft. Present procurement plans are for another 48 F-14As to be acquired by the Navy.

The first F-14A made its first flight on December 21, 1970, but was lost on its second flight. Testing resumed on May 24, 1971, and seven more of the test aircraft flew during that year. Development of an F-14B version had been planned, with more powerful F401-P-400 engines, but rising costs have cast doubts on the completion of planned procurement of 179 of this model. The first two F-14A squadrons were commissioned at NAS Miramar on October 12, 1972.

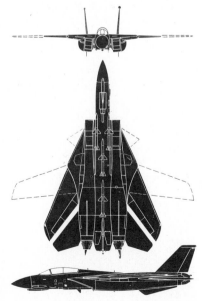

Grumman OV-1 Mohawk
U.S.A.

Two-seat observation aircraft, in service.
Data and photograph: OV-1D. Silhouette: OV-1B.

Powered by: Two 1,150eshp Lycoming T53-L-701 turboprops.
Span: 48ft 0in (14.63m).
Length: 41ft 0in (12.50m).
Empty weight: 12,054lb (5,467kg).
Gross weight: 18,109lb (8,214kg).
Max. speed: 308mph (496km/h) at 5,000ft (1,520m).
Range: 1,010 miles (1,625km) with external tanks.
Armament: Six wing strong-points allow for pylon-mounted bombs, rockets, etc., if required.

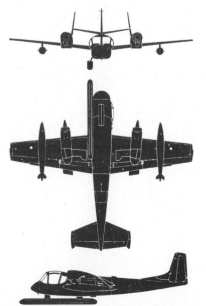

Designed originally to meet joint US Army and Marine Corps requirements, the Mohawk is now exclusively an Army aircraft, and was the first turboprop-engined type to go into service with the US Army. The primary mission for which it was designed (as the Grumman G-134) was tactical observation and battlefield surveillance in direct support of Army operations, flying from unprepared fields and having a STOL performance. Initial contracts were for nine test aircraft designated YAO-1AF (later YOV-1A); the first of these flew on April 14, 1959. Production models were the OV-1A, primarily for photographic reconnaissance; the OV-1B with SLAR (side-looking airborne radar) in a long container under the fuselage, and the OV-1C with infra-red mapping gear. Deliveries to the Army began in 1961 and production of the three models totalled 64, 101 and 133 respectively. During 1968, four Mohawks were completed to OV-1D standard, as described above, with provision for conversion between SLAR and infra-red modes; this version also added a third photographic system, comprising a vertical, panoramic camera. Production of 37 OV-1Ds followed successful evaluation of the prototypes. One OV-1B was evaluated by the *Luftwaffe* in 1964, but no procurement followed.

Grumman S-2 Tracker   *U.S.A.*

Four-seat carrier-based anti-submarine attack aircraft, in service.
Data and silhouette: S-2E. Photograph: CS2F-2.

Powered by: Two 1,525hp Wright R-1820-82WA piston-engines.
Span: 72ft 7in (22.13m).
Length: 43ft 6in (13.26m).
Empty weight: 18,750lb (8,505kg).
Gross weight: 29,150lb (13,222kg).
Max. speed: 265mph (426km/h) at sea level.
Ferry range: 1,300 miles (2,095km).
Armament: 60 echo-sounding depth charges in fuselage; one Mk.101 or Mk.57 nuclear depth bomb or similar store in bomb bay; 32 sonobuoys in nacelles; four float lights; six underwing pylons for 5-inch rockets, torpedoes, etc.

First flown on December 4, 1952, the S2F-1 (as the Grumman G-89 was originally designated) went into production for the US Navy for combined "hunter-killer" operations in the anti-submarine role. Of

755 S-2As built, over 100 were for export to Argentina, Brazil, Italy, Japan, the Netherlands, Taiwan, Thailand and Uruguay, and are still serving with all these nations. The S2F-1T (later TS-2A) was used as a trainer. The 60 S-2Cs (S2F-2s) had enlarged bombbays to accommodate two homing torpedoes and have mostly been converted to US-2C utility aircraft. The S-2D (originally S2F-3) had an 18in (45cm) front fuselage extension, a 35in (89cm) greater span, a wider cockpit and improved equipment. Production totalled 119, and deliveries began in May 1961. In October 1962, the S-2E succeeded the S-2D, with more advanced ASW equipment. Similar equipment added to early S-2As changed their designation to S-2B and, with further modifications, to S-2F. In 1972, Martin Marietta produced a prototype S-2G and kits for 49 more to be converted by the USN, this version having updated equipment for interim use until the S-3A enters service.

Production of the S-2E ended in 1968 with a batch of 14 for the RAN. The Royal Canadian Navy obtained 100 Trackers built by D.H. Canada, of which 17 later went to the Netherlands; the first 43, starting in January 1957, were CS2F-1s and the final 57, starting in October 1958, were CS2F-2s, with improved equipment.

Based on the S-2D, Grumman developed the TF-1 Trader as a nine-seat transport for COD duty; the 87 built were later redesignated C-1A and four TF-1Qs became EC-1As. Another derivative of the Tracker was the E-1B (originally WF-2) Tracer, with APS-82 search radar in a large radome above the fuselage, and new tail unit. Production totalled 88; most have been replaced by E-2 Hawkeyes.

Handley Page Victor

Great Britain

Five-seat flight refuelling tanker, in service.
Photograph and data: Victor K.Mk.2.
Silhouette: Victor K.Mk.1A.

Powered by: Four 20,600lb (9,344kg) st Rolls-Royce Conway R.Co.17 Mk.201 turbojets.
Span: 120ft 0in (36.6m).
Length: 114ft 11in (35.0m).
Gross weight: Over 170,000lb (77,110kg).
Max. speed: Over Mach 0.92 (600mph; 966km/h) at 40,000ft (12,000m).
Max. range: 4,600 miles (7,400km).
Armament: None.

Developed to a similar specification to that for the Hawker Siddeley Vulcan, the prototype Victor (WB771) flew on December 24, 1952, and was followed by a second (WB775) on September 11, 1954; both had early type Sapphire turbojets. The first production Victor B.Mk.1 bomber flew on February 1, 1956, and differed from the prototypes by having a lengthened fuselage, no dorsal fin and 11,000lb (4,990kg) st Sapphire 200s. Deliveries to the RAF began in 1958, production of 50 aircraft being sufficient to equip four squadrons. Late production aircraft were designated B.Mk.1A, signifying equipment changes and the addition of ECM radar in the rear fuselage, and all were eventually converted to this standard. Subsequently, six were modified to B(K)1A two-point flight refuelling tankers and 25 others to K.1 or K.1A three-point tankers. The B.Mk.2 (first flown on February 20, 1959) had Rolls-Royce Conway turbojets and the wing span increased from 110ft (33.5m) to 120ft. Deliveries to No. 139 Squadron began late in 1961 and this was the first Victor unit to become operational with the Blue Steel missile in February 1964, 21 of the 34 production B.2s being converted for this role. Another eight were modified for strategic reconnaissance duties as Victor SR.2, with No. 543 Squadron, and were still in service in 1972, although earmarked for replacement by Vulcans. Twenty-nine B.Mk.2s are under conversion to K.Mk.2 tanker configuration by Hawker Siddeley.

Hawker Hunter

Great Britain

Single-seat fighter and two-seat trainer, in service.
Data, photograph and silhouette: Hunter FGA.Mk.9.

Powered by: One 10,000lb (4,540kg) st Rolls-Royce Avon 207 turbojet.
Span: 33ft 8in (10.26m).
Length: 45ft 10½in (13.98m).
Gross weight: 24,000lb (10,885kg).
Max. speed: Mach 0.92 (710mph; 1,140km/h) at sea level.
Range: 1,840 miles (2,965km) with external tanks.
Armament: Four 30mm cannon in nose; underwing attachments for two 1,000lb bombs, or two packs each containing up to 37 × 2in rockets, or 12 × 3in rockets on inner pylons, plus up to 24 × 3in rockets outboard.

As the Hawker P.1067, the prototype Hunter (WB188) first flew on July 20, 1951. The Avon-powered F.Mk.1 made its first flight on May 16, 1953, and aircraft of this mark equipped the first RAF squadron, No. 43, in mid-1954. This version is no longer in service; nor are the Sapphire-powered F.Mk.2 and 5. The Mk.1 was superseded in production by the F.Mk.4, with Avon 115, more internal fuel and provision for underwing weapons or fuel tanks, and this mark saw service in Denmark (F.Mk.51) and Peru (F.Mk.52). It was followed by the F.Mk.6 (prototype first flown January 22, 1954), with Avon 203, and export versions are still flying in India (FGA.Mk.56), Switzerland (F.Mk.58), Iraq (F.Mk.6), Lebanon, Jordan and Saudi Arabia. Final version in RAF service is the FGA.Mk.9, a ground attack development of the Mk.6 with tail parachute and increased weapon load, equipping two squadrons. Versions of the Mk.9 serve with the Rhodesian, Jordanian (FGA.Mk.73), Chilean (FGA.Mk.71), Iraqi (FGA.Mk.59) and Kuwait (FGA.Mk.57) Air Forces. Singapore has twelve FGA.74s and four FR.74s, with more on order; the Sheikhdom of Abu Dhabi acquired ten FGA.Mk.76 and FR.Mk.76As, and two two-seat T.Mk.76As. Four Mk.78 have been supplied to Qatar. Other side-by-side two-seat trainer versions of the Hunter include the RAF's T.Mk.7 and Royal Navy's T.Mk.8, and variants delivered to the Netherlands, Denmark (T.Mk.53), Peru (T.Mk.62), India (T.Mk.66), Iraq (T.Mk. 69), Chile, Kuwait (T. Mk.67), Jordan (T.Mk. 66B) and Singapore (T.Mk.75). The Royal Navy's GA.Mk.11 was a conversion of the Mk.4 for use as a single-seat advanced ground attack trainer. Late in 1970 Switzerland ordered 30 refurbished Hunters, for final assembly by the Federal Aircraft Factory, with delivery starting in late 1972. Thirty more have been ordered subsequently.

Hawker Siddeley Andover   *Great Britain*

Short/medium-range turboprop transport, in service.
Data, photograph and silhouette: Andover C.Mk.1.

Powered by: Two 3,245ehp Rolls-Royce Dart R.Da.12 Mk.201 turboprops.
Span: 98ft 6in (30.02m).
Length: 78ft 0in (23.77m).
Gross weight: 50,000lb (22,680m).
Max. speed: 302mph (486km/h) at 15,000ft (4,570m).
Range: 1,158 miles (1,865km) with max. fuel at 258mph (415km/h).
Accommodation: Crew of two or three; 44 troops, 30 paratroops, 18 stretchers and attendants or 15,350lb (6,963kg) of freight.

The Andover C.Mk.1 is a rear-loading military transport developed from the Hawker Siddeley 748 commercial airliner. The prototype of the commercial 748 Series 1 flew on June 24, 1960, and was followed on November 6, 1961, by the prototype Series 2 with more powerful (2,105ehp) Dart R.Da.7.Mk.531 engines. Specially-equipped Series 2s are operated by The Queen's Flight (two) and for passenger-carrying duties with the RAF (four), under the designation Andover CC.Mk.2 (see page 192).

The prototype Andover C.Mk.1 was built by extending the fuselage of the original prototype 748 and adding the revised tail, with straight-in loading ramp, and other modifications. It flew for the first time on December 21, 1963. The first of 31 genuine Andover C.Mk.1s made its first flight on July 9, 1965. No. 46 Squadron in No. 46 Group, Strike Command, is operating the type, which was also a mainstay of Air Forces Gulf until the British withdrawal in 1971.

The Andover C.Mk.1 has a variable landing gear, which allows the position of the cabin floor to be adjusted easily, in both the horizontal and vertical planes, to line up with the tail-board of the loading or unloading vehicle.

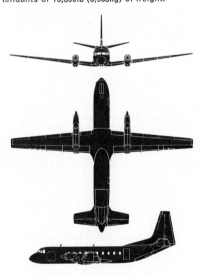

Hawker Siddeley Buccaneer   *Great Britain*

Two-seat carrier-borne and land-based low-level strike aircraft, in production and service.
Data, photograph and silhouette: Buccaneer S.Mk.2.

Powered by: Two 11,100lb (5,035kg) st Rolls-Royce RB.168 Spey Mk.101 turbofans.
Span: 44ft 0in (13.41m).
Length: 63ft 5in (19.33m).
Max. gross weight: 62,000lb (28,123kg).
Max. speed: Mach 0.85 (646mph; 1,038km/h) at 200ft (60m).
Typical strike range: 2,300 miles (3,700km).
Armament: Internal weapons-bay, with rotating door, for nuclear or conventional (four 1,000lb bombs, or camera pack; four underwing atttachments for Bullpup or Martel missiles, 1,000lb bombs (three on each pylon) or rocket packs. Max. weapon load 16,000lb (7,257kg).

Work on what was then known as the Blackburn B.103 began in the early 'fifties to meet the requirements of the Naval specification NA.39 for a carrier-launched aircraft capable of flying at transonic speed close to the ground or sea to strike at enemy objectives. A pre-production batch of 20 B.103s was ordered in July 1955 and the first of these flew on April 30, 1958. The name Buccaneer S.Mk.1 was adopted in August 1960.

A production order for 50 aircraft was placed in October 1959, and the first 40 of these were delivered as S.Mk.1s to equip Nos. 801, 809 and 800 Squadrons, starting in July 1962. The final 10 aircraft were completed as S.Mk.2s, with Speys replacing the 7,100lb (3,220kg) st Gyron Junior 101s in the first version. The prototype S.Mk.2 flew on May 17, 1963, followed by the first production model on June 6, 1964. Orders for 74 more S.Mk.2s were placed by the Royal Navy, and the type entered service with No. 801 Squadron in October 1965. Nos. 809, 800 and 803 were also equipped. Those remaining in Navy service are now designated S.Mk.2C (without Martel capability) or S.Mk.2D.

In 1968, the RAF ordered 26 Buccaneer S.Mk.2Bs, with revised equipment, a bomb-door fuel tank and provision for carrying Martel missiles, followed by a second contract for 16 in 1972. About 60 ex-Navy aircraft are being converted to S.Mk.2A (without Martel capability) or S.Mk.2B for the RAF. The first RAF Buccaneer squadron, No. 12, became operational in July 1970 and is one of four assigned to Strike Command. The first of three squadrons to fly the Buccaneer in Germany, No. 15, formed in October 1970. The South African Air Force has 13 Buccaneer S.Mk.50s with 8,000lb (3,630kg) st BS.605 twin-chamber auxiliary rocket engine.

67

Hawker Siddeley/HAL Gnat *Great Britain*

Data and silhouette: Gnat T.Mk.1.
Photograph: HAL Gnat Mk.1.
Two-seat advanced trainer, in service.

Powered by: One 4,400lb (1,996kg) st Bristol Siddeley Orpheus 101 turbojet.
Span: 24ft 0in (7.32m).
Length: 37ft 10in (11.51m).
Gross weight: 9,145lb (4,148kg).
Max. speed: Mach 0.95 (635mph; 1,023km/h) at 31,000ft (9,450m).
Range: 1,180 miles (1,900km) with external tanks.

The original single-seat Gnat lightweight fighter was evolved by the Folland Aircraft company as a private venture. The prototype flew for the first time on July 18, 1955, and this version, armed with two 30mm cannon and underwing racks for two 500lb bombs or 12 × 3in rockets, was supplied to the British Ministry of Aviation (6), India (25 and 15 sets of components), Finland (12) and Yugoslavia (2). The Gnat Mk.1 is also first-line equipment in India, where over 200 have so far been built under licence by Hindustan Aeronautics Ltd (HAL). In 1972, HAL gave details of its Gnat Mk.2 development, which will feature integral fuel tanks in the wings so that extra weapons can be carried under the wings in place of external fuel tanks.

Development of the Gnat two-seat trainer began in 1958, when an evaluation quantity of 14 was ordered for the RAF, and the first of these flew on August 31, 1959. The trainer is some 15 per cent bigger all round than the fighter, the increased wing area being necessary to give the low-speed handling characteristics needed in a trainer, and the lengthened fuselage making room for a second cockpit in tandem. The evaluation batch was followed by 91 production T.Mk.1s, the first of which were delivered in November 1962. These aircraft are standard equipment at No. 4 Flying Training School, RAF Training Command; as the mounts for the official aerobatic team of the RAF, the Red Arrows, they have become well-known throughout the world.

Hawker Siddeley Harrier   *Great Britain*

Single-seat V/STOL strike and reconnaissance aircraft, in production and service.
Data and silhouette: Harrier GR.Mk.1.
Photograph: AV-8A, Harrier GR.Mk.1 and T.Mk.2.

Powered by: One 19,000lb (8,620kg) st Rolls-Royce Bristol Pegasus 101 vectored-thrust turbofan.
Span: 25ft 3in (7.70m).
Length: 45ft 6in (13.87m).
Gross weight: VTOL approx. 16,000lb (7,257kg); STOL approx. 23,000lb (10,433kg); max. over 25,000lb (11,339kg).
Max. speed: over 737mph (1,186km/h).
Typical radius of action: 500 miles (805km).
Armament: Three under-fuselage and four underwing attachments for 5,000lb (2,268kg) of stores. Typical load includes a 1,000lb bomb and two 30mm gun pods under fuselage; two pods of nineteen 68mm SNEB rockets and two 1;000lb bombs under wings.

The Harrier is the operational development of the P.1127 Kestrel, first aircraft to utilise the Pegasus vectored-thrust turbofan. The four rotating exhaust nozzles on this engine make possible either vertical take-off and landing or, where a forward run is possible, short take-off with a heavier weapon load. The first of six pre-production Harriers made its first hovering flight on August 31, 1966, and all six were flying by mid-1967. The first of 77 single-seat Harrier GR.1s for the RAF flew on December 28, 1967, powered by the Pegasus 101 engine. Engines of this type were later modified to the more powerful Pegasus 102 standard, the aircraft being then designated GR.1As: a further change of engine to Pegasus 103 changes the designation to GR.3.

The RAF also acquired 13 tandem two-seat Harrier T.Mk.2s with revised front fuselage and tail unit; the first two two-seaters flew on April 24 and July 14, 1969, respectively. The same engine changes as described above change the designations to T.Mk. 2A and T.Mk. 4 respectively.

Deliveries to the RAF's Harrier Conversion Team began in April 1969, and No. 1 Squadron, the only Harrier unit in No. 38 Group of Strike Command, began working up on the type in the latter half of that year. Three Harrier squadrons are assigned to RAF Germany (Nos. 3, 4 and 20). The US Marine Corps received on January 6, 1971, the first of 90 Harriers ordered as AV-8As, and plans to buy 20 more. The first ten had Pegasus 10 (F402-RR-400) engines; the remainder have the 21,500lb st Pegasus 11 (F402-RR-401). Single-seat export models have Hawker Siddeley designation Harrier Mk. 50. The single Mk.52 is a two-seat demonstrator.

Hawker Siddeley Nimrod   *Great Britain*

Four-engined long-range anti-submarine aircraft, in production and service.

Powered by: Four 11,500lb (5,217kg) st Rolls-Royce Spey Mk.250 turbofans.
Span: 114ft 10in (35.0m).
Length: 126ft 9in (38.63m).
Gross weight (typical): 192,000lb (87,090kg).
Max. speed: 575mph (926km/h).
Typical ferry range: 5,755 miles (9,265km).
Armament: Mines, bombs, depth charges and torpedoes in weapon-bay. Two AS.12 or other missiles under wings.

First pure-jet aircraft built for anti-submarine duties anywhere in the world, the Nimrod has an airframe basically similar to that of the Comet 4C airliner, with an unpressurised pannier containing a huge weapon-bay added under the fuselage. The centre fuselage is fitted out as a navigational and tactical centre for the men who operate the wide range of submarine detection devices; these include sonar equipment, air-to-surface radar, Autolycus ionisation detector which "sniffs" the presence of any shipping below, magnetic anomaly detection (MAD) equipment in a tail "sting" which detects any metallic object on or under the water, and sonobuoys. There is a searchlight in the front of the fuel pod on the starboard wing leading-edge and an electronic countermeasures pod on the fin-tip. The 12-man crew includes three men on the flight deck, and two navigators and seven sensor operators in the forward cabin. Up to 45 passengers can be carried when the Nimrod is operated in its secondary trooping role.

The first of two prototype Nimrods, converted from Comet transports, flew on May 23, 1967. A total of 46 MR.Mk.1 production models has been ordered to replace the RAF's Shackletons and the first of these (XV226) flew on June 28, 1968. Deliveries to No. 201 Squadron of Strike Command, at Kinloss, began on October 2, 1969. Nimrods now equip five Strike Command squadrons, (Nos. 42, 120, 201, 203 and 206) and the OCU (No. 37). Three additional aircraft, designated Nimrod R.Mk.1, serve in an electronic reconnaissance role with No. 51 Squadron at RAF Wyton.

Hawker Siddeley Vulcan
Great Britain

Five-seat medium bomber, in service. Data, photograph and silhouette: Vulcan B.Mk.2.

Powered by: Four 20,000lb (9,072kg) st Rolls-Royce Bristol Olympus 301 turbojets.
Span: 111ft 0in (33.83m).
Length: 99ft 11in (30.45m).
Gross weight: Over 180,000lb (81,650kg).
Max. cruising speed: Over Mach 0.94 (625mph; 1,006km/h) at 50,000ft (15,250m).
Combat radius: 1,725-2,875 miles (2,780-4,630km.
Armament: No guns. Mk.2 can carry Blue Steel stand-off bomb, nuclear free-fall weapons or 21 × 1,000lb high-explosive bombs.

The prototype Avro 698 (VX770) made its first flight on August 30, 1952, and was powered by Rolls-Royce Avons. The second prototype (VX777) flew on September 3, 1953, and had Olympus 100 engines and the later-standard visual bomb-aiming station under the nose. Production Vulcan B.Mk.1s (45 built, commencing XA889) began to appear in February 1954, with Olympus 101, 102 or 104 engines. Deliveries to the RAF began in mid-1956, and Mk.1 and 1A (with electronics in bulged tailcone) eventually equipped three operational squadrons of RAF Bomber Command. On August 31, 1957, VX777 flew as the aerodynamic test vehicle for the Mk.2, with enlarged and modified wing. The first production Mk.2 (XH533) flew in August 1958 and deliveries to the RAF began on July 1, 1960, the first squadron equipped being 83. Following transfer of responsibility for Britain's nuclear deterrent to the Royal Navy's Polaris submarine force, only one squadron of Strike Command is now equipped with Vulcan Mk.2s armed with the Blue Steel stand-off bomb, this being No. 617 at Scampton, intended primarily for attack at low level. The other remaining Vulcan B.Mk.2 squadrons of Strike Command are Nos. 44 and 101, based at Waddington, and Nos. 9 and 35 at Akrotiri, Cyprus; these are intended primarily for tactical support duties. Conversion of some Vulcans for the strategic reconnaissance role was planned in 1973.

Hindustan HF-24 Marut   *India*

Single-seat fighter, in production and limited service.
Data apply to Marut Mk.1.

Powered by: Two 4,850lb (2,200kg) st Rolls-Royce Bristol Orpheus 703 turbojets.
Span: 29ft 6¼in (9.00m).
Length: 52ft 0¾in (15.87m).
Gross weight: 24,048lb (10,908kg).
Max. speed: Mach 1.02 (673mph; 1,083km/h) at 40,000ft (12,200m).
Normal range: 750 miles (1,200km).
Armament: Four 30mm cannon in nose and retractable pack of 48 air-to-air rockets in fuselage aft of nose-wheel bay; four 1,000lb bombs or rockets under wings.

First supersonic fighter designed in any Asian country except the Soviet Union, the HF-24 Marut was developed initially under the leadership of Professor Kurt Tank, whose earlier products included the wartime Focke-Wulf Fw 190 fighter. Design studies were started in 1956, to meet an Indian Air Force requirement, and early research work included flight testing of a full-scale wooden glider version of the HF-24. The prototype HF-24 Mk.1 fighter, as described and illustrated above, flew for the first time on June 17, 1961. It was followed by a second prototype and then by the first of a production batch of more than 60 Mk.1s in March 1963. The initial flight of Mk.1s was accepted formally by the Indian Air Force on May 10, 1964, and three squadrons existed in 1972.

They are expected to be followed from 1975 by some 200 Mk.2s, with a reheat version of the Orpheus 703 turbojet, and about 25 of a tandem two-seat training version, the Mk.1T, which flew for the first time on April 30, 1970. These are intended to be followed by the HF-24 Mk. 3, designed for Mach 2 performance and probably powered by two Turbo-Union RB.199 turbofans without afterburning.

One HF-24 was sent to Egypt as a flying test-bed for the Helwan E-300 afterburning turbojet and flew with this engine on March 29, 1967; but the E-300 was subsequently abandoned.

Ilyushin Il-18 (NATO code-name: Coot)

U.S.S.R.

Troop and personnel transport, in production and service.

Powered by: Four 4,250shp Ivchenko AI-20M turboprops.
Span: 122ft 8½in (37.40m).
Length: 117ft 9in (35.90m).
Gross weight: 141,100lb (64,000kg).
Max. payload: 29,750lb (13,500kg).
Cruising speed: 388mph (625km/h).
Range: 2,300 miles (3,700km) with max. payload.

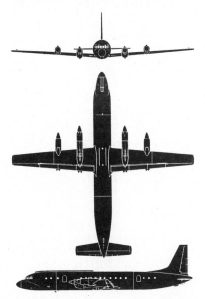

Well-known as one of Russia's standard airliners and one which has been exported widely to countries in the Soviet sphere of influence, the Il-18 appeared quite late in military service, although a prototype was seen in Soviet Air Force markings as early as 1958. The Il-18 first flew in July 1957 and entered airline service less than two years later. In commercial operation it carries up to 122 passengers and can probably carry about the same number of troops when used in the military role. At least one Il-18 is serving as an executive transport, this being operated by the Yugoslav Air Force as a Presidential aircraft. Others are used as VIP transports in Russia, and it is thought that China, as well as the air forces of Afghanistan, Algeria, Bulgaria, Czechoslovakia, Poland and Yugoslavia, has the type in military transport service.

Also in service with Soviet air forces is an anti-submarine version of the Il-18, designated Il-38 and known by the NATO codename of *May*. This is described separately (see page 75).

Ilyushin Il-28 (NATO code-names: Beagle and Mascot)

U.S.S.R.

Four-seat tactical bomber, reconnaissance and ECM (electronic countermeasures) aircraft, in service.

Powered by: Two 5,950lb (2,700kg) st Klimov VK-1 turbojets.
Span: 64ft 0in (19.50m).
Length: 58ft 0in (17.68m).
Gross weight: 43,000lb (19,500kg).
Max. speed: 580mph (933km/h) at 15,000ft (4,575m).
Range: 1,500 miles (2,400km) with max. bombload.
Armament: Two 20mm cannon in nose; two 23mm cannon in tail turret; 4,500lb (2,050kg) of bombs.

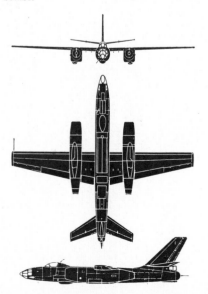

Russia's counterpart to the Canberra, the Il-28 was first shown publicly on May Day, 1950, when it took part in fair numbers in the annual fly-past over Moscow. Several thousand were built, in Czechoslovakia as well as in the Soviet Union, and Il-28s have served as light attack/reconnaissance/ECM aircraft in the air forces of Russia, Poland, Czechoslovakia, Hungary, East Germany, Afghanistan, Algeria, Iraq, North Korea, Morocco, Nigeria, Syria, North Vietnam, Yemen, Indonesia, China and Egypt, although replacement with Su-7 fighter-bombers has taken place in many of these countries. Finland has two, which are used primarily for target-towing.

The Il-28 is powered by two VK-1 turbojets, which are developed versions of the Rolls-Royce Nene. Construction is conventional, with the straight wing/swept tail design that characterised the first generation of Soviet jet-bombers. Some 2,620 gallons (11,900 litres) of fuel are stowed internally, and wing-tip tanks can be carried, although they seldom are. The blister usually seen under the front fuselage houses the scanner of a radar navigation and blind-bombing system of rather limited value.

In addition to the bomber, there is an operational trainer version designated Il-28U (NATO code-name *Mascot*) which has a second pilot's cockpit below and forward of the standard fighter-type canopy. It lacks the under-nose radar blister and forward-firing guns of the Il-28 bomber, but is otherwise similar in construction and performance.

Ilyushin Il-38 (NATO code-name: May)

U.S.S.R.

Maritime reconnaissance and anti-submarine aircraft, in service.

Powered by: Four 4,250shp Ivchenko AI-20 turboprops.
Span: 122ft 8½in (37.4m).
Length: 129ft 10in (39.6m).
Weights: Probably similar to those of Il-18.
Max. cruising speed: 400mph (645km/h).
Max. range: 4,500miles (7,250km).

This Soviet maritime patrol aircraft bears the same relationship to the Il-18 (page 73) as does the Lockheed P-3 Orion to the Electra transport. To fit it for its important role it has an MAD tail "sting", an under-nose radome, other ASW (anti-submarine warfare) electronics and weapon-carrying capability. The main cabin has few windows on each side. Concentration of equipment and weapons in the forward area has changed the centre of gravity so much that the wing has had to be moved forward considerably by comparison with the Il-18.

Il-38s were in service with Soviet units based in Egypt until the Summer of 1972, sometimes displaying Egyptian insignia, and have also been seen in the vicinity of NATO naval forces during exercises in more northern waters.

Kaman H-2 Seasprite

U.S.A.

Ship-based ASW and missile defence helicopter, in production and service. Data, photograph and silhouette: SH-2D

Powered by: Two 1,350shp General Electric T58-GE-8F turboshafts.
Rotor diameter: 44ft 0in (13.41m).
Length, nose and blades folded: 38ft 4in (11.68m).
Gross weight: 12,800lb (5,805kg).
Max. speed: 168mph (270km/h).
Range: 445 miles (716km).
Armament: MK-46 homing torpedoes on fuselage-side mountings.

The prototype Seasprite flew on July 2, 1959, and deliveries of the original UH-2A version to Helicopter Utility Squadron 2 of the US Navy began on December 18, 1962. Eighty-eight were built, each powered by a 1,250shp T58-GE-8B engine. The 102 UH-2Bs differed in having a lower standard of electronic equipment for VFR operation only. All As and Bs were converted subsequently to UH-2C configuration, with two T58-GE-8F engines, deliveries of the updated aircraft beginning in August 1967. Six were modified further to HH-2C standard, for search and rescue missions in Southeast Asia, with a chin Minigun turret, side-firing machine-guns, armour plating, four-blade (instead of three-blade) tail rotor, dual main wheels, and increased overload gross weight of 12,800lb. Sixty-seven HH-2D conversions were similar but without armament and armour.

In 1971, two HH-2Ds were modified for evaluation in an ASW role as part of the Navy's LAMPS (Light Airborne Multi-Purpose System) programme. Two others became YSH-2Es (first flown March 7, 1972) with Texas Instruments APS-122 surface search radar in a domed chin housing, forward of a boat-shape fairing housing other advanced avionics. All 115 Seasprites in the US Navy's inventory are expected to be converted to **SH-2D/F LAMPS** standard for ASW and ASMD (anti-ship missile defence) duties, carrying nose radar (initially Marconi LN 66, later APS-122), magnetic anomaly detector, sonobuoys, smoke markers, flares and homing torpedoes. The first SH-2D flew on March 16, 1971. Twenty had been delivered for service with the Atlantic and Pacific Fleets by late 1972, with conversion of 25 more under way.

Kamov Ka-25 (NATO code-name: Hormone)

U.S.S.R.

Anti-submarine and general-purpose helicopter.
Data based on that for Ka-25K.

Powered by: Two 900shp Glushenkov GTD-3 turboshaft engines.
Rotor diameter: 51ft 8in (15.74m).
Length: 32ft 0in (9.75m).
Gross weight: 16,100lb (7,300kg).
Max. speed: 137mph (220 km/h).
Accommodation: Probably crew of three or four. Twelve passengers in transport version.
Armament: Internal weapons bay in cabin undersurface for stores, including torpedoes.

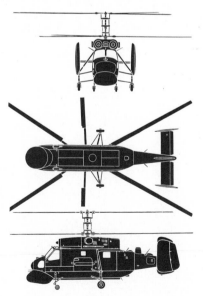

The Ka-25—NATO code-name *Hormone*—was first seen in prototype form in the Soviet Aviation Day display over Moscow on July 9, 1961. It then carried two dummy air-to-surface missiles, on outriggers on each side of its cabin. No such installation has been seen on production Ka-25s, which serve on board ships of the Soviet Navy, including the helicopter carriers *Moskva* and *Leningrad*, but there is a weapons bay in the cabin undersurface. Equipment includes an under-nose search radar, optional equipment pod at the base of the central tail-fin and cylindrical housing above the tail-boom, and inflatable pontoons on each wheel of the undercarriage. The Ka-25 has a commercial counterpart in the Ka-25K which was exhibited at the 1967 Paris Aero Show, and is itself used for similar transport and general-purpose duties. It is a product of the design team headed by Nikolai Kamov, which has been producing helicopters with co-axial rotors for many years, one of the earliest being a "strap-on" type for individual use. Several of the later designs, such as the Ka-10 lightweight observation type and the two-seat Ka-15, were used by the Soviet Navy.

Kawasaki C-1 *Japan*

Twin-turbofan troop and freight transport, under development.

Powered by: Two 14,500lb (6,575kg) st Pratt & Whitney JT8D-9 turbofans.
Span: 100ft 4¾in (30.60m).
Length: 95ft 1¾in (29.00m).
Empty weight: 51,035lb (23,150kg).
Gross weight: 85,320lb (38,700kg).
Max. speed: 507mph (815km/h) at 25,000ft (7,620m).
Range: 2,050 miles (3,300km) with 5,730lb (2,600kg) payload.
Accommodation: Crew of five, 60 troops, 45 paratroops, 36 litters and attendants, or 17,640lb (8,000kg) of freight.
Armament: None.

This medium-size troop and cargo transport was developed by Nihon Aeroplane Manufacturing Company (NAMC) to replace the Air Self-Defence Force's present fleet of Curtiss C-46s. Design work began in 1966 and the first of two XC-1 flying prototypes made its first flight on November 12, 1970, followed by the second on January 16, 1971. Two C-1 pre-production aircraft were ordered in the 1971 Fiscal Year, with Kawasaki now designated as prime contractor for the programme. Eleven production C-1s are to be ordered initially, with the first one scheduled to fly in 1973–74. Total production is expected to be about 24 aircraft. Kawasaki will build the front fuselage and wing centre-section, and will be responsible for final assembly and flight testing. The outer wings will be built by Fuji; the centre and rear fuselage and tail unit by Mitsubishi; the flaps, ailerons, engine pylons and pods by Nihon Hikoki; the undercarriage by Sumitomo; and the cargo loading system by Shin Meiwa.

Kawasaki P-2J

Japan

Twelve-seat anti-submarine and maritime patrol bomber, in production and service.

Powered by: Two 2,850shp General Electric T64-IHI-10 turboprops and two 3,085lb (1,400kg) st Ishikawajima-Harima J3-IHI-7C auxiliary turbojets.
Span: 101ft 3½in (30.87m).
Length: 95ft 10¾in (29.23m).
Empty weight: 42,500lb (19,277kg).
Gross weight: 75,000lb (34,019kg).
Cruising speed: 230mph (370km/h).
Max. range: 2,765 miles (4,450km).
Armament: Attachments for sixteen 5in rockets under wings. Internal stowage for 8,000lb (3,630kg) of bombs, depth charges or torpedoes.

The P-2J is a development of the P-2H Neptune (see page 84), of which Kawasaki manufactured 48 for the Japanese Maritime Self-Defence Force in 1959–65. Work on the prototype began in 1965, after four years of design effort, and it flew for the first time on July 21, 1966. Although produced by conversion of a standard P-2H, only the wings and tail unit remained substantially unchanged, apart from an increase in rudder chord. The fuselage was lengthened by 50in (1.27m) forward of the wing to accommodate improved electronic equipment, almost up to the standard of that carried by the P-3 Orion. The undercarriage was redesigned to have twin-wheel main units. Biggest change of all was to the power plant, with the original piston-engines replaced by T64 turboprops built under licence by Ishikawajima-Harima. These give less take-off power than the piston-engines, but make possible a saving of 10,000lb (4,535kg) in the aircraft's weight by comparison with the P-2H. Fuel capacity is increased, and an additional crew member, known as the combat co-ordinator, is carried. The first of an initial series of 46 production P-2Js flew on August 8, 1969, and was delivered to the JMSDF on October 7 that year. The first P-2J squadron had 10 in service by February 1971, and orders are to be increased to cover a total of 91 aircraft.

Lockheed C-5A Galaxy   *U.S.A.*

Heavy strategic transport, in service.

Powered by: Four 41,000lb (18,600kg) st General Electric TF39-GE-1 turbofans.
Span: 222ft 8½in (67.88m).
Length: 247ft 10in (75.54m).
Empty weight: 325,244lb (147,528kg).
Gross weight: 764,500lb (346,770kg).
Max. speed: 571mph (919km/h) at 25,000ft (7,600m).
Range: 6,333 miles (10,191km) with 112,600lb (51,074kg) payload.
Armament: None.

The design of the massive Lockheed C-5A began in 1963 when MATS (now MAC) put out to industry a requirement for an out-size logistics transport which could carry a 125,000lb (56,700kg) load for 8,000 miles (12,875km), and could operate from the same airfields as those used by the C-141 Star-Lifter (see page 82). Development contracts went to Boeing, Douglas and Lockheed in May 1964 and to Pratt & Whitney and General Electric for engine development. During 1965, Lockeed's L500 design—the work of the company's Georgia Division—was selected, together with General Electric GE1/6 engines, to meet the requirement. An initial contract for 58 aircraft was placed with Lockheed, with first and second options for 57 and 85 more. First flight of the first C-5A was made on June 30, 1968; the first operational model (the ninth C-5A built) was delivered to MAC on December 17, 1969. Production plans were limited subsequently to a total of 81 aircraft, because of rising costs; these equip four squadrons, one at Charleston AFB, one at Dover AFB and two at Travis AFB. During development, a C-5A took off at a world record weight of 798,200lb (362,064kg).

Lockheed C-130 Hercules   *U.S.A.*

Multi-purpose transport, in production and service.
Data: C-130E. Photograph: Hercules C-130H. Silhouette: HC-130H.

Powered by: Four 4,050eshp Allison T56-A-7A turboprops.
Span: 132ft 7in (40.41m).
Length: 97ft 9in (29.78m).
Empty weight: 72,892lb (33,063kg).
Normal gross weight: 155,000lb (70,310kg).
Max. cruising speed: 368mph (592km/h).
Range: 2,420-4,700 miles (3,895-7,560km).
Accommodation: Crew of four and 92 troops or 64 paratroops or 74 stretchers or freight.

First flight of the YC-130 Hercules was made on August 23, 1954 and delivery of the C-130A tactical transport began in December 1956. It was followed by the C-130B with higher weight and better range, production of the two versions totalling 461.

The C-130E, first flown on August 25, 1961, was developed as an interim turbine transport for MAC, with more underwing fuel. Special versions of the Hercules include C-130A drone carriers; 16 RC-130As for aerial survey duties; 10 JC-130Bs for air-snatch satellite recovery; a single STOL NC-130B with BLC by air-blowing over all control surfaces; 12 C-130Ds with skis for Arctic operations. Also in service are twelve HC-130Bs for USCG search and rescue duties; the EC-130E for the USCG; WC-130E for the USAF; 46 KC-130Fs used by the Marine Corps; seven US Navy C-130Fs; and LC-130F/R ski-planes used by the Navy in the Antarctic. On December 8, 1964, Lockheed flew the first of 66 HC-130Hs, with 4,910eshp Allison T56-A-15 engines and special recovery equipment on the nose; 20 of these became HC-130Ps with provision to air-refuel helicopters and to recover parachute-borne loads in mid-air. Fifteen HC-130Ns are similar to the HC-130H, with advanced direction-finding equipment. The current production C-130H is basically an E with T56-A-15 engines. The C-130K, similarly powered, was selected for RAF Transport Command and delivery of 66 began in 1967. Eight EC-130Qs are operated by US Navy squadron V.Q-4 for command communications. Other export customers for the Hercules have included the Argentine, Australia, Belgium, Brazil, Canada, Chile, Colombia, Indonesia, Iran, Italy, Libya, New Zealand, Norway, Pakistan, Peru, Saudi Arabia, South Africa, Sweden, Turkey and Venezuela. LTV modified seven Hercules as AC-130E Gunships for the interdiction role in Vietnam following trials with an armed prototype AC-130A. Orders for all versions totalled more than 1,200 at the beginning of 1972, with over 1,150 delivered.

Lockheed C-141A StarLifter   *U.S.A.*

Long-range strategic freighter, in service.

Powered by: Four 21,000lb (9,525kg) st Pratt & Whitney TF33-P-7 turbofans.
Span: 159ft 11in (48.74m).
Length: 145ft 0in (44.20m).
Empty weight: 133,773lb (60,678kg).
Gross weight: 316,600lb (143,600kg).
Max. cruising speed: 564mph (908km/h).
Max. range: 6,140 miles (9,880km).
Accommodation: Crew of four-six plus 154 troops, 123 paratroops, 80 stretchers and 16 sitting casualties, or freight.

Lockheed won a hotly contested design competition in March 1961 with this design, laid out to meet the USAF's Specific Operational Requirement 182. The requirement was for a jet freighter to modernize the MAC fleet of piston-engined and turbo-prop transports. On March 16, 1961, following selection of the Lockheed design, procurement authorization was issued to allow production of the new freighter to begin, and this was followed on August 16 by the contract for the first five aircraft. The original requirement was for 132 aircraft and later orders brought the total built to 284 by the time production ended late in 1967. The first of the evaluation aircraft flew on December 17, 1963 and delivery of operational aircraft to the USAF began in 1965. The StarLifter is the flying element of the Logistics Support System 476L, and is built round an 81ft (24.7m) long cargo compartment, 10ft by 9ft (3.12m by 2.77m) in cross-section, with straight-in rear loading at truck-bed height and provision for air-dropping. Some aircraft have been modified to carry the Minuteman ICBM in a special container, and have structural strengthening for the 86,207lb (39,103kg) weight of this load.

The C-141A is equipped with an all-weather landing system. It set up a world record for heavy cargo drops by parachuting a load of 70,195lb (31,840kg), and was the first jet transport from which US Army paratroops jumped.

Lockheed F-104 Starfighter   *U.S.A.*

Single-seat all-weather tactical strike and reconnaissance fighter, in production and service. Silhouette: F-104G. Photograph and data: F-104S.

Powered by: One 17,900lb (8,120kg) st (with afterburning) General Electric J79-GE-19 turbojet.
Span: 21ft 11in (6.68m) without tip-tanks.
Length: 54ft 9in (16.69m).
Empty weight: 14,900lb (6,760kg).
Gross weight: 31,000lb (14,060kg).
Max. speed: Mach 2.2 (1,450mph; 2,330km/h) at 36,000ft (11,000m).
Combat radius: 775 miles (1,247km) with max. fuel.
Armament: One 20mm M-61 Vulcan rotary-barrel cannon and up to 4,000lb (1,815kg) of external stores. Normally, two AIM-7 Sparrow III and two AIM-9 Sidewinder air-to-air missiles for interceptor role.

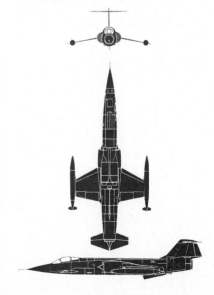

Lockheed's Model 83 Starfighter was built in limited quantities for the USAF Tactical and Air Defense Commands after protracted development, following the first flight of the prototype on February 7, 1954. The single-seat F-104A and two-seat F-104B were used by ADC for North American air defence, and some were supplied to China and Pakistan; the F-104C and F-104D were TAC equivalents. A major re-design produced the F-104G multi-mission version with a 15,800lb (7,167kg) st (with afterburning) J79-GE-11A engine, which became the subject of an intra-European production programme, with production lines in Germany, Italy, Holland and Belgium which produced 977 aircraft plus a further 50 ordered by the Luftwaffe late in 1968; similar versions were built in Canada (for the CAF and export) and in Japan. Lockheed built another 179 F-104Gs, including one each for Italy and Belgium, 96 for Germany and 81 under USAF contract for supply under MAP to other nations. European nations which received F-104Gs from US and Canadian production comprise Denmark, Greece, Norway, Spain and Turkey. Lockheed also built the two-seat F-104DJ for Japan, F-104F for Germany and TF-104G for Germany, Belgium, Italy, Netherlands, Denmark and other European air forces. Current production version is the F-104S (data above) with nine external stores points and provision for Sparrow missiles. The Italian Air Force ordered 165 of this version, and the first of two prototypes built by Lockheed flew in 1966. Production is by Aeritalia at Turin, where the first production model was flown for the first time on December 30, 1968. About 95 had been delivered by mid-1972.

Lockheed P-2 Neptune   *U.S.A.*

**Maritime patrol bomber, in service.
Data and silhouette: P-2H. Photograph: AP-2E.**

Powered by: Two 3,500hp Wright R-3350-32W piston-engines and two 3,400lb (1,540kg) st Westinghouse J34 turbojets.
Span: 103ft 10in (31.65m).
Length: 91ft 8in (27.94m).
Empty weight: 49,935lb (22,650kg).
Gross weight: 79,895lb (36,240kg).
Max. speed: 403mph (648km/h).
Range: 3,685 miles (5,930km) with ferry tanks.
Accommodation: Crew of up to seven, comprising two pilots, navigator/bombardier, radar operator and gunners.
Armament: Optional dorsal turret with two 0.50in machine-guns. Sixteen 5in rocket projectiles under wings. Internal stowage for 8,000lb (3,630kg) of bombs, depth charges or torpedoes.

Work on the Lockheed Model 26 began in September 1941 to produce an aeroplane to meet US Navy requirements for an anti-submarine and anti-shipping patrol bomber. Design proposals were accepted by the US Navy in 1944 and orders for two prototypes and 15 production aircraft were placed. Production continued for 20 years, to bring the total built to more than 1,000 by the time the Lockheed production line closed in April 1962. The Neptune was initially designated P2V and variants from P2V-1 to P2V-7 were produced. Progressive modifications accounted for the changes in designation, with the P2V-7 (now P-2H) introducing two jet engines under the wing to boost its performance. This became a retrospective modification on several earlier Neptune models. As well as the US Navy, several overseas Services operate the Neptune, including the RAAF and R.Neth. Navy and the Air Forces or Navies of Argentina, Brazil, France, Japan and Portugal. In Japan, Kawasaki built 48 P-2H Neptunes under licence and then evolved the P-2J which has 2,850shp General Electric T64-IHI-10 turboprops in place of piston-engines, and 3,085lb (1,400kg) st IHI J3-7C underwing jets (see page 79). Illustrated is an AP-2E of the U.S. Army, used for special duties in South-east Asia.

Lockheed P-3 Orion

U.S.A.

Twelve-seat anti-submarine recon-naissance aircraft, in production and service.
Data for P-3C. Photograph: EP-3E.

Powered by: Four 4,910eshp Allison T56-A-14 turboprops.
Span: 99ft 8in (30.37m).
Length: 116ft 10in (35.61m).
Empty weight: 61,491lb (27,890kg).
Gross weight: 135,000lb (61,235kg).
Max. speed: 473mph (761km/h) at 15,000ft (4,570m).
Mission radius: 1,550 miles (2,494km) with 3 hours on station at 1,500ft (450m).
Armament: Torpedoes, mines, depth charges and bombs (including nuclear weapons) in internal weapons bay; wing-mounted weapons on ten pylons. Max. total weapons load 20,000lb (9,070kg).

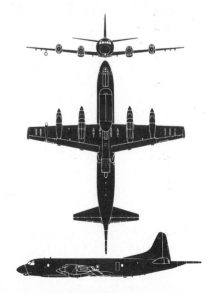

The US Navy's standard land-based anti-submarine aircraft, the Orion was designed to Type Specification No. 146, issued in August 1957. As required by the specification, Lockheed based its proposal on a derivative of a production aircraft—the Electra transport. Lockheed was announced winner of the design competition on April 24, 1958; a research and development contract was awarded on May 8, 1958 and a pre-production contract on October 7, 1958. An Electra was modified as an aerodynamic prototype and flew on August 19, 1958. An operational prototype, the YP3V-1, flew on November 25, 1959, and the first production P3V-1 for service trials flew on April 15, 1961. The designation was changed to P-3A in July 1962, and on August 13 Navy Squadron VP-8 formally accepted the first three Orions for service at Patuxent River NAS. After more than 100 P-3As had been delivered, with 4,500eshp T56-A-10W engines, production for the US Navy switched to the P-3B with 4,910eshp T56-A-14 engines. In addition, the RAAF acquired ten P-3Bs, the RNZAF five and the Royal Norwegian Air Force five. Three are to be delivered to the Spanish Air Force. Latest US Navy version is the P-3C, with A-NEW data processing system, which flew for the first time on September 18, 1968; Iran has ordered four. The WP-3A, equipped for weather reconnaissance, is also operated by the US Navy, as are 12 EP-3E special reconnaissance aircraft with radomes above and below the fuselage, converted from P-3As (10) and EP-3Bs (2). A single RP-3D is used by the US Naval Oceanographic Office for mapping the Earth's magnetic field.

Lockheed S-3A Viking   *U.S.A.*

Four-seat carrier-borne anti-submarine aircraft, under development.

Powered by: Two General Electric TF34-GE-2 turbofans, each rated at approx. 9,000lb (4,082kg) st.
Span: 68ft 8in (20.93m).
Length: 53ft 4in (16.26m).
Empty weight (approx.): 26,600lb (12,065kg).
Gross weight: 42,500lb (19,277kg).
Max. speed: 506mph (814km/h).
Combat range: more than 2,300 miles (3,705km).
Armament: Torpedoes, depth charges, mines, missiles, rockets and special weapons in internal bomb-bays and under wings.

This new carrier-based anti-submarine aircraft is being developed to replace the S-2 Tracker in service with the US Navy. Lockheed-California was awarded an initial $461 million contract for the S-3A in August 1969, after a design competition, and flew the first of eight research and development aircraft ahead of schedule on January 21, 1972. All eight were flying by the Spring of 1973. Deliveries to the fleet of the first batches of 48 production aircraft so far authorised are planned to begin in 1974.

The crew of the S-3A consists of a pilot, co-pilot, tactical operator and acoustic sensor operator. The co-pilot is responsible for non-acoustic sensors, such as radar and infra-red devices. Improved sonobuoys and MAD equipment enhance the capability of finding the quieter, deeper-diving submarines now in service. The airframe is stressed for an increase in gross weight up to 50,000lb (22,680kg) and the fuselage will take a 50 per cent expansion of the present electronics. The basic design could be adapted easily for future variants, such as tanker, utility transport, ASW command and control, and electronic countermeasures aircraft.

Lockheed SR-71

U.S.A.

Two-seat strategic reconnaissance aircraft, in service.
Data, photograph and silhouette: SR-71A.

Powered by: Two 32,500lb (14,740kg) st (with afterburning) Pratt & Whitney J58 turbojets.
Span: 55ft 7in (16.95m).
Length: 107ft 5in (32.74m).
Gross weight: 170,000lb (77,110kg).
Max. speed: More than Mach 3.0 (2,000mph; 3,220km/h).
Range: 2,982 miles (4,800km) at Mach 3.0 at 78,750ft (24,000m).
Accommodation: Crew of two.
Armament: Unarmed.

Developed in strict secrecy and with remarkable speed, the basic Lockheed A-11 is reported to have first flown in 1961 but was not revealed publicly until February 1964. The original requirement is believed to have been for a "U-2 replacement", an aircraft capable of flying at sufficient altitude and speed to be virtually un-interceptable if used on long-range strategic reconnaissance flights. The initial batch of three A-11s were modified during 1964 for evaluation as YF-12As in the role of air defence fighters, carrying eight Hughes AIM-47A missiles in internal bays. The similar but longer SR-71A was first flown on December 22, 1964 and went into limited production to equip the 9th Strategic Reconnaissance Wing of SAC, which received its first SR-71s in January 1966. The SR-71B had a raised rear cockpit and was used as a trainer by the 9th Wing. When it crashed, it was replaced by one of the YF-12As converted for the training role and designated SR-71C.

World records set up by a YF-12A on May 1, 1965, included a speed of 2,070mph (3,331 km/h) over a 15/25-km course and a sustained height of 80,258ft (24,462m). These still stood as absolute records in 1973.

McDonnell F-101 Voodoo   *U.S.A.*

Data and silhouette: F-101B. Photograph: CF-101B.

Two-seat long-range interceptor fighter, in service.

Powered by: Two 14,880lb (6,750kg) st (with afterburning) Pratt & Whitney J57-P-55 turbojets.
Span: 39ft 8in (12.09m).
Length: 67ft 5in (20.55m).
Gross weight: 46,500lb (21,100kg).
Max. speed: Mach 1.85 (1,220mph; 1,963km/h) at 40,000ft (12,200m).
Max. range: 1,550 miles (2,495km).
Armament: Three Falcon missiles in internal weapon bay plus two Genie missiles under fuselage.

The Voodoo was derived from an earlier McDonnell design, the XF-88, only two prototypes of which were built. A production order for the developed design, the F-101, was placed in 1951 to provide Strategic Air Command with a single-seat escort fighter for its B-36s. This requirement was later dropped and production of the F-101 was continued for Tactical Air Command. The first flight was made on September 29, 1954 and three squadrons were equipped with F-101As (77 built) before the F-101C (47 built) succeeded it, with improved load-carrying ability. During 1967 and 1968, many of these aircraft were converted to reconnaissance fighters for ANG squadrons, with nose-mounted cameras, as RF-101Gs and RF-101Hs respectively. The RF-101A and RF-101C also carried cameras in a lengthened nose, production totals being 35 and 166 respectively. For service with Air Defense Command, the F-101B was developed as a two-seat long-range interceptor, with all-weather capability; this version first flew on March 27, 1957. Production totalled 480, including some with full dual control, designated TF-101B. Fifty-six Voodoo two-seaters were supplied to the RCAF after service with ADC, plus ten with dual control, these being designated F-101F and TF-101F respectively by the USAF, and CF-101B and CF-101F by the Canadian Armed Forces. Since 1970, the 58 remaining CF-101B/F aircraft have been exchanged for 66 refurbished aircraft of similar type with updated electronics and other refinements. Four RF-101Cs serve with the Nationalist Chinese Air Force.

McDonnell Douglas A-4 Skyhawk   *U.S.A.*

Photograph and data: A-4M. Silhouette: A-4F.

Single-seat carrier-based light attack bomber, in production and service.

Powered by: One 11,200lb (5,080kg) st Pratt & Whitney J52-P-408A turbojet.
Span: 27ft 6in (8.38m).
Length: 40ft 3¼in (12.27m).
Empty weight: 10,465lb (4,747kg).
Gross weight: 24,500lb (11,113kg).
Max. speed: 645mph (1,038km/h) with 4,000lb (1,814kg) bombs.
Range: 2,055 miles (3,307km) with external fuel.
Armament: Two 20mm cannon in wings; fuselage crutch and four wing strong points carry maximum 10,000lb (4,535kg) load of assorted bombs, rockets or other stores.

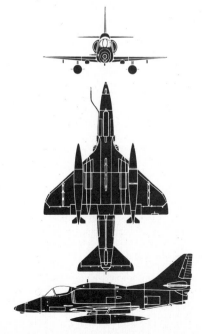

The prototype XA4D-1 flew on June 22, 1954, with a Wright J65-W-2 engine. The 166 initial production A-4As had J65-W-4 engines and entered service in October 1956. They were followed by the A-4B, first flown on March 26, 1956; this had a J65-W-16A and other improvements. Equipment for all-weather operation, including terrain-clearance radar in a lengthened nose, produced the A-4C, first flown on August 21, 1958. Douglas built 542 A-4Bs and 638 A-4Cs. The A-4E, which first flew on July 12, 1961 had more payload and range, with a J52-P-6A engine; 499 were built. The first prototype TA-4E trainer, with lengthened fuselage for tandem seating and a J52-P-8A engine, flew on June 30, 1965, and production models, redesignated TA-4F, began to reach the US Navy in May 1966. On August 31, 1966, Douglas flew the prototype A-4F, and deliveries of 146 of this version began in June 1967, with a J52-P-8A turbojet, avionics in a saddle bay behind the pilot and other changes. The TA-4J is a simplified trainer for the US Navy with P-6 engine. A-4Cs modified to an equipment standard comparable with that of the A-4F, for service with USN Reserve carrier air wings, are designated A-4L. The A-4M (data above), first flown on April 10, 1970, is a USMC derivative of the A-4F with J52-P-408A and other improvements. The RAN has purchased eight A-4G and two TA-4G; Israel operates the A-4E, A-4H and TA-4H; the RNZAF bought ten A-4Ks and 4 TA-4Ks; Argentina acquired 66 surplus A-4B Skyhawks, redesignated A-4Q (Navy) and A-4P (Air Force) after modification; and Singapore has 40 A-4Bs. Latest version is the A-4N Skyhawk II, with P-408A engine, uprated avionics and 30mm guns, first flown on June 12, 1972, and in production for Israel.

McDonnell Douglas F-4 Phantom II   *U.S.A.*

Two-seat multi-mission land and carrier-based fighter and fighter-bomber, in production and service.
Data: Phantom F-4EJ. Photograph: FGR.Mk.2.

Powered by: Two 17,900lb (8,120kg) st (with afterburning) Pratt & Whitney J79-GE-17 turbojets.
Span: 38ft 5in (11.70m).
Length: 63ft 0in (19.20m).
Empty weight: 30,073lb (13,641kg).
Gross weight: 57,400lb (26,037kg).
Max. speed: Mach 2.2 (1,450mph; 2,330km/h) at 36,000ft (11,000m).
Max. range: 1,860 miles (3,000km).
Armament: Basic armament of four Sparrow III missiles on semi-submerged mountings under fuselage and two Sparrow III or four Mitsubishi AAM-2 or Sidewinder missiles on two wing pylons. Alternative armament includes bombs exceeding 16,000lb (7,250kg) in weight, gun pods, rocket pods, etc.

Development of the Phantom II began in September 1953 under the designation AH-1 as a high-performance attack two-seater for the USN. The designation was changed to F4H after the specification had been altered to include air-to-air armament, and the first XF4H-1 was flown on May 27, 1958. US Navy Squadron VF-101 received its first production aircraft in December 1960. Trials in the ground attack role led to USAF adoption, and basic Navy and USAF versions became the F-4B and F-4C respectively. The first F-4C flew on May 27, 1963, the first YRF-4C (reconnaissance version) on August 9, 1963 and the first production RF-4C on May 18, 1964. The RF-4B reconnaissance version for the USN flew on March 12, 1965. Production totalled 696 F-4A/Bs, 46 RF-4Bs, 583 F-4Cs and 481 RF-4Cs by early 1972. Later USAF versions are the F-4D (flown December 8, 1965; 825 built) with improved avionics, and F-4E with nose-mounted M-61 gun. The Navy acquired one squadron of F-4Gs with improved avionics, followed by full production F-4Js with J79-GE-10 engines and many improvements. F-4K and F-4M are Spey-engined Phantom FG.Mk.1 (48 ordered) and FGR.Mk.2 (120 ordered) respectively. The RN received 28 Phantom FG.Mk.1s, and has one operational squadron. The other aircraft are operated by the RAF in the UK and Germany, in ground attack, interceptor and reconnaissance roles. Iran is receiving 144 F-4D/Es, and delivery of 18 F-4Ds to South Korea began in mid-1969. Israel received the first of many F-4Es and RF-4Es in the latter half of 1969. Germany has 88 RF-4E reconnaissance fighters, which are being followed by 175 F-4Fs (modified to have leading-edge slats, also being retro-fitted to all F-4Es); and Japan ordered 104 F-4EJs in 1968. Other operators of the F-4E include the Turkish and Greek Air Forces, which have ordered 40 and 36 respectively. Spain has 36 F-4Cs in service as C-12s. The USN is updating 178 F-4Bs as F-4Ns.

McDonnell Douglas F-15 Eagle   *U.S.A.*

Single-seat air superiority fighter, under development.

Powered by: Two 29,000lb (13,155kg) st Pratt & Whitney F100-PW-101 afterburning turbofans.
Span: 42ft 9¾in (13.05m).
Length: 63ft 9¾in (19.45m).
Max. speed: above Mach 2.
Armament: One internally-mounted M-61 20mm multi-barrel gun in fuselage, to be replaced later by a Philco-Ford 25mm gun. AIM-9L advanced Sidewinder air-to-air missiles on wing stations. Four AIM-7F advanced Sparrow air-to-air missiles on lower corners of air intake trunks. Provision for carrying electronic warfare pods on outboard wing stations.

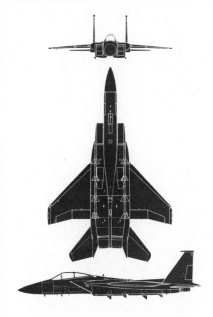

When Russia's MiG-25 was first shown in public in 1967, the USAF began the urgent development of an air superiority fighter capable of fighter sweep, escort and combat air patrol duties in areas where the new Soviet fighter might be met. McDonnell Douglas was selected to design and build the new aircraft, as the F-15, in December 1969. Cost of the initial stages of the programme, including the manufacture of 20 aircraft for development testing, was estimated at some £480 million. From the start, emphasis was placed on high manoeuvrability, rate of climb and acceleration, and the ability to locate, engage and destroy enemy aircraft at any range. This led to selection of engines that would give the aircraft a thrust-to-weight ratio of better than one-to-one, and the same kind of twin-tail configuration as the MiG-25 and Grumman F-14. Extreme speed and high-flying ability were considered less important, as the enemy would have to "come down to fight". Close-range destructive power was planned around the use of new "dogfight" versions of the Sidewinder missile and a specially developed multi-barrel cannon.

The first single-seat F-15A was named Eagle at its roll-out on June 22, 1972. It flew for the first time on July 27, and was to be joined in the flight test programme by 17 more F-15As and two TF-15 two-seat trainers. Production of the first 30 of a planned total of 729 for Tactical Air Command is under way in 1973.

Martin and General Dynamics B-57 Canberra

U.S.A.

Data and silhouette: B-57B. Photograph: RB-57F.

Two-seat light tactical bomber, in service.

Powered by: Two 7,200lb (3,265kg) st Wright J65-W-5 turbojets.
Span: 64ft 0in (19.51m).
Length: 65ft 6in (19.96m).
Gross weight: 55,000lb (24,950kg).
Max. speed: 582mph (937km/h) at 40,000ft (12,200m).
Range: 2,300 miles (3,700km).
Armament: 6,000lb (2,720kg) bomb load in rotary bomb-bay; 16 underwing points for rockets; eight fixed forward-firing 0.50in guns in nose.

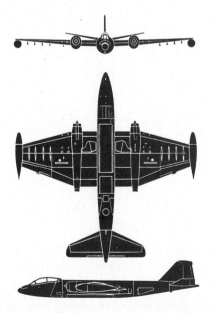

The Canberra originated in Britain (see page 48) as an English Electric design. Martin built under licence eight B-57As and then 67 RB-57As with cameras in the rear of the bomb-bay. Their principal version was the B-57B, with extensively revised front fuselage to accommodate nose armament, crew in tandem and rotary bomb-bay; 202 were built, and served from 1955 to 1959. The 38 B-57Cs were similar but had dual control, and the B-57E also was similar with the addition of target towing gear; 68 of the latter were built. Most B-57Bs had been retired from active service by the early 1960s, but were recalled from ANG squadrons in 1964 for operations in Vietnam. Some have since been modified to B-57Gs, with special sensors for night interdiction; others serve in the electronic countermeasures role as EB-57Bs and EB-57Es.

Extensive modifications were made in the 20 RB-57Ds, used for high-altitude strategic reconnaissance, with extended span, wing and fuselage radomes and J57 engines. Six of the RB-57Ds were two-seaters and the remainder single-seaters, with varying standards of reconnaissance equipment, some later becoming EB-57Ds in the ECM role.

A further development for ultra-high-altitude strategic reconnaissance was the RB-57F, with a 122ft (37.18m) span, two 18,000lb (8,165kg) st Pratt & Whitney TF33-P-11 turbofans plus two 3,300lb (1,500kg) st Pratt & Whitney J60-P-9 turbojets in underwing pods, and many other changes. Twelve were converted by General Dynamics at Forth Worth. Some B-57Bs and RB-57Ds were supplied to the Chinese Nationalist Air Force. Others went to Pakistan and South Vietnam.

Mikoyan/Gurevich MiG-17 (NATO code-name: Fresco)

U.S.S.R.

Single-seat fighter, in service.
Data and photograph: *Fresco-C.* **Silhouette:** *Fresco-E.*

Powered by: One 6,990lb (3,170kg) st (with afterburning) Klimov VK-1A turbojet.
Span: 31ft 0in (9.45m).
Length: 36ft 4in (11.10m).
Gross weight (clean): 12,500lb (5,670kg).
Max. speed: 700mph (1,125km/h) at sea level.
Max. range with external tanks and bombs: 750 miles (1,205km).
Armament: Three 23mm NR-23 cannon; four eight-rocket pods or two 550lb (250kg) bombs.

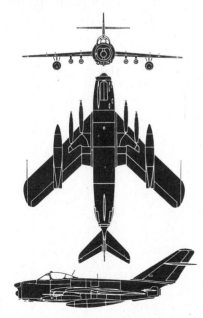

The MiG-17 was developed from the MiG-15, which it began to supersede in production in 1953. In an effort to achieve supersonic performance, the design was considerably refined, with a thinner wing section, increased wing sweep (47° inboard, 43° outboard) and lengthened rear fuselage; but the MiG-17 remained subsonic in level flight. Five versions of the MiG-17 are known to have been produced. The initial model, known to NATO as *Fresco-A*, had a 5,950lb (2,700kg) st VK-1 turbojet, without afterburner, narrow dive-brakes at the tail like the MiG-15 and an armament of one 37mm and two 23mm cannon. In *Fresco-B*, the dive-brakes were enlarged and moved to just aft of the wing trailing-edge. This was probably unsuccessful, as the next version, *Fresco-C*, retained the larger brakes but had them repositioned at the tail; it also introduced an afterburner, an additional 23mm cannon in place of the 37mm gun, and underwing armament. *Fresco-D* is a limited all-weather fighter version of the *C* with radar in a central bullet in its air intake and in a lip over the intake, and sometimes carries four air-to-air missiles instead of cannon. *Fresco-E* is similar but without afterburner. *Fresco-C* was built in Czechoslovakia (as S-104), Poland (as LiM-5) and China, as well as in Russia. Many remain in service, especially with air forces in Asia and Africa which have received aid from the USSR. Reported Soviet designations are MiG-17P for *Fresco-B*, MiG-17F for *Fresco-C*, MiG-17PF for *Fresco-D* and MiG-17PFU for *Fresco-E*.

Mikoyan MiG-19 (NATO code-name: Farmer. Chinese designation: F-6) *U.S.S.R.*

Single-seat fighter, in service.
Data: *Farmer-C.*
Photograph and silhouette: *Farmer-D.*

Powered by: Two 7,165lb (3,250kg) st (with afterburning) Klimov RD-9B turbojets.
Span: 29ft 6in (9.00m).
Length: 42ft 11in (13.10m).
Gross weight: 19,180lb (8,700kg).
Max. speed: 902mph (1,450km/h) at 33,000ft (10,000m).
Armament: Three 30mm cannon and underwing rocket pods, missiles, etc.

With the MiG-19, Mikoyan finally achieved supersonic performance in level flight. He retained the basic mid-wing, nose-intake layout of the MiG-15 and 17, but mounted two new Klimov small-diameter turbojets side-by-side in the rear fuselage, more than doubling the available thrust. The initial version (*Farmer-A*) entered service early in 1955, with an armament of one 37mm cannon under the nose and two 23mm cannon in the wing-roots, plus underwing rockets, missiles and drop tanks. *Farmer-B* was similar, but with radar in a bullet radome in the air intake and in a lip over the intake for limited all-weather operations. The most widely-used version (*Farmer-C*) introduced an under-fuselage air-brake, supplementing the original air-brakes on the sides of the rear fuselage, and was fitted with three improved cannon of 30mm calibre. *Farmer-D* is the limited all-weather counterpart of the *C*, with radar in nose bullet and lip fairing and only the wing-root guns. Some *D*s have been seen with four underwing missiles (code-name *Alkali*) and no guns. Soviet designations are reported to be MiG-19S for early *Farmer-C*s with Klimov AM-5 turbojets, MiG-19SF for later RD-9B-powered *Farmer-C*s, MiG-19PF for *Farmer-D* and MiG-19PM for the *D* with *Alkali* missiles. Before its break with the USSR, China received full manufacturing data for the MiG-19 and put the type into production, under the designation F-6. This is standard equipment in the Chinese Air Force and has been supplied to the Pakistan Air Force. Tanzania is also expected to receive a squadron of F-6s in 1973. Several East European air forces still fly Soviet-built MiG-19s, as well as countries such as Iraq, Cuba and Egypt which have received Soviet military aid.

Mikoyan MiG-21 (NATO code-names: Fishbed and Mongol)

U.S.S.R.

Single-seat fighter and two-seat trainer, in production and service.
Data, photograph and silhouette: MiG-21 MF.

Powered by: One 14,550lb (6,600kg) st (with afterburning) Tumansky RD-11-300 turbojet.
Span: 23ft 5½in (7.15m).
Length: 51ft 8½in (15.76m).
Gross weight: 20,725lb (9,400kg).
Max. speed: Mach 2.1 (1,385mph; 2,230km/h) at 36,000ft (11,000m).
Range (clean): 683 miles (1,100km).
Armament: One under-belly twin-barrel 23mm cannon. Four underwing pylons for K-13 (*Atoll*) missiles, packs of 16 rockets or drop tanks.

First seen in prototype form in the 1956 Aviation Day fly-past over Moscow, the MiG-21 is standard equipment in the air forces of the Soviet Union, Afghanistan, Algeria, Bulgaria, Cuba, Czechoslovakia, Egypt, Finland, East Germany, Hungary, India, Indonesia, Iraq, North Korea, North Vietnam, Poland, Romania, Syria and Yugoslavia. The original MiG-21F production version (*Fishbed-C*) was built also in Czechoslovakia and, probably in modified form without licence rights, in China. It is a comparatively short-range interceptor, with limited all-weather capability and an armament of one 30mm cannon and two rocket pods or *Atoll* infra-red homing missiles very like the American Sidewinder. Also in widespread use is the later MiG-21PF (*Fishbed-D*) with a lengthened nose of larger diameter, housing more effective radar. Cannon armament is deleted on the PF, which has a repositioned pitot boom, and an RD-11 turbojet uprated from the former 12,500lb (5,670kg) st to 13,120lb (5,950kg). A wider-chord fin on the interim *Fishbed-E* was supplemented on the MiG-21PFM (*Fishbed-F*) by a sideways-hinged canopy instead of the original one-piece windscreen/canopy, and improved radar. MiG-21SPS aircraft of the Czech Air Force have an added flap-blowing system. The MiG-21FL is an export PF, of which some have been built by HAL in India with an external twin-cannon pod. Latest major version in the Soviet Air Force is the MiG-21MF (*Fishbed-J*), with uprated engine, heavier armament, deeper dorsal spine fairing and other changes (data above). *Fishbed-H* is similar, with an under-fuselage pack for a reconnaissance camera or ECM equipment, and optional wingtip ECM pods. *Fishbed-K* is fitted with tail-warning radar and is being supplied to Warsaw Pact air forces. Tandem two-seat training versions have the NATO code-name *Mongol*.

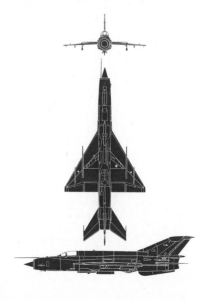

Mikoyan MiG-23 (NATO code-name: Flogger)

U.S.S.R.

Single-seat variable-geometry fighter, in service.

Powered by: One turbojet with afterburning.
Span (estimated): 50ft 0in (15.25m) spread; 29ft 6in (9.00m) swept.
Length (estimated): 57ft 0in (17.40m).
Normal gross weight (estimated): 28,000lb (12,700kg).
Max. speed (estimated): Mach 2.3 (1,520mph; 2,450km/h) at 36,000ft (11,000m) with external stores.
Combat radius (estimated): 600 miles (960km).

The prototype of this "swing-wing" fighter made its first public appearance in the 1967 Aviation Day display at Domodedovo Airport, Moscow, but did not land there. Change of wing sweep, from fully-forward to fully-aft, was accomplished in flight in about four seconds, and the aircraft looked very workmanlike. The fillets forward of the wing-root leading-edges can be expected to offer a considerable increase in lift, and the Phantom-type air intakes, with splitter plates, should prove simple and efficient. The commentator at Domodedovo announced that this aircraft could fly at supersonic speed at ground level and Mach 2 at medium and high altitudes. No armament, or stores attachments, could be discerned on the prototype. Several squadrons of MiG-23s were believed to be operational by the beginning of 1973.

Mikoyan MiG-25 (NATO code-name: Foxbat)

U.S.S.R.

Single-seat supersonic fighter, in production and service.

Powered by: Two afterburning turbojets, each giving 24,250lb (11,000kg) st at take-off.
Span (estimated): 40ft 0in (12.20m).
Length (estimated): 69ft 0in (21.00m).
Gross weight (estimated): 64,200lb (29,120kg).
Max. speed: Mach 3.2 (2,110mph; 3,400km/h) at 36,000ft (11,000m).
Combat radius: 700 miles (1,130km).

The existence of a new Soviet aircraft designated E-266 was revealed in April 1965 when an aircraft of this type, flown by Alexander Fedotov, set a 1,000km closed-circuit record with a 2,000kg payload at 1,441.5mph (2,320km/h). This flight was probably made in a prototype, and no more of the E-266 was heard until October 5, 1967, when the same pilot established a height record of 98,349ft (29,997m) carrying a 2,000kg payload, after a rocket-assisted take-off. Photographs released at the time showed that the E-266 was the new twin-fin, twin-jet aircraft of which four examples had taken part in the Aviation Day air display over Moscow in July 1967. They were later found to be designated MiG-25; and when further record attempts in 1967, probably with a pre-production aircraft, included a speed of 1,852mph (2,981km/h) over a 500km circuit, there seemed little doubt that the MiG-25 would be the world's fastest combat aircraft in service. It is primarily a high-altitude interceptor and reconnaissance aircraft, with four underwing attachments for air-to-air missiles. There are, in addition, weapon bays in the forward part of each air-intake trunk.

At least six MiG-25s were airlifted to Egypt in An-22 freighters in the Spring of 1971. Before withdrawal of the Soviet forces from that country in the Summer of 1972, these MiGs made a number of reconnaissance sorties off the coast of Israel and over Sinai, against which the Israeli defences proved ineffective.

MIL Mi-4 (NATO code-name: Hound) *U.S.S.R.*

Transport, ASW and general-purpose helicopter, in service.

Powered by: One 1,700hp ASh-82V piston-engine.
Rotor diameter: 68ft 11in (21.00m).
Fuselage length: 55ft 1in (16.80m).
Max. gross weight: 17,200lb (7,800kg).
Max. speed: 130mph (210km/h) at 5,000ft (1,500m).
Range: 250 miles (400km) with 8 passengers.
Accommodation: Crew of two and 14 troops or 3,525lb (1,600kg) of freight or vehicles.
Armament: Army support version has a machine-gun in the front of the under-fuselage nacelle and can carry air-to-surface rockets. The ASW version has an under-nose search radar, MAD towed "bird" stowed against the rear of the fuselage pod, and racks for flares, markers or sono-buoys on each side of the cabin.

In service with the Soviet Air Force since 1953, the Mi-4 was the second Soviet helicopter produced in quantity, after the smaller Mi-1. Although an original design with a number of exclusive features, the Mi-4 bears a strong overall resemblance to the Sikorsky S-55, which clearly influenced the approach of the Mil design bureau. One of the special features of the Mi-4 is the use of clam-shell rear loading doors beneath the tail boom to allow small military vehicles, such as the GAZ-69 command truck, or a 76mm anti-tank gun to be carried. Another feature which distinguishes the military Mi-4 from the Sikorsky design is the fairing under the front fuselage which can house a navigator or observer, and carries a machine-gun for army support duties. Several thousand Mi-4s have been built. They serve throughout Soviet Army and Air Force commands, and have been supplied to a number of foreign Air Forces, including those of Afghanistan, Albania, Algeria, Bulgaria, Cambodia, China, Cuba, Czechoslovakia, Egypt, Finland, East Germany, Hungary, India, Indonesia, Iraq, North Korea, Mali, Mongolia, North Vietnam, Poland, Romania, Syria, the Yemen and Yugoslavia. Also in service is the Soviet Navy's anti-submarine version.

MIL Mi-6 (NATO code-name: Hook) *U.S.S.R.*

Heavy transport and assault helicopter, in production and service.

Powered by: Two 5,500shp Soloviev D-25V (TB-2BM) turboshaft engines.
Rotor diameter: 114ft 10in (35.00m).
Length: 108ft 10½in (33.18m).
Empty weight: 60,055lb (27,240kg).
Max. gross weight: 93,700lb (42,500kg).
Max. speed: 186mph (300km/h).
Range: 652 miles (1,050km) with 9,480lb (4,300kg) payload.
Accommodation: Crew of 5 and 65 passengers, 41 stretcher patients or assorted military loads.
Armament: Provision for gun in nose.

First revealed in 1957, the Mi-6 was still the largest helicopter in standard service in 1972, although dwarfed by the Mi-12 prototypes. Developed by Russia's most experienced helicopter design team, the Mi-6 broke completely new ground, and was the first turbine-powered helicopter to achieve large-scale production in Russia. Soviet reports suggested that the design was based on the requirements for geological surveys in Siberia; but the initial production batch of Mi-6s went to the Soviet Air Force to serve as assault transports, carrying troops, supplies or complete missile systems. A few examples were delivered to Indonesia early in 1965, by which time the Mi-6 was also reported to be in service with Aeroflot, carrying passengers and freight in remote areas. Others have been supplied to the Bulgarian, Egyptian and North Vietnamese Air Forces. The NATO code-name of the Mi-6 is *Hook*: a "crane" version, with minimum fuselage, is known as the Mi-10 (*Harke*).

Mil Mi-8 (NATO code-name: Hip)   *U.S.S.R.*

General-purpose and assault transport helicopter, in production and service.

Powered by: Two 1,700shp Isotov TV2-117A turboshaft engines.
Rotor diameter: 69ft 10¼in (21.29m).
Fuselage length: 60ft 0¾in (18.31m).
Max. gross weight: 26,455lb (12,000kg).
Max. speed: 155mph (250km/h).
Range: 233 miles (375km) with 28 passengers.
Accommodation: Crew of two or three and 28–32 passengers, 12 stretchers and a medical attendant, 8,820lb (4,000kg) of internal freight or 6,614lb (3,000kg) of externally-slung freight in standard transport versions.
Armament: Twin-rack for external stores on outrigger structure on each side of cabin.

Similar in overall size to the Mi-4, and able to use Mi-4 rotor blades and secondary gearboxes in an emergency, the Mi-8 is used extensively in commercial form by Aeroflot and other operators. Examples in service with the Soviet Air Force were first seen during 1967 and, although the type has not yet matched the worldwide military operations of the Mi-4, it is known to serve with the air forces of Bulgaria, Czechoslovakia, Egypt, Ethiopia, East Germany, Hungary, India, Iraq, Pakistan, Sudan and Syria.

When the Mi-8 made its first public appearance in 1961 it had a single 2,700shp Soloviev turboshaft engine, but production models have two Isotov engines side-by-side above the cabin. The first flight of the twin-turbine model was made on September 17, 1962. A rear-loading ramp facilitates the loading of bulky freight or small wheeled vehicles. The military version has circular cabin windows instead of the square windows of the commercial model.

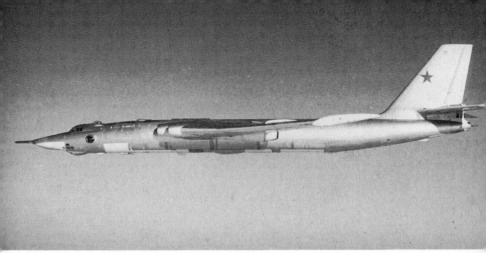

Myasishchev Mya-4 (NATO code-name: Bison)

U.S.S.R.

Four-jet long-range reconnaissance· bomber, in service.
Photograph: *Bison-C*. **Data and silhouette**: *Bison-B*.
The following data are estimated:

Powered by: Four 19,180lb (8,700kg) st Mikulin AM-3D turbojets.
Span: 170ft 0in (51.82m).
Length: 162ft 0in (49.38m).
Loaded weight: 350,000lb (158,750kg).
Max. speed: 560mph (900km/h) at 36,000ft (11,000m).
Unrefuelled range: 7,000 miles (11,265km) at 520mph (837km/h) with 10,000lb (4,535kg) of bombs.

This huge bomber, which was designed by V. M. Myasishchev, was described as Russia's answer to the American B-52 Stratofortress nuclear bomber. It was designed for the same task of carrying thermo-nuclear weapons over intercontinental ranges, with the help of flight refuelling in extreme cases. But it was probably contemporary with rather than an "answer" to the B-52, because it first put in an appearance over Moscow in May 1954, and was believed to be coming off the assembly lines at a rate of 15 a month by early 1956.

In contrast with the B-52's four pairs of podded turbojets, the Mya-4 has only four engines in a Comet-type buried installation. Its operational height is believed to be little more than 45,000ft (13,700m), which explains the heavy defensive armament. On the original bomber version (*Bison-A*), this included ten 23mm cannon in twin-gun turrets in the tail, above the fuselage fore and aft of the wing and under the fuselage fore and aft of the bomb-bay. A modified version (*Bison-B*) with refuelling probe in the nose and new electronic equipment appeared in the maritime reconnaissance role in 1964, and a further development (*Bison-C*) has a lengthened nose as shown in the photograph. Armament on these later versions is reduced to six 23mm guns.

Nord 2501/2504 Noratlas   *France*

Twin-engined medium-range transport, in service.
Data, silhouette and photograph: Nord 2501.

Powered by: Two 2,040hp SNECMA (Bristol) Hercules 738 or 758 piston-engines.
Span: 106ft 7in (32.50m).
Length: 72ft 0in (21.96m).
Gross weight: 45,415lb (20,600kg).
Max. speed: 273mph (440km/h).
Range: 1,550 miles (2,500km) with a 4½-ton payload.
Armament: None.

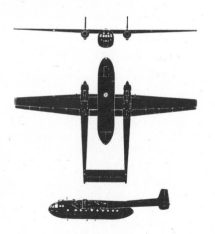

The original prototype Nord 2500 (first flown September 10, 1949) had 1,600hp Gnome-Rhone 14R engines. The second prototype, designated Nord 2501 and first flown on November 28, 1950, switched to Hercules engines and 200 aircraft of this type were built for the French Air Force; 30 were supplied to Israel and 12 entered service with the Portuguese Air Force. Twenty-five were built for Federal Germany, where a further 161 were produced under licence by Flugzeugbau Nord. The first German-built Noratlas flew on August 6, 1958. Few remain in Luftwaffe service. Four have been transferred to the air force of Niger, about 24 to Greece, and others to commercial operators. Some French aircraft have been supplied to Chad. Others have been fitted with a nose radome (as illustrated) and serve with the French Air Force as flying classrooms.

Maximum payload of the Nord 2501 is about 7½ tons of cargo or 45 passengers, including paratroops. Other military variants were the 2504, of which five were supplied to the French Navy as flying classrooms for anti-submarine crews, with wingtip Marboré turbojets; and the 2508 transport, of which two were built with 2,500hp Pratt & Whitney R-2800 engines and wingtip-mounted Marborés, and were taken over by the German Air Force in 1963 to flight test equipment under development for the Transall C-160 transport.

North American F-86 Sabre *U.S.A.*

Single-seat tactical fighter and fighter-bomber, in service.
Data and photograph: F-86F.
Silhouette: F-86K

Powered by: One 5,970lb (2708kg) st General Electric J47-GE-27 turbojet.
Span: 39ft 1in (11.91m).
Length: 37ft 6½in (11.44m).
Empty weight: 11,125lb (5,046kg).
Max. gross weight: 20,610lb (9,350kg).
Max. speed: 687mph (1,105km/h) at sea level.
Range: 925 miles (1,488km) at 530mph (853km/h).
Armament: Six 0.50in machine-guns, plus two Sidewinder missiles, two 1,000lb bombs or eight rockets.

The Sabre first flew on October 1, 1947, and was produced as the USAF's first swept-wing fighter. It was widely used in the Korean War and was licence-built in Australia, Canada, Italy and Japan. North American built more than 6,000 of the F-86A, D, E, F, H and K versions. Of these, the F-86A, E, F and H were day fighters and fighter-bombers. The F-86D was an all-weather interceptor with radar in a nose radome above the air intake and an afterburning engine. The F-86K, built by Fiat in Italy, was similar, for service with NATO air forces in Europe; and the F-86L, of which 981 were completed, was a conversion of the D with more advanced electronics. Although no longer operational with the USAF, versions of the Sabre serve with some 20 other air forces, and surplus USAF Sabres were being converted to QF-86 target drones in 1973.

Canadair built 1,815 Sabres under licence between 1950 and 1958, for the RCAF, RAF and foreign air forces. The last version built was the Sabre Mk.6 with Orenda 14 turbojet, and this remains in first-line service as an interceptor in the South African and Pakistani Air Forces.

A version of the F-86 with Rolls-Royce Avon engine was ordered by the RAAF from the Commonwealth Aircraft Corporation in 1951, and a prototype flew on August 3, 1953. This was followed by 111 production aircraft known as Sabre 30, 31 and 32. They were superseded in the RAAF by Mirage IIIs, but sufficient Avon-Sabre 32s to equip a single fighter-bomber squadron were transferred to the Royal Malaysian Air Force in 1970 and 16 others have gone to the Indonesian Air Force.

North American F-100 Super Sabre   *U.S.A.*

Interceptor and fighter-bomber, in service.
Data and silhouette: F-100D. Photograph: F-100F.

Powered by: One 17,000lb (7,710kg)st Pratt & Whitney J57-P-21A afterburning turbojet.
Span: 38ft 9in (11.81m).
Length: 54ft 3in (16.53m).
Empty weight: 21,000lb (9,525kg).
Gross weight: 34,832lb (15,800kg).
Max. speed: Mach 1.3 (864mph; 1,390km/h) at 36,000ft (11,000m).
Range: 1,500 miles (2,410km) with two external tanks.
Accommodation: Pilot only.
Armament: Four 20mm cannon in fuselage; six underwing pick-up points for bombs, rockets, air-to-air or air-to-surface missiles, etc.

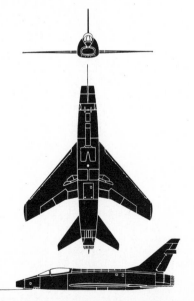

First of the USAF's "Century Series" of fighters (so called because the "F" designations were 100 and above), the Super Sabre began life, as the name suggests, as a development of the F-86 Sabre. An official contract was placed in November 1951 and the prototype YF-100A flew on May 25, 1953. The first production model F-100A flew on October 29, 1953, and three aircraft were delivered to the USAF in the following month. The three principal variants were the F-100A interceptor, the F-100C fighter-bomber with a strengthened wing and the F-100D, also a fighter-bomber, with improved equipment and other changes. The F-100F was a two-seater with lengthened fuselage, capable of use as a trainer or an operational fighter. Sidewinder and Bullpup missiles were added to F-100s still in service in the late 'fifties, and these aircraft played a prominent part in the war in Vietnam in its early years. F-100s of all production variants were supplied under MDAP to a number of NATO nations, including Denmark, Turkey and France, all of which continue to operate the type. Others were made available to the Nationalist Chinese air force.

North American T-28 Trojan and Sud-Aviation Fennec
U.S.A./France

**Data, photograph and silhouette: T-28D.
Two-seat basic trainer and light ground
attack aircraft, in service.**

Powered by: One 1,425hp Wright R-1820-
56S piston-engine.
Span: 40ft 7½in (12.38m).
Length: 32ft 10in (10.00m).
Empty weight: 6,521lb (2,958kg).
Gross weight: 8,495lb (3,853kg).
Max. speed: 380mph (611km/h).
Range: Over 500 miles (805km) with full weapon
load.
Armament: Two 0.50in machine-gun packs,
plus bombs, rockets, napalm, etc., on six under-
wing racks.

The North American NA-159 design,
winner of a USAF competition in 1948
for a new trainer, bridged the gap between
the earlier primary trainers of considerably
lower power and the *ab initio* jet trainers
now in use. At the time of its introduction
into service, the T-28 was the most powerful
aircraft ever used for primary training and
was adopted by both the USAF and the
US Navy. Production trainers for the
USAF, with an 800hp Wright R-1300 engine,
were designated T-28A; the prototype flew
on September 26, 1949. With a 1,425hp
R-1820 engine, the US Navy's T-28B was
similar; the T-28C had deck landing arrester
gear for training purposes. Trainer versions
continue in service with the US Navy and
many foreign air forces. In addition, several
hundred surplus T-28s were adapted for
ground attack duties. Carrying bombs,
rockets and gun packs under the wings, the
T-28D was evolved as a US version for
operation in South Vietnam and the Congo,
and still serves with several air forces, some
designated AT-28D as attack trainers. A
similar variant produced by Sud-Aviation
in France was called the Fennec and was
used in Algeria; Fennecs continue in first-
line service in the Argentine Navy, with the
ability to operate from its carriers. To
develop a more potent ground attack and
counter-insurgency aeroplane, the YAT-
28E was developed with a 2,445shp Lycoming YT55 turboprop. The first of three
prototype conversions flew on February 15,
1963, but no production of this variant
ensued.

North American Rockwell B-1A   *U.S.A.*

Powered by: Four 30,000lb (13,600kg) st General Electric F101-GE-100 augmented turbofans.
Span: 137ft 0in (41.75m) spread; 78ft 0in (23.77m) swept.
Length: 143ft 0in (43.58m).
Gross weight: 350,000–400,000lb (158,750–181,450kg).
Max. speed: approx. Mach 2.2 (1,450mph; 2,333km/h) at 50,000ft (15,000m).
Max. range: 6,100 miles (9,800km) at Mach 0.85 (560mph; 900km/h) at high altitude.

The first of three B-1A flying prototypes is expected to make its first flight in the Spring of 1974. It will be a variable-geometry (swing-wing) design, with a blended wing/body structure, and will carry up to 50,000lb (22,680kg) of weapons, including SRAM missiles and SCAD armed decoys packed on a rotary dispenser. After cruising to the target at subsonic speed, the B-1A would make a supersonic over-the-target dash at either high or low altitude, protected by electronic jamming equipment, infra-red countermeasures and other devices.

Tupolev Tu-? (NATO code-name: Backfire)   *U.S.S.R.*

Gross weight: 272,000lb (123,350kg).
Max. over-target speed: Mach 2.25 to 2.5 (1,650mph; 2,655km/h).
Max. range: 5,500-6,000 miles (8,850-9,650km) at high altitude.

Russia's counterpart to the B-1A, this formidable swing-wing bomber was spotted first by Western intelligence sources as long ago as July 1970, near the Tupolev works at Kazan in Central Asia. Two prototypes and a pre-production batch

of *Backfires* have since undergone considerable flight testing, including impressive flight refuelling trials. After one such refuelling, a *Backfire* is said to have remained airborne for ten hours. Only the outer wing panels have variable sweep, as on *Fitter-B* (page 128). The engines are believed to be basically similar to the 38,580lb (17,500kg) st turbofans used in the Tu-144 supersonic airliner, making possible low-level penetration of enemy airspace at supersonic speed.

North American Rockwell OV-10 Bronco

U.S.A.

Data and photograph: OV-10A.
Observation and COIN aircraft, in service.

Powered by: Two 715shp Garrett AiResearch T76-G-410/411 turboprops.
Span: 40ft 0in (12.19m).
Length: 41ft 7in (12.67m).
Empty weight: 6,969lb (3,161kg).
Gross weight: 14,466lb (6,563kg).
Max. speed: 281mph (452km/h) clean at sea level.
Combat radius: 228 miles (367km) with max. weapon load, no loiter.
Armament: Four 0.30in machine-guns in sponsons, which also carry maximum of 2,400lb external ordnance; provision for one Sidewinder AAM under each wing, and for 1,200lb load under fuselage. Max. weapon load 3,600lb (1,633kg).

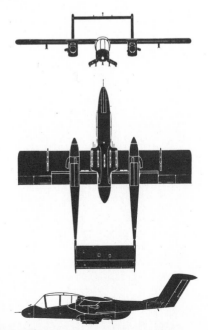

Post-war experience in limited warfare persuaded the US Navy of the need for a light multi-purpose counter-insurgency aircraft. The North American NA300 won a design competition, against entries from eight other companies. Seven prototypes were ordered, under the designation YOV-10A; and the first of these flew on July 16, 1965. These early aircraft had 660shp T76-GE-6/8 (handed) engines, span of 30ft (9.14m), max. weight of 12,364lb (5,608kg) and "straight" sponsons. The seventh YOV-10A was evaluated with Pratt & Whitney T74 turboprops, and the sixth was modified in 1967 to production configuration with a 10ft increase in wing span, up-rated engines as shown above, anhedral on the sponsons and a number of smaller modifications. The first production contracts were placed in October 1966 and deliveries began early in 1968. The USAF acquired 157 OV-10As for forward air control and secondary ground support duties; the US Marine Corps received 114 similar aircraft, of which 18 were loaned to the US Navy for light armed reconnaissance, helicopter escort and forward air control duties in Vietnam. Production for the US services ended in April 1969; but the Thai Air Force has ordered 32 OV-10Cs, while the Federal German government ordered 18 OV-10Bs for target towing duties. Twelve of the latter have a General Electric J85 auxiliary turbojet mounted above the fuselage to boost their max. speed to 393mph (632km/h), in which form they are redesignated OV-10B(Z) (first flown on September 21, 1970). Two YOV-10Ds (converted OV-10As) are armed night observation gunships for the US Marines. Sixteen OV-10Es ordered by Venezuela are similar to the OV-10A.

North American Rockwell RA-5C Vigilante

U.S.A.

Carrier-based reconnaissance aircraft, in service.

Powered by: Two General Electric J79-GE-10 turbojets, each rated at 17,859lb (8,118kg) st with afterburning.
Span: 53ft 0in (16.15m).
Length: 76ft 7½in (23.35m).
Empty weight: 40,900lb (18,552kg).
Gross weight: 66,800lb (30,300kg).
Max. speed: Mach 2.1 (1,385mph; 2,230km/h) at 40,000ft (12,200m).
Range: 3,000 miles (4,825km).
Accommodation: Crew of two in tandem.
Armament: Four underwing pylons for nuclear or conventional bombs, missiles or external fuel tanks.

First flown on August 31, 1958 (as the XA3J-1), the Vigilante was designed primarily to deliver any type of bomb after operating from the deck of an aircraft carrier and to have a Mach 2 speed. A unique feature was the "linear" bomb bay, comprising a tunnel running the length of the fuselage, from which bombs were ejected at the aft end. As originally designed, the A3J-1 was to have had an XLR46-NA-2 rocket motor in addition to the jet engines but this scheme was abandoned. The A-5A Vigilante (57 delivered) entered service with VAH-7 in 1961, and was first operational at sea on board the USS *Enterprise* in February 1962. The A-5B Vigilante (six built, prototype first flown on April 29, 1962) was a long-range version of the A-5A with additional fuel in a "saddleback" fairing on the fuselage, but the attack role was abandoned before this version entered production and the RA-5C was adopted instead in the reconnaissance role. The RA-5C (59 originally ordered) is externally similar to the A-5B, with four under-wing attachments for 333-gallon (1,515 litre) fuel tanks, bombs or missiles, and carries cameras, side-looking radar and other reconnaissance equipment in a long ventral fairing. The first RA-5C flew on June 30, 1962, and deliveries to the USN began in 1964. In addition to new production, many A-5As and Bs were converted to RA-5C standard. Then, in 1969, the type was re-instated in production to meet Vietnam needs, a total of 46 additional aircraft being completed, as described above. Earlier RA-5Cs have 17,000lb (7,710kg) st J79-GE-8 engines.

Northrop F-5 and F-5E Tiger II $\qquad$ *U.S.A.*

Lightweight fighter, in production and service.

Data: F-5E Tiger II. Photograph: RF-5A. Silhouette: F-5A.

Powered by: Two 5,000lb (2,267kg) st General Electric J85-GE-13 afterburning turbojets.
Span: 26ft 8in (8.13m).
Length: 48ft 3¾in (14.73m).
Empty weight: 9,558lb (4,335kg).
Gross weight: 21,820lb (9,897kg).
Max. speed: Mach 1.6 (1,055mph; 1,700km/h) at 35,000ft (11,000m).
Max. range: 2,314 miles (3,720km).
Accommodation: Pilot only.
Armament: Two 20mm cannon in nose. One Sidewinder air-to-air missile on each wingtip; five pylons under fuselage and wings for assorted stores up to a total of 7,000lb (3,175kg).

The F-5 was the outcome of a project begun by Northrop in 1954 to develop a small, lightweight supersonic fighter which would be substantially cheaper than its contemporaries of similar performance. Construction of three N-156Fs began in May 1958 as a private venture which was subsequently backed by the US Department of Defense, and the first of these flew on July 30, 1959. Production contracts were placed by the Department of Defense for N-156s to be supplied as the F-5A and RF-5A (single-seat) and F-5B (two-seat), under mutual aid programmes, to such nations as Greece, Turkey, Morocco, Nationalist China, the Philippines, Thailand, South Vietnam, Iran, Ethiopia, Libya and South Korea. The R Norwegian AF ordered 108, including F-5Gs, camera-equipped RF-5Gs and F-5Bs for training. Spain acquired 36 SF-5As and 34 SF-5Bs, assembled by CASA and operated by the Spanish Air Force as C-9s and CE-9s respectively. Canadair built 89 CF-5A single-seaters and 26 two-seat CF-5Ds for the Canadian Armed Forces, plus 75 NF-5As and 30 NF-5Bs for the RNethAF. Sixteen of the CF-5As and two CF-5Bs have been transferred to Venezuela. Following flight trials of a YF-5B-21 prototype, with uprated engines, manoeuvring flaps and other improvements, the USAF ordered a production version for supply to America's allies under the designation F-5E Tiger II. The first F-5E flew on August 11, 1972. Deliveries will be made primarily to countries in Southeast Asia which receive MAP assistance, including South Vietnam, South Korea, Taiwan and Thailand. In addition, Saudi Arabia and Iran have ordered Tiger IIs.

Panavia MRCA   *Great Britain/Germany/Italy*

Two-seat multi-role combat aircraft, under development.

Powered by: Two 14,500lb (6,577kg) st Turbo-Union RB.199-34R afterburning turbofans.
Span: (estimated): 44ft 3½in (13.50m) spread; 27ft 10½in (8.50m) swept.
Length: (estimated): 54ft 2in (16.50m).
Weights and performance: Secret.
Armament: Secret, but will include guided and semi-active homing air-to-air missiles, "scatter-weapons", and all types of air-to-surface weapons, according to version, on pylons under the fuselage and wings. Built-in armament comprises two 25mm cannon.

Panavia Aircraft GmbH was set up in Munich in March 1969 to design and build a multi-role combat aircraft (MRCA) for service with the air forces of Great Britain, West Germany and Italy from 1977. Shareholders are British Aircraft Corporation (42½%), Messerschmitt-Bölkow-Blohm (42½%) and Aeritalia (15%). A second company named Turbo-Union was established by Rolls-Royce (40%), MTU (40%) and Fiat (20%) to supply engines for the MRCA, which will be a compact, swing-wing type able to fulfil five major duties: close air support/battlefield interdiction, interdictor strike, air superiority, naval operations, and reconnaissance. In addition, all three member nations in the project will require a trainer version. First flight is scheduled for late 1973, with four development aircraft being assembled in the UK, three in Germany and two in Italy. The RAF is expected to acquire 385 initially, to replace the Vulcan, Buccaneer and Phantom for overland strike, reconnaissance, air defence and maritime strike tasks. The German Air Force and Navy require about 322 and Italy 100 to replace Starfighters and Aeritalia G91s.

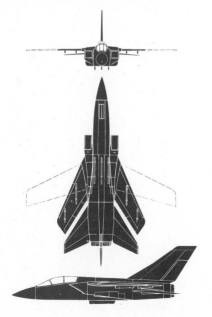

Republic F-105 Thunderchief   *U.S.A.*

Data and photograph: F-105D. Silhouette: F-105F.
Single-seat long-range tactical fighter-bomber, in service.

Powered by: One 26,500lb (12,030kg) st Pratt & Whitney J75-P-19W afterburning turbojet.
Span: 34ft 11¼in (10.65m).
Length: 67ft 0¼in (20.43m).
Empty weight: 27,500lb (12,475kg).
Gross weight: 52,545lb (23,835kg).
Max. speed: Mach 2.1 (1,385mph; 2,230km/h) at 36,000ft (11,000m).
Max. range: Over 2,000 miles (3,220km).
Armament: One General Electric 20mm Vulcan multi-barrel gun, plus more than 14,000lb (6,350kg) of stores under fuselage and wings.

Development of the F-105 was started in 1951. Two prototypes, designated YF-105A, had J57-P-25 turbojets, and the first of these flew on October 22, 1955. A switch to the more powerful J75-P-3 or -5 engine changed the designation to F-105B on the next 75 aircraft, these being the first to feature the Thunderchief's unique swept-forward air intakes. Three trials aircraft were laid down in the reconnaissance role as RF-105Bs, but this version was not developed. Principal production version was the F-105D (600 built) with many improvements, and this variant equips TAC Wings in the US and the Far East. A proposed two-seat version, the F-105E, was dropped, but 143 F-105Fs were ordered in 1962 for use as operational trainers. These have a 31-inch longer fuselage, second cockpit with dual controls, and taller fin; the first F-105F flew on June 11, 1963. The F-105D and F-105F played a major part in the air war in Vietnam. Continuous updating enabled these aircraft to carry the latest missiles and equipment, including advanced electronic countermeasures devices. About 30 F-105Ds have been modified to carry the T-Stick II bombing system, including electronics in a "saddle-back" fairing above the fuselage. The first flight of a T-Stick II version was made on August 9, 1969. The F-105Gs were Fs converted for the suppression of surface-to-air missile sites in Vietnam, with an ECM pod mounted on the under-fuselage.

Saab-32 Lansen

Sweden

Two-seat attack fighter and photographic reconnaissance aircraft, in service.
Data, photograph and silhouette: A32A.

Powered by: One 9,920lb (4,500kg) st Svenska Flygmotor R.M.5A2 (Rolls-Royce Avon) afterburning turbojet.
Span: 42ft 7¾in (13.00m).
Length: 48ft 0¾in (14.65m).
Empty weight: 16,500lb (7,485kg).
Gross weight: 22,000–28,660lb (9,980–13,000kg).
Max. speed: 700mph (1,125km/h) at sea level.
Max. range: 2,000 miles (3,220km).
Armament: Four 20mm cannon and underwing racks for two RB04 air-to-surface missiles, 2,200lb (1,000kg) of bombs or up to 24 rockets.

One of the first two-seat aircraft in the world able to exceed Mach 1 (in a dive), the Lansen (first of four prototypes flown November 3, 1952) was designed primarily for all-weather attack duties against targets at sea and ashore. The prototypes had British-built Avons, but these were replaced by Swedish-built Avon RA.7Rs (R.M.5A2) with reheat on the first production series, designated A32A, of which deliveries began in 1955. About 280 were built for service with four attack wings (10 squadrons). Replacement with Viggens began in 1971.

Next to enter production was the J32B two-seat night and all-weather fighter (first flown January 7, 1957). Although similar to the A in appearance, it has a 15,190lb (6,890kg) st Swedish-built 200-series Avon with afterburning, designated R.M.6B, and was produced with much heavier armament. The 20mm cannon were replaced by four 30mm guns, supplemented by underwing racks for Sidewinder missiles or rocket pods. This version, of which about 150 were built, entered service in July 1958. It is no longer operational as a fighter, but a few J32Bs are used for ECM training and special duties. Others are replacing J29s for target towing.

Third version of the Lansen is the R.M.5-engined S32C reconnaissance aircraft, carrying cameras in a modified nose, which first flew on March 26, 1957. About 35 were built to equip two squadrons, with which they still fly.

Saab-35 Draken

Sweden

Single-seat fighter, reconnaissance aircraft and two-seat trainer, in production and service.
Data and photograph: Saab-35XD.
Silhouette: J35F.

Powered by: One 17,650lb (8,000kg) st Volvo Flygmotor R.M.6C (Avon 300-series) afterburning turbojet.
Span: 30ft 10in (9.40m).
Length: 50ft 4in (15.35m).
Gross weight: 33,070lb (15,000kg).
Max. speed: Mach 2 (1,320mph; 2,125km/h) at 36,000ft (11,000m).
Armament: Two 30mm cannon (optional). Racks under fuselage and wings for four Sidewinder air-to-air missiles, 2,200lb (1,000kg) of bombs, or rockets.

Like the Lansen, the Draken was designed to operate from auxiliary air-strips formed by sections of Sweden's main roads. The large area of its "double delta" wing helps to give it short take-off and landing runs. The first of three prototypes flew on October 25, 1955, with an imported Avon. The first production J35A interceptor for the Swedish Air Force flew on February 15, 1958, with a 15,200lb (6,895kg) st Swedish-built R.M.6B (200-series Avon) and this version entered service in 1960. It was followed by the J35B (first flown on November 29, 1959) with a more advanced fire-control system for collision-course tactics. This version entered service in 1961, but most J35As and Bs were converted subsequently to J35D standard, with 17,200lb (7,800kg) st R.M.6C engine, an improved autopilot and extra fuel. The prototype J35D flew on December 27, 1960, and this version became operational in 1964. Some J35As were also converted into SK35C two-seat dual-control trainers, to supplement new production. The S35E is a reconnaissance version with cameras in its nose.

Final production version for the Swedish Air Force was the J35F, basically similar to the D but with improved fire-control system and armament of one 30mm gun and two or four Falcon air-to-air missiles. The F was manufactured in greater numbers than any of its predecessors and 20 Swedish all-weather fighter squadrons now operate Drakens.

First export order for the Draken was for 46 Saab-35XDs, with greatly increased weapon load and range, for Denmark, made up of 20 F-35 fighter-bombers, 20 RF-35 reconnaissance/fighters and 6 TF-35 trainer/fighters. They were followed by 12 Saab-35S single-seaters for Finland. Overload take-off weight of these export single-seaters, with nine 1,000lb bombs, is 35,275lb (16,000kg).

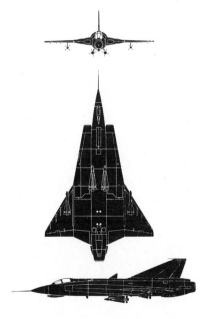

Saab-37 Viggen   *Sweden*

Single-seat multi-mission combat aircraft and two-seat trainer, in production and service.
Photograph, data and silhouette: AJ37.

Powered by: One 26,450lb (12,000kg) st Volvo Flygmotor R.M.8 (P. & W. JT8D-22) afterburning turbofan.
Span: 34ft 9¼in (10.60m).
Length: 53ft 5¾in (16.30m).
Normal gross weight: approx. 35,275lb (16,000 kg).
Max. speed: Mach 2 (1,320mph; 2,125km/h) at 36,000ft (11,000m).
Combat radius: 310–620 miles (500–1,000km).
Armament: Three attachments under fuselage and two under each wing, for RB04 or RB05 air-to-surface missiles, plus alternative 30mm gun packs, bombs, rockets or mines.

The Viggen is a multi-mission combat aircraft, intended to replace the whole range of A32A Lansens, J32B Lansens, J35 Drakens and S32C Lansens used at present by the Swedish Air Force for attack, interception, and reconnaissance duties. After pioneering the double-delta configuration with the Draken, Saab have turned to an even more advanced aerodynamic shape for the Viggen, which uses a foreplane, fitted with flaps, in combination with a main delta wing. This, together with the great power of its engine, gives it STOL capability and it is able to operate from roads and runways only 550 yards (500m) long. The first of seven prototypes flew on February 8, 1967, and all were completed by July 2, 1970, when the SK37 tandem two-seat trainer version made its first flight. The initial production contract, announced in March 1967, was for 83 of the AJ37 single-seat attack version and 17 SK37 trainers; a further 75 AJ37s were ordered in April 1968. As its designation implies, the AJ37 can be used also as an interceptor. Other versions, under development, are the JA37 single-seat interceptor, which can be used also for attack, and the S37 single-seat reconnaissance aircraft. The first production AJ37 flew on February 23, 1971, and deliveries to F7 Wing of the Swedish Air Force began in June 1971. Orders for all versions of the Viggen are expected to total 500 in due course.

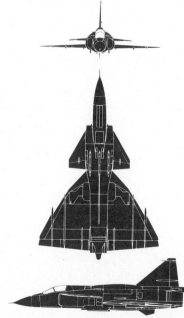

Saab-105

Sweden

**Two-seat basic trainer and light attack aircraft, in production and service.
Data and photograph: Saab-105G.
Silhouette: SK60C.**

Powered by: Two 2,850lb (1,293kg) st General Electric J85-GE-17B turbojets.
Span: 31ft 2in (9.50m).
Length: 35ft 5in (10.80m).
Empty weight: 6,801lb (3,085kg).
Max. gross weight: 14,330lb (6,500kg).
Max. speed: 603mph (970km/h) at sea level.
Range: 1,677 miles (2,700km) at 40,000ft (12,000m) with external tanks.
Armament: Six underwing attachments for up to 5,180lb (2,350kg) of Minigun or 30mm gun packs, rockets, rocket packs, bombs, Sidewinder missiles, or reconnaissance packs.

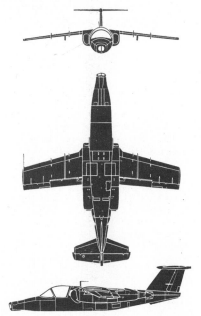

Although it is operated mainly as a two-seater in its military roles, the Saab-105 is a multi-purpose light twin-jet aircraft capable of accommodating two more people on rear seats behind the crew. It was developed as a private venture, the first of two prototypes flying for the first time on June 29, 1963. Early in the following year, Saab received a Royal Swedish Air Board contract for 130 production models, each powered by two 1,640lb (743kg) st Turboméca Aubisque turbofans. Subsequently, a further 20 were ordered. The first production model flew on August 27, 1965, and deliveries of the basic SK60A trainer to the Swedish Air Force began in the spring of 1966. Some were returned to Saab to be fitted with attachments for weapons and a gunsight, in which form they are designated SK60B; although still used mainly for training, they are now capable of quick conversion to attack configuration. In addition, a small number of the As that were modified to B standard were fitted with a permanent panoramic reconnaissance camera installation in the nose, as shown in the silhouette drawings. The prototype of this version, the SK60C, flew on January 18, 1967; full attack capability is retained. Austria has 40 Saab-105Os (developed from the prototype Saab-105XT) with General Electric J85 turbojets, higher performance and much increased weapon load. The first of these flew on February 17, 1970 and deliveries began soon afterwards. The Saab-105G (data above) is a further development with increased armament, more advanced avionics and refined controls. It first flew on May 26, 1972.

SEPECAT Jaguar

Great Britain/France

Data, silhouette and photograph:
Jaguar S.
Single-seat light tactical support air-
craft, in production.

Powered by: Two 7,140lb (3,238kg) st Rolls-
Royce/Turboméca Adour 102 afterburning
turbofans.
Span: 28ft 6in (8.68m).
Length: 50ft 11in (15.52m).
Max. gross weight: 32,600lb (14,500kg).
Max. speed: Mach 1.6 (1,056mph; 1,700km/h) at
36,000ft (11,000m).
Max. range: 2,614 miles (4,210km) with external
tanks.
Armament: Two 30mm Aden guns in lower
fuselage. One attachment under fuselage and
four under wings for up to 10,000lb (4,500kg) of
stores (Martel missiles, 1,150lb bombs, napalm
tanks, rocket pods, etc). Provision for air-to-air
missiles at wing-tips.

Evolved from Breguet's Br 121 project, the
Jaguar is a lightweight dual-role aircraft that
is being built in four main versions: Jaguar
A is a single-seat tactical support aircraft
for the French Air Force; its RAF counterpart is the Jaguar S, and Jaguar M is a
single-seater proposed for service with the
French Navy; Jaguar E is a two-seat advanced trainer for the French services, its
RAF counterpart being the Jaguar B.
Jaguar K identifies the proposed export
standard. Development is entrusted to an
international company known as SEPECAT,
formed by BAC and Dassault/Breguet.
Development of the Jaguar began in 1965,
and the first of two prototypes of the Jaguar
E was first flown on September 8, 1968. It
was followed by the second E on February
11, 1969 and the two prototype Jaguar As on
March 29 and May 27, 1969. The Jaguar M
prototype flew on November 14, 1969 and
the two British single-seat prototypes on
October 12, 1969 and June 12, 1970. The
final prototype, a Jaguar B, flew for the first
time on August 30, 1971. The first production Jaguar E flew on November 2, 1971, and
deliveries of this version began in 1972.
The RAF will have 165 Ss, designated
Jaguar GR.Mk.1 in service, sufficient for
nine first-line squadrons, and the first of
these flew on October 11, 1972. The full
production standard includes a laser range-
finder in the nose and a special electronics
pack near the tip of the fin. In addition, 35
Jaguar T.Mk.2 two-seaters will be used for
operational conversion and continuation
training. France will also acquire 200
Jaguars.

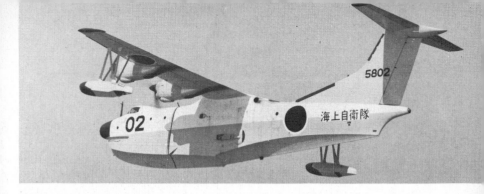

Shin Meiwa PS-1 *Japan*

Four-turboprop STOL anti-submarine flying-boat, in production and service.

Powered by: Four 3,060shp Ishikawajima-Harima (General Electric) T64-IHI-10 turboprops.
Span: 108ft 8¾in (33.14m).
Length: 109ft 11in (33.50m).
Empty weight: 58,000lb (26,300kg).
Gross weight: 94,800lb (43,000kg).
Max. speed: 340mph (547km/h) at 5,000ft (1,525m).
Ferry range: 2,948 miles (4,744km) at 196mph (315km/h).
Accommodation: Crew of ten, comprising two pilots, a flight engineer, two sonar operators, navigator, MAD operator, radio and radar operators, and a tactical co-ordinator.
Armament: Two underwing pods, between each pair of engine nacelles, each contain two homing torpedoes; six 5in rockets on attachments under wingtips; four 330lb anti-submarine bombs in weapon-bay.

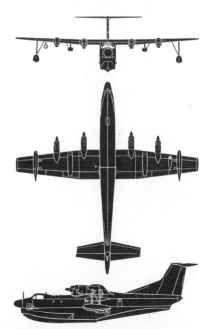

This big new flying-boat is a rarity at a time when most anti-submarine aircraft are land-based or carrier-borne. It has many novel features, including a built-in tricycle beaching gear which enables it to move on the ground under its own power. A 1,400shp General Electric T58-IHI-10 shaft-turbine is housed in the upper centre portion of the hull to provide compressed air for the "blown" flaps and tail surfaces which help to give the PS-1 STOL capability. It will take off from a calm sea in 820ft (250m) and land in 590ft (180m). It has been designed to operate in winds of up to 25 knots and waves 13ft (4m) high, which represent the normal maximum rough sea conditions in the Pacific near Japan. The PS-1 is designed to land and take off repeatedly, to dip its large sonar deep into the sea while searching for submarines. Other operational equipment includes a searchlight, search radar in nose, magnetic anomaly detector (MAD), sono-buoys and electronic countermeasures installation. The prototype, known as the PX-S, flew on October 5, 1967, and was followed by a second in mid-1968. They were delivered to a Maritime Self-Defence Force test squadron in 1968, and were joined in service by two PS-1 pre-production aircraft in 1972. The first ten production PS-1s are scheduled for delivery by March 1974, with 9 more PS-1s and three PS-1S amphibious search and rescue models planned under the follow-up defence budget. The PS-1S will accommodate up to 20 survivors (18 on stretchers) or 69 passengers in a transport role.

Short Belfast C.Mk.1

Great Britain

Heavy strategic transport, in service.

Powered by: Four 5,730eshp Rolls-Royce Tyne R.Ty.12 turboprops.
Span: 158ft 9½in (48.42m).
Length: 136ft 5in (41.69m).
Max. gross weight: 230,000lb (104,300kg).
Max. cruising speed: 352mph (566km/h) at 24,000ft (7,300m).
Max. range: 5,300 miles (8,530km) at 336mph (540km/h).
Accommodation: Crew of five; up to 78,000lb (35,400kg) of freight, including the largest types of guns, vehicles and guided missiles used by the British Army and RAF.
Armament: None.

In December 1960, the RAF finalised its contract with Short Brothers & Harland for ten strategic freighters for which the name Belfast was then adopted, in place of Britannic by which the design had been known previously. The design was based originally on that of the Bristol Britannia airliner, but little of the latter airframe is left except for some basic wing structure. Highly-complex equipment includes an automatic landing system for use in bad weather, and in January 1970 the Belfast became the first military transport in the world to be cleared for "hands-off" automatic landing in fully-operational conditions. Construction of the first Belfast began in October 1959 and it flew for the first time on January 5, 1964. Deliveries to the RAF began on January 20, 1966, when the first Belfast was handed over to No. 53 Squadron at RAF Brize Norton. This squadron, now part of Strike Command, operates its Belfasts primarily as freighters, although the aircraft was designed for easy conversion into a transport for 150 troops, or up to 250 with a removable upper deck fitted.

Sikorsky S-58 (H-34 Seabat, Choctaw, Seahorse)

U.S.A.

General-purpose and anti-submarine helicopter, in service.

Powered by: One 1,525hp Wright R-1820-84 piston-engine.
Rotor diameter: 56ft 0in (17.07m).
Fuselage length: 46ft 9in (14.25m).
Empty weight: 7,750–8,275lb (3,515–3,754kg).
Gross weight: 14,000lb (6,350kg).
Max. speed: 123mph (198km/h) at sea level.
Range: 280 miles (450km) at 98mph (158km/h).
Accommodation: 12 passengers (CH-34, UH-34); 4 crew (SH-34).
Armament: Provision for anti-submarine weapons in SH-34 only.

The US Navy contracted on June 30, 1952 for Sikorsky to produce a prototype helicopter for anti-submarine duties. Designated XHSS-1, this prototype flew on March 8, 1954 and was the first example of the Sikorsky S-58 to be built; production eventually totalled 1,821, more than any other single Sikorsky type. US Navy versions were the SH-34G Seabat; SH-34J with automatic stabilisation equipment and other improvements; SH-34H, a single prototype with two General Electric T58 turboshaft engines, and the LH-34D equipped for cold-weather operation. The US Marines used the UH-34D Seahorse utility transport, plus the UH-34E with amphibious gear and the VH-34D executive transport. The Navy versions were also used later in a utility role, as UH-34G and UH-34J. Six HH-34Fs were supplied for Coast Guard use. US Army variants (many still in service) were the CH-34A and CH-34C Choctaw. Sikorsky supplied many S-58s to foreign services, including those of the Argentine, Brazil, Canada, Chile, Germany, Italy, Israel, Japan, the Netherlands and Thailand. For the French Army and Navy, Sud-Aviation built 166 S-58s, plus five for Belgium. Westland in the UK built the S-58 as the Wessex (see page 142).

Sikorsky is offering to S-58 operators a turbine engine retrofit modification, based on the installation of an 1,800shp Pratt & Whitney PT6 Twin-Pac twin-engine unit. The prototype conversion, designated S-58T, flew for the first time on August 19, 1970. Deliveries of production conversions and kits began in the following year.

Sikorsky S-61B (H-3 Sea King)   *U.S.A.*

Anti-submarine and transport helicopter, in production and service.
Data and silhouette: SH-3D. Photograph: SH-3H.

Powered by: Two 1,400shp General Electric T58-GE-10 turboshafts.
Rotor diameter: 62ft 0in (18.90m).
Fuselage length: 54ft 9in (16.69m).
Empty weight: 11,865lb (5,382kg).
Gross weight: 18,626lb (8,449kg).
Max. speed: 166mph (267km/h) at sea level.
Range: 625 miles (1,005km).
Accommodation: Crew of four (SH-3D).
Armament: 840lb (381kg) of homing torpedoes, depth charges, etc. (SH-3D only).

The Sikorsky S-61 was developed initially to provide the US Navy with an anti-submarine helicopter combining the "hunter" and "killer" roles. It was designed around two T58 turboshaft engines, with a watertight hull to permit operations on and off water. The prototype, designated XHSS-2, first flew on March 11, 1959, and deliveries to operational anti-submarine units began in September 1961. The HSS-2 designation was changed to SH-3A Sea King (255 built), in July 1962, this version having 1,250shp T58-GE-8B engines. Nine SH-3As were modified to RH-3A by the addition of mine-sweeping gear. Other conversions include HH-3A armed search and rescue helicopters, SH-3G utility helicopters, and SH-3H multi-purpose helicopters for ASW and missile defence duties. Ten specially-equipped versions, originally HSS-2Z and now VH-3A, are operated by the Executive Flight Detachment based in Washington for VIP duties; five are operated by the Marines and five by the Army. Forty-one CHSS-2s (similar to SH-3As) were delivered to the Canadian Armed Forces. Eighty-three HSS-2s have been ordered by the Japanese Navy, for assembly by Mitsubishi. With uprated engines, the SH-3D appeared in 1965; 74 were built by Sikorsky and others by Agusta for the Italian Navy and Iran. In Britain, Westland is building a version with Gnome engines (see page 140). The Spanish Navy has 10 Sikorsky-built SH-3Ds, the Brazilian Navy four and the Argentine Navy four (designated S-61D-4). The Royal Danish Air Force acquired nine S-61A transports (similar to SH-3A) for long-range air/sea rescue. The Royal Malaysian Air Force has sixteen 31-seat S-61A-4 Nuri transports.

Sikorsky S-61R (H-3)

U.S.A.

Data, photograph and silhouette: CH-3.
Troop transport, assault and rescue helicopter, in production and service.

Powered by: Two 1,500shp General Electric T58-GE-5 turboshafts.
Rotor diameter: 62ft 0in (18.90m).
Fuselage length: 57ft 3in (17.45m).
Empty weight: 13,255lb (6,010kg).
Gross weight: 22,050lb (10,000kg).
Max. speed: 162mph (261km/h) at sea level.
Range: 465 miles (748km) at 144mph (232km/h).
Accommodation: Crew of 2–3; 30 troops, 15 litters or 5,000lb (2,270kg) of cargo.
Armament: None.

This version of the S-61 (see also page 120) was developed to meet USAF requirements for a general-purpose helicopter. Purchase of the CH-3C (S-61R) followed USAF experience using six "borrowed" HSS-2s (S-61As), redesignated CH-3Bs, for missile site support and drone recovery duties. The CH-3C retained amphibious capability and the original 1,300shp T58-GE-1 engines, but had new stabilising sponsons, a hydraulically-operated rear-loading ramp and a built-in auxiliary power unit. The initial USAF order for 22 CH-3Cs, placed on February 8, 1963, was followed by contracts for 19 more after the type had been selected in July 1963 to fill a new USAF requirement for a long-range rotary-wing support system. The first S-61R flew on June 17, 1963 and this civil prototype was followed a few weeks later by the first CH-3C. Deliveries to the USAF began on December 30, 1963 and in February 1966 production was switched to the CH-3E with 1,500shp T58-GE-5s, 42 being built to this standard. All aircraft delivered as CH-3C were later modified to CH-3E standard and 50 new HH-3Es were similar, the latter going to the USAF Aerospace Rescue and Recovery Service, with defensive armament, armour-plating, jettisonable fuel tanks and rescue hoist. The HH-3F is an unarmed version for extended search and rescue operations by the US Coast Guard, who have ordered a total of 40, with the name of Pelican.

Sikorsky S-64 Skycrane (CH-54 Tarhe)

U.S.A.

Heavy-lift helicopter, in production and service.

Data: CH-54A.

Powered by: Two 4,500shp Pratt & Whitney T73-P-1 turboshafts.
Rotor diameter: 72ft 0in (21.95m).
Fuselage length: 70ft 3in (21.41m).
Empty weight: 19,234lb (8,724kg).
Max. gross weight: 42,000lb (19,050kg).
Max. speed: 127mph (204km/h) at sea level.
Range: 253 miles (407km).
Armament: None.

The highly-functional Skycrane consists basically of a "backbone" structure carrying a cab for the three crew members at the front, two turboshaft engines and the main rotor system above the centre of gravity, and the tail rotor system at the rear. The underside of the backbone is flattened, so that bulky cargoes can be clamped up tight underneath it, between the stalky main undercarriage legs. The payload can be slung from strong points, but is often accommodated in interchangeable Universal Military Pods, each accommodating 45 combat-equipped troops, 24 litters, a surgical unit or field command or communications post. The first of three prototypes of the S-64A flew on May 9, 1962; the second and third machines were delivered to Germany for evaluation by the Federal armed forces. In June 1963, the US Army ordered six, under the designation CH-54A, to evaluate the heavy lift concept as an aid to battlefield mobility. Five of these aircraft were delivered to the 478th Aviation Company in June 1964 and after a full operational trial of these helicopters in Vietnam, the Army placed orders for about 60 production CH-54As. In Vietnam, loads carried by these helicopters have included 20,000lb (9,072kg) armoured vehicles and up to 87 troops in a detachable van. They had retrieved more than 380 damaged aircraft by mid-1970. Two CH-54Bs, with 4,800shp T73-P-700 engines, high-lift rotor blades and gross weight of 47,000lb (21,319kg), were acquired by the Army in 1969, for evaluation, and eight more were delivered in 1970/71.

Sikorsky S-65A (H-53 Sea Stallion) *U.S.A.*

Heavy assault transport helicopter, in production and service.
Data for CH-53D. Photograph: S-65-Oe.

Powered by: Two 3,925shp General Electric T64-GE-413 turboshafts.
Rotor diameter: 72ft 2¾in (22.02m).
Fuselage length: 67ft 2in (20.47m).
Empty weight: 23,485lb (10,653kg).
Max. gross weight: 42,000lb (19,050kg).
Max. speed: 196mph (315km/h) at sea level.
Range: 257 miles (413km).
Accommodation: Crew of 3; up to 64 troops, 24 stretchers or internal or external cargo.
Armament: None.

Based on S-64 experience, Sikorsky designed the S-65 to meet a Marine requirement for a heavy assault transport. A contract was placed in August 1962, and the first prototype flew on October 14, 1964 under the designation CH-53A. Deliveries of this version, with 2,850shp T64-GE-6 engines, began in mid-1966 and CH-53As served in Vietnam from January 1967. Their primary mission is to carry cargo, including such things as a 1½-ton truck and trailer, or a 105mm howitzer. Rear cargo doors under the tail boom provide direct access to the fuselage, which is sealed and provided with sponsons to permit emergency water landings. In September 1966, the USAF adopted an armed version with 3,080shp T64-GE-3 engines, external jettisonable fuel tanks, a flight refuelling probe and rescue hoist, for the Aerospace Rescue and Recovery Service. An order was placed for eight, designated HH-53B, and the first of these flew on March 15, 1967. They were followed in production by 58 HH-53Cs, each with 3,435shp T64-GE-7 engines. A later production version for the Marines was the CH-53D, as described above. The German armed forces are equipping with 110 similar CH-53Gs, assembled and partially manufactured in Germany. Israel has eight CH-53s, and the Austrian Air Force has two S-65-Oes for rescue duties in the Alps. Latest US production version is the RH-53D, of which 30 have been ordered for mine countermeasures duties, following US Navy operation of nine borrowed CH-53As in this role. The RH-53D will have uprated engines, improved blades and a loaded weight of 50,000lb (22,680kg). Production of the CH-53A and D versions for the USN totalled 265, and of HH-53s for the USAF, 66.

Soko J-1 Jastreb

Yugoslavia

Single-seat light attack aircraft, in production and service.

Powered by: One 3,000lb (1,360kg) st Rolls-Royce Bristol Viper 531 turbojet.
Span: 38ft 4in (11.68m) with wingtip tanks.
Length: 35ft 1½in (10.71m).
Empty weight: 6,217lb (2,820kg).
Gross weight: 10,287lb (4,666kg).
Max. speed: 510mph (820km/h) at 20,000ft (6,100m).
Max. range: 945 miles (1,520km).
Armament: Three 0.50in Colt-Browning machine-guns in nose; eight underwing attachments for two bombs of up to 550lb each, and 57mm or 127mm rockets.

The Jastreb is a light attack version of the Galeb two-seat basic trainer described on page 227, with modified wings, more powerful engine and heavier armament provisions. Its electrical system has been augmented to make the aircraft independent of ground supply for engine starting. Optional equipment includes identification radar and assisted take-off rockets. Two prototypes were flying by early 1968, when the type was already in production for the Yugoslav Air Force and available for export. Four Jastrebs have been supplied to Zambia.

Soko P-2 Kraguj

Yugoslavia

Single-seat lightweight close-support aircraft, in service:

Powered by: One 340hp Lycoming GSO-480-B1A6 piston-engine.
Span: 34ft 11in (10.64m).
Length: 26ft 0½in (7.93m).
Empty weight: 2,491lb (1,130kg).
Gross weight: 3,580lb (1,624kg).
Max. speed: 183mph (295km/h) at 5,000ft (1,500m).
Max. range: 500 miles (800km).
Armament: Two 7.7mm machine-guns in wings; two underwing attachments for 220lb bombs, napalm tanks or 12-round rocket pods; four underwing attachments for 57mm or 127mm rockets.

The Kraguj resurrects the concept of a light piston-engined attack aircraft that was pioneered by the US Fletcher Defender in the early 1950s. It is very similar to the Defender in configuration and performance, but is slightly larger, with a more powerful engine. The idea was to provide an aircraft that can be flown by pilots who have received minimum training, for use in areas where heavy ground anti-aircraft defences and interceptor fighters are not likely to be encountered. Construction is all-metal and the Kraguj is designed to operate from rough airstrips or fields. It will take off and land in under 400ft (122m).

The prototype of the Kraguj flew in about 1966 and squadrons of the Yugoslav Air Force are believed to have been equipped with the type by 1968.

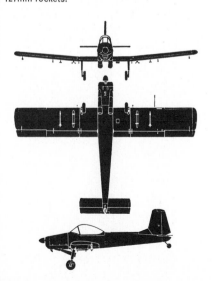

Sud-Aviation S.O.4050 Vautour   *France*

Twin-engined bomber and all-weather fighter, in service.
Data, photograph and silhouette: Vautour IIN.

Powered by: Two 7,720lb (3,500kg) st SNECMA Atar 101E-3 turbojets.
Span: 49ft 6½in (15.10m).
Length: 51ft 1in (15.57m).
Gross weight: 45,635lb (20,700kg).
Max. speed: Mach 0.9 (686mph; 1,105km/h) at sea level.
Range: 2,485 miles (4,000km).
Armament: Four 30mm cannon. Two packs containing total of 232 rockets. Underwing attachments for four Matra R.511 or R.530 and Sidewinder air-to-air missiles.

The prototype Vautour flew on October 16 1952. Production orders were placed for a total of 140 Vautour IIs, made up of 30 Mk. IIA single-seat ground attack aircraft, 40 Mk.IIB two-seat bombers and 70 Mk.IIN two-seat all-weather fighters. The IIBs and Ns were delivered to the French Air Force and remain in service. Twenty-five of the IIAs were supplied to Israel, and those remaining still form an important part of that country's attack force.

The Vautour IIA is armed with four 30mm cannon and carries three 1,000lb or six 750lb bombs internally, plus four bombs of up to 1,000lb each under its wings. The Mk.IIB carries the same weapon load as the IIA, except that the nose guns are deleted to make way for the glazed bomb-aimer's position. All versions are supersonic in a dive.

Sukhoi Su-7B (NATO code-names: Fitter-A and Moujik)

U.S.S.R.

Single-seat ground-attack fighter, in production and service.

Powered by: One 22,050lb (10,000kg) st Lyulka AL-7F (TDR 31) afterburning turbojet.
Span: 29ft 3½in (8.93m).
Length: 57ft 0in (17.37m).
Max. gross weight: 29,750lb (13,500kg).
Max. speed: Mach 1.6 (1,055mph; 1,700km/h) at 36,000ft (11,000m).
Max. range: 900 miles (1,450km).
Armament: Two 30mm cannon in wing roots; attachments under wings for bombs (usually two 750kg and two 500kg) or rocket pods.

This sweptwing fighter is standard equipment in Soviet ground attack squadrons and has also been supplied to the Cuban, Czech, Polish, East German, Hungarian, North Vietnamese, Egyptian and Indian air forces. Its fuselage, power plant and tail unit appear to be almost identical with those of the delta-wing Su-9, with the same provision for carrying two external fuel tanks under the centre-fuselage. The Su-7 was one of four single-seat fighter aircraft seen for the first time, in prototype form, at the 1956 Tushino display, the others being the MiG-21, the Su-9 and a sweptwing counterpart of the MiG-21 which was allocated the NATO code-name *Faceplate*. It seems probable that the Su-7 and *Faceplate* were evaluated in competition to find a new fighter for close-support duties, and that the Sukhoi design was chosen, as *Faceplate* did not enter service. When first seen, the Su-7 had its pitot boom mounted centrally above the air intake; but current versions have the boom offset to starboard. Very large area-increasing wing-flaps are fitted, extending from the root to more than mid-span. Wing sweep is approximately 60°, with fences at about mid-span and just inboard of the tip of each wing. A tandem two-seat version is used for training and has the NATO code-name *Moujik*.

Sukhoi Variable-Geometry Su-7 (NATO code-name: Fitter-B)

U.S.S.R.

Single-seat ground-attack fighter, in service.

Powered by: One 22,050lb (10,000kg) st Lyulka AL-7F afterburning turbojet.
Span: 41ft 0in (12.50m) spread; 29ft 6in (9.00m) swept.
Length: 56ft 0in (17.00m).
Max. gross weight: 29,750lb (13,500kg).
Max. speed: Mach 1.6 (1,055mph; 1,700km/h) at 36,000ft (11,000m).
Armament: Two 30mm cannon in wing roots; attachments under main wing fences for external stores.

The prototype of this ground-attack fighter is believed to have been the first variable-geometry aircraft test-flown in the Soviet Union. When it appeared at the 1967 Aviation Day display at Domodedovo Airport it was regarded as a test-bed, built to evaluate the merits of a swing-wing as economically as possible. It differed from the standard Su-7 only in having the outer 13ft (4.0m) of each wing pivoted, with one very large fence and two smaller ones near the tip of each inner, fixed panel. There was a full-span leading-edge slat on each outer panel.

Photographs taken at Domodedovo suggested that this prototype had weapon attachments built into the bottom of its two large wing fences. The significance of these was subsequently made clear by evidence that at least one or two squadrons of similar aircraft are in front-line service with the Soviet Air Force. They can be assumed to have improved take-off performance and range compared with the standard Su-7, at the cost of comparatively modest airframe modifications.

Sukhoi Su-9 (NATO code-names: Fishpot and Maiden)

U.S.S.R.

Single-seat all-weather fighter, in service.
The following data are estimated:

Powered by: One 22,050lb (10,000kg) st Lyulka AL-7F afterburning turbojet.
Span: 26ft 0in (7.90m).
Length: 56ft 0in (17.00m).
Max. speed: Mach 1.8 (1,190mph; 1,915km/h) at 36,000ft (11,000m).
Armament: Two *Anab* infra-red and/or radar homing air-to-air missiles under wings.

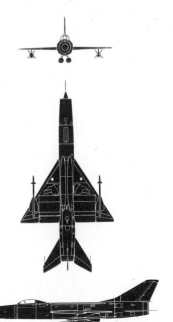

In its prototype form, as seen in the 1956 Soviet Aviation Day display in Moscow, this delta-wing all-weather fighter had a small conical radome above its air intake. On production aircraft (code-named *Fishpot* by NATO), the radome forms a centre-body in the circular air intake. The resulting fighter bears a superficial resemblance to the MiG-21, but is considerably heavier and has a much more powerful engine. It is a generally cleaner design, with a more sturdy-looking undercarriage and with no cut-out at the roots of the tailplane trailing-edge. *Fishpot* probably has a greater range and better all-weather capability than the MiG-21. It is normally seen with a pair of external fuel tanks side-by-side under the centre-fuselage. A developed version, seen at Tushino in 1961, had a new forward fuselage of longer and less-tapered form, with enlarged centre-body, and this is now known to be the standard version in service, together with some Su-9 operational trainers (NATO *Maiden*) with tandem cockpits like those of the Su-7 trainer (NATO *Moujik*).

Up to the present, *Fishpot* has been identified in service only with the Soviet Air Force.

Sukhoi Su-II (NATO code-name: Flagon)

U.S.S.R.

Data, photograph and silhouette:
Flagon-A.
Single-seat interceptor, in production and service.

Powered by: Two turbojets with afterburning.
Span (estimated): 30ft 0in (9.15m).
Length (estimated): 68ft 0in (20.50m).
Gross weight (estimated): 35,275lb (16,000kg).
Max. speed (estimated): Mach 2.3 (1,520mph; 2,450km/h) at 36,000ft (11,000m).

One of several Soviet aircraft making their first public appearance at the Domodedovo flying display in July 1967 was this high-performance interceptor, a product of the Sukhoi design bureau and now known to be designated Su-11. In addition to a single aircraft in which Vladimir Ilyushin performed aerobatics, nine of these fighters appeared in formation, apparently indicating that the Su-11 had reached squadron service. Some of these aircraft carried an *Anab* air-to-air missile beneath each wing. The standard fighter has the NATO code-name *Flagon-A*. Also shown at Domodedovo was a variant known as *Flagon-B*, which has STOL performance through the addition of lift-jets amidships. These engines are located aft of the cockpit and between the jet pipes of the two propulsion engines. Doors in the top of the fuselage hinge up to form air intakes for the lift-jet engines when they are in use. *Flagon-B*, which was a development aircraft rather than a service type, had extended wing-tips with reduced sweepback on the leading-edge of the outer panels. In other respects, it appeared to be a standard *Flagon-A*.

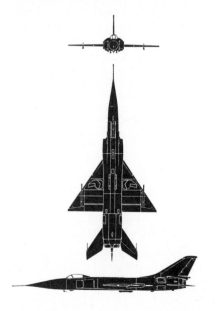

Transall C-160

France/Germany

Twin-turboprop medium-range transport, in service.

Powered by: Two 6,100shp Rolls-Royce Tyne R.Ty.20 Mk.22 turboprops.
Span: 131ft 3in (40.0m).
Length: 106ft 3½in (32.40m).
Empty weight: 63,400lb (28,758kg).
Gross weight: 108,250lb (49,100kg).
Max. speed: 333mph (536km/h) at 15,000ft (4,500m).
Range: 2,832 miles (4,558km) with 8-ton payload.
Accommodation: Crew of four, 93 troops, 61–81 paratroops, 62 litters or 35,270lb (16,000kg) freight.
Armament: None.

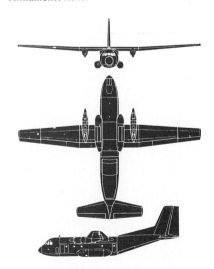

The Transall (Transporter Allianz) C-160 is one of the results of design collaboration between the aircraft industries of western Europe. Its development began in January 1959, when French and German companies undertook the joint production of a medium transport to meet the requirements of the *Armée de l'Air* and *Luftwaffe*, with possible commercial applications also. The Rolls-Royce Tyne engines were built by a British/French/Belgian/German consortium and equipment includes a Smith's flight control system which is being used as the basis of an automatic landing system. Operation from semi-prepared surfaces was one of the original requirements of the design, and there is provision for fitting two auxiliary turbojets under the outer wings to reduce the take-off run.

The first of three flying prototypes was assembled in France by Nord-Aviation (now part of Aérospatiale) and flew on February 25, 1963. The second, assembled in Germany by VFW (now VFW-Fokker), flew on May 25, 1963. The third, assembled in Germany by Hamburger Flugzeugbau (now part of Messerschmitt-Bölkow-Blohm), flew on February 19, 1964. Nord began flight testing the first of six C-160A pre-production aircraft, with a 20-inch longer fuselage, on May 21, 1965. The first production C-160s were completed in 1967. Subsequent deliveries totalled 50 C-160Fs for France, 110 similar C-160Ds to replace the *Luftwaffe*'s Noratlas, and nine C-160Zs for the South African Air Force. Twenty of the C-160Ds have been transferred to the Turkish Air Force. Production ended in October 1972.

Tupolev Tu-16 (NATO code-name: Badger)

U.S.S.R.

Twin-jet medium bomber, in service.
Photograph: *Badger-D.* **Silhouette:**
Badger-C.
The following data are estimated:

Powered by: Two 20,950lb (9,500kg) st Mikulin AM-3M turbojets.
Span: 110ft 0in (33.50m).
Length: 120ft 0in (36.50m).
Gross weight: 150,000lb (68,000kg).
Max. speed: 587mph (945km/h) at 35,000ft (10,700m).
Range: 3,975 miles (6,400km) at 480mph (770km/h) with 3 tons of bombs.
Accommodation: Crew of about seven.
Armament: *Badger-A* has seven 23mm cannon, in pairs in dorsal, ventral and tail turrets and singly on starboard side of nose, plus nine tons of bombs in bomb-bay. *Badger-B/G* is similar except that two jet-propelled *Kennel* or rocket-powered *Kelt* air-to-surface anti-shipping missiles are carried under wings, instead of bombs. *Badger-C* has a large nose radome, precluding fitment of the nose cannon, and carries a *Kipper* air-to-surface missile under the fuselage.

First seen in a Moscow fly-past in 1954, the Tu-16 has been a standard Soviet medium-range reconnaissance-bomber ever since. It is the aircraft from which the Tu-104 airliner was evolved. Some 2,000 appear to have been built, of which several hundred are still in service with the Soviet Long-Range Aviation force and about 200 with the Naval Air Fleet. About 20 of the standard bomber version (*Badger-A*) were supplied to Egypt and represented the most potent bomber force in the Middle East then destroyed in the June 1967 war. Replacements have been seen over the Mediterranean with both Egyptian and Soviet markings. Six *Badger-As* were supplied to the Iraqi Air Force.

Indonesia received an estimated 20 *Badger-Bs*, carrying jet-powered aeroplane-type anti-shipping missiles (NATO code-name *Kennel*), but these were grounded in 1972.

The Soviet Naval Air Fleet appears to use *Badger-As* as long-range reconnaissance-bombers, but also has *Badger-Bs* and possibly *Badger-Cs*. This last version was shown in the 1961 Tushino display and can be identified by a large radome built into its nose. The *Kipper* anti-shipping missile that it carries is something like the American Hound Dog, with underslung engine, but has conventional swept wings and tail instead of a tail-first delta layout. *Badger-G* differs from the *B* in carrying two rocket-powered *Kelt* missiles.

Badger-D (with nose radome) has under-fuselage electronic blisters, as does *Badger-E* (with glazed nose); while *Badger-F* has electronic pods on underwing pylons and windows in its bomb-bay doors for a battery of reconnaissance cameras. All versions can refuel in flight from other *Badgers*, using a unique wingtip-to-wingtip hose technique.

Tupolev Tu-22 (NATO code-name: Blinder)

U.S.S.R.

Photograph: *Blinder-C.* **Silhouette:** *Blinder-A.*

Twin-jet supersonic bomber, in service. The following data are estimated:

Powered by: Two unspecified turbojets with afterburners, rated at about 26,000lb (11,800kg) st each.
Span: 90ft 10½in (27.70m).
Length: 132ft 11½in (40.53m).
Gross weight: About 185,000lb (83,900kg).
Max. speed: Mach 1.4 (920mph; 1,480km/h) at 40,000ft (12,000m).
Max. range: 1,400 miles (2,250km).
Accommodation: Crew of three.
Armament: *Blinder-B* carries *Kitchen* missile semi-recessed in fuselage under-surface; radar-controlled tail gun.

This rear-engined bomber was first shown at the 1961 Tushino air display prior to which time it was unknown to the West. Ten examples flew overhead on that occasion: of these, nine appeared to be reconnaissance-bombers, with a fairly small internal weapon-bay and a pointed nose radome. The tenth carried a *Kitchen* (NATO code-name) air-to-surface missile under its belly and was fitted with a considerably larger and more heart-shaped radome. In both cases there were, surprisingly, large windows in the bottom of the fuselage, immediately aft of the radome, for visual bomb-aiming or cameras.

At the 1967 air display over Domodedovo, a total of 22 Tu-22s appeared, most of them carrying *Kitchen* air-to-ground stand-off missiles. All these aircraft had flight refuelling probes and the wider radome of the single example seen previously. This version is now identified as *Blinder-B*, while the version carrying internally-housed free-fall weapons is *Blinder-A*. A third version, *Blinder-C*, can be identified by the windows for reconnaissance cameras in its bomb-bay doors. There is also a trainer version, with an extra cockpit above and to the rear of the standard position. The Tu-22 is in service with units of the Soviet Navy as a shore-based attack bomber and reconnaissance aircraft, and an ECM version has been reported.

Tupolev Tu-28P (NATO code-name: Fiddler)

U.S.S.R.

Two-seat all-weather fighter, in service. The following data are estimated:

Powered by: Two unidentified turbojets with afterburners; rating about 27,000lb (12,250kg) st each.
Span: 65ft 0in (20.00m).
Length: 85ft 0in (26.00m).
Gross weight: About 100,000lb (45,000kg).
Max. speed: Mach 1.75 (1,150mph; 1,850km/h) at 36,000ft (11,000m).
Armament: Four large infra-red and/or radar-homing air-to-air missiles (NATO code-name *Ash*) under wings.

This formidable-looking long-range interceptor was first seen at the 1961 Tushino air display. Its evolution can be traced back to the Tu-16 (*Badger*) through the Tu-98 (*Backfin*) prototypes which were produced in 1955 to provide a long-range all-weather interceptor capable of defending the USSR against British and American strategic bombers. The examples of *Fiddler* seen in 1961 each carried two *Ash* missiles, but three Tu-28Ps displayed in 1967 each carried four of these missiles and dispensed with the large ventral fairing of the earlier versions.

Tupolev Tu-95 (NATO code-name: Bear)

U.S.S.R.

Four-turboprop long-range bomber, in service.
Photograph: *Bear-D.* **Data and silhouette:** *Bear-A.*
The following data are estimated:

Powered by: Four 14,795shp Kuznetsov NK-12MV turboprops.
Span: 159ft 0in (48.50m).
Length: 155ft 10in (47.50m).
Gross weight: 340,000lb (154,220kg).
Max. speed: 500mph (805km/h) at 41,000ft (12,500m).
Range: 7,800 miles (12,550km) with 11 tons of bombs.
Armament: Six 23mm cannon, in pairs in dorsal, ventral and tail turrets. *Bear-A* carries up to 25,000lb (11,340kg) of bombs in internal bay. *Bear-B* has nose radome and carries *Kangaroo* air-to-surface missile under fuselage.

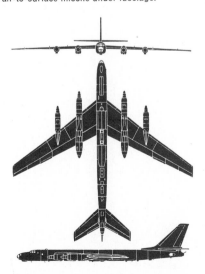

Unique among heavy bombers in that it is powered by turboprop engines, the Tu-95 was first seen in the 1955 Aviation Day display, when seven flew over Moscow escorted by several MiG-17 fighters. It is the aircraft from which the huge Tu-114 transport aircraft was evolved (see page 136). The four NK-12MV turboprops make the Tu-95 the fastest propeller-driven aircraft in military service, with a cruising speed matching that of the twin-jet Tu-16 and a greater range and bomb-carrying capacity than the Myasishchev Mya-4. It is believed that more than 100 of the original strategic bomber version (*Bear-A*) were built—some sources suggest as many as 300. By 1961, a modernisation programme was under way, based on the employment of a long-range jet-powered air-to-surface missile (code-name *Kangaroo*). The updated aircraft (redesignated *Bear-B* by NATO) took part in the Tushino air display that year and have since been seen many times, minus missile, on long-range reconnaissance flights to photograph NATO fleet movements at sea. *Bear-B* has a large nose radome and optional flight refuelling probe. Another reconnaissance version, identified in 1964, is the *Bear-C* with different electronic equipment. *Bear-D*, first seen in 1967, has an under-nose radome like that of the Canadair Argus and a huge under-belly radome; it is able to take over control of anti-shipping missiles launched from other aircraft or ships, and guide them into their targets.

Bear-E is generally similar to the *A* but carries reconnaissance cameras in its bomb-bay. *Bear-F* has enlarged fairings at the rear of its undercarriage pods.

135

Tupolev Tu-114 (NATO code-name: Moss)

U.S.S.R.

Airborne early warning and fighter control aircraft, in service.

Powered by: Four 14,795shp Kuznetsov NK-12MV turboprops.
Span: 167ft 8in (51.10m).
Armament: None.

This AWACS (airborne warning and control system) aircraft caused quite a stir when it was first seen in a Soviet documentary film in 1968, because the USAF was at that time only beginning to consider development of a similar machine based on the Boeing 707 transport (see page 169). *Moss* (its Soviet military designation is unknown) is based on the Tu-114 transport and has the usual four Kuznetsov NK-12MV turboprop engines, driving contra-rotating propellers. Changes centred mainly on the fuselage, which has only a few windows in the electronics-packed cabin and a great number of added excrescences, including a flight refuelling nose-probe, ventral tail-fin and many external antennae and fairings. The rotating "saucer" radome above the fuselage is able to detect incoming attack aircraft over long ranges, so that *Moss* can direct interceptor fighters towards them. Aircraft of this type have been encountered frequently during NATO exercises, and the accompanying photograph was taken during an encounter between *Moss* and RN Phantom fighters from HMS *Ark Royal*. Its specification should be similar to that of the Tu-114, which is 177ft 6in (54.10m) long, with a gross weight of 376,990lb (171,000kg), maximum speed of 540mph (870km/h) and maximum range of 5,560 miles (8,950km).

Vought A-7 Corsair II

U.S.A.

Data: A-7D. Photograph A-7E. Silhouette: A-7A.
Single-seat light attack aircraft, in production and service.

Powered by: One 14,250lb (6,465kg) st Allison TF41-A-1 (Rolls-Royce Spey) turbofan.
Span: 38ft 9in (11.80m).
Length: 46ft 1½in (14.06m).
Empty weight: approx. 19,500lb (8,845kg).
Gross weight: 42,000lb (19,050kg).
Max. speed: 698mph (1,123km/h) at sea level.
Max. ferry range: more than 3,340 miles (5,375km).
Armament: One M-61 20mm multi-barrel cannon in fuselage. Two fuselage and six wing strong-points for external load of more than 15,000lb (6,805kg) of missiles, bombs, rockets, gun packs or fuel tanks.

Winner of a 1963 design contest for a light-weight attack aircraft for the US Navy, the A-7A Corsair II was derived from the F-8 Crusader fighter. Differences from the original design included a shorter fuselage, a fixed (as opposed to variable-incidence) wing, revised control surfaces for subsonic operations, and the installation of an 11,350 lb (5,150kg) st Pratt & Whitney TF30-P-6 non-afterburning turbofan for greater range and endurance. An initial contract for three prototypes was placed in March 1964, and the first of these aircraft made its first flight on September 27, 1965. Deliveries to a Corsair II training unit began in October 1966 and the first operational unit, VA-147, was commissioned in February 1967; it was deployed to the Vietnam theatre in December 1967. Vought Aeronautics built 199 A-7As. The first A-7B (196 built) flew on February 6, 1968, with a 12,200lb (5,534kg) st TF30-P-8 engine. In October 1966 the USAF ordered the A-7D, with more advanced avionics and an Allison TF41 (Rolls-Royce Spey) engine. The first Spey-powered A-7D flew on September 26, 1968, following earlier trials with two A-7D airframes powered by TF30 engines. Deliveries began in December 1968. The US Navy's A-7E also has more advanced avionics and features of the A-7D. The first 67 had TF30-P-8 engines (first flown November 25, 1968) and were retrospectively designated A-7C to avoid confusion with subsequent A-7Es which have a 15,000lb (6,805kg) st TF41-A-2. The YA-7H Corsair II-2 (first flown August 29, 1972) is a private-venture tandem two-seat training/combat conversion of an A-7E, with an overall length of 48ft 5in (14.76m).

137

Vought F-8 Crusader

U.S.A.

Data: **F-8E.** Photograph: **F-8E(FN).**
Silhouette: **RF-8A.**
Single-seat carrier-based day fighter, in service.

Powered by: One 18,000lb (8,165kg) st Pratt & Whitney J57-P-20 turbojet.
Span: 35ft 8in (10.87m).
Length: 54ft 6in (16.61m).
Max. gross weight: 34,000lb (15,420kg).
Max. speed: Nearly Mach 2.
Armament: Four 20mm cannon. Four Sidewinder missiles on fuselage; wing racks for two 2,000lb bombs or two Bullpup A or B missiles or 24 Zuni air-to-ground rockets.

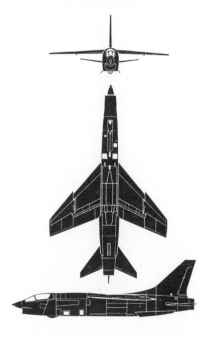

The Crusader was winner of a 1953 design competition for a deck-landing supersonic fighter. An unusual feature of the design was the high wing position, adopted to permit the wing incidence to be increased for low approach speeds without high angles of incidence on the fuselage. The original designation for the Crusader series was F8U, changed to F-8 in 1962. First flight of the prototype was on March 25, 1955 and deliveries of the F-8A (with 16,000lb; 7,257kg st J57-P-12) to VF-32 Squadron began in March 1957. Later As had a J57-P-4A of 16,200lb (7,327kg) st. The F-8B was similar with J57-P-4A and improved radar; production of these first two models totalled 318 and 130 respectively, plus 144 camera-equipped RF-8As. The single two-seat NTF-8A first flew on February 6, 1962, having earlier served as the prototype F-8E. Distinguished by two ventral fins, the F-8C introduced the 16,900lb (7,665kg) st J57-P-16 and first flew on August 20, 1958. Production totalled 187 before the F-8D appeared. First flown on February 16, 1960, this introduced the P-20 engine and limited all-weather capability with a Vought push-button auto-pilot; 152 were built. With higher-performance radar and a three-inch longer nose radome, the F-8E prototype first flew on June 30, 1961 and went into service in February 1962. Production ended in mid-1964 when 286 F-8Es had been built. The French Navy purchased 42 F-8E(FN)s with provision for Matra 530 missiles; the first of these flew on June 26, 1964. In post-production modification and modernisation programmes, 73 RF-8As have become RF-8G and a total of 89 F-8Ds and 136 F-8Es were updated to F-8H and F-8J respectively, with attack capability and other improvements. Subsequently, 87 F-8Cs were modified to F-8K and 61 F-8Bs to F-8L. Surviving F-8As are now designated TF-8A.

Westland Lynx (WG.13)   *Great Britain*

Twin-engined multi-purpose helicopter, in production.
Photograph and silhouette: Lynx AH. Mk.1. Data: Lynx HAS. Mk.2.

Powered by: Two 900shp Rolls-Royce BS.360-07-26 turboshafts.
Rotor diameter: 42ft 0in (12.80m).
Fuselage length: 38ft 3¼in (11.67m).
Empty weight: 5,352lb (2,427kg).
Gross weight: 8,000lb (3,628kg).
Max. cruising speed: 184mph (296km/h) at sea level.
Range: 173–489 miles (278–788km).
Accommodation: Basic crew of two; or pilot and up to 10 troops or 2,000lb (907kg) of internal freight, or three stretchers and two seated casualties.
Armament: Provision for 20mm cannon or two Miniguns in cabin; or racks for pods of guns or rockets, or six AS.11 or four AS.12 or Swingfire missiles.

The Lynx is one of the three types of helicopter covered by the Anglo-French helicopter agreement, the others being the SA330 Puma and SA341 Gazelle. Five prototype aircraft were built initially, under the design leadership of Westland, and the first of these flew on March 21, 1971, followed by the first in Army configuration on April 12, 1972, and the first in Navy configuration on May 25, 1972. Earlier, the Lynx's semi-rigid main rotor had been flight tested on a Scout.

Basic versions of the Lynx are an all-weather general-purpose aircraft for the British Army and Marines (Lynx AH.Mk.1) with advanced electronics, and frigate-borne anti-submarine hunter-killer versions for the Royal Navy (HAS.Mk.2) and French Navy, to replace types such as the Wasp. Two of the latter version have been ordered by the Argentine Navy. A training version for the RAF has also been projected as the Lynx HT.Mk.3.

Armament and equipment will vary according to role. Dual controls are optional, as are avionics such as Decca Doppler and navigation computer with roller map display. The ASW version will have provision for carrying two Mk.44 homing torpedoes, AS.12 or BAC CL384 missiles and search radar. Seven pre-production Lynx's will be used in the military development programme. During a series of record attempts in 1972, the prototype British Army Lynx achieved a speed of 200mph (322km/h) over a 15/25km course.

Westland Sea King

Great Britain

Anti-submarine and general-purpose helicopter, in production and service.

Powered by: Two 1,500shp Rolls-Royce Bristol Gnome H.1400 turboshafts.
Rotor diameter: 62ft 0in (18.90m).
Fuselage length: 55ft 9¾in (17.01m).
Typical empty weight: 15,474lb (7,019kg).
Gross weight: 20,500lb (9,300kg).
Normal operating speed: 131mph (211km/h).
Max. ferry range: 1,105 miles (1,778km).
Accommodation: Crew of four in anti-submarine role. Provision for carrying up to 22 troops or nine stretchers and two attendants.
Armament: Four Mk.44 homing torpedoes, bombs or four Mk.11 depth charges, etc. Provision for machine-gun in starboard cabin doorway.

This is the Sikorsky SH-3D Sea King (see page 120) as built under licence by Westland for the Royal Navy. It differs from the US version in having Gnome engines; an automatic flight control system of the kind installed in the Wessex HAS.Mk.3; long-range sonar, with Doppler processing and bathythermograph facilities; a tactical display provided by AW391 search radar in a dorsal hump fairing and an associated Doppler navigation system. In addition to its basic ASW role, the Sea King is used for tactical and logistic operations, and search and rescue duties. Four imported SH-3D airframes were converted to Sea King standard by Westland Helicopters Ltd during 1967. The first of 56 Sea King HAS Mk.1s ordered by the Royal Navy made its first flight on May 7, 1969 and No. 700S Squadron was commissioned as the first RN Sea King unit on August 19. It was followed by Nos. 824 and 826 operational squadrons, and production for the RN was completed in mid-1972.

Export orders have included 22 Sea King Mk.41s (first flown March 6, 1972) for search and rescue duties with the Federal German Navy; nine ASW Sea King Mk.42s for No. 330 Squadron of the Indian Navy (first flight October 14, 1970), and ten Mk.43 search and rescue models for the Norwegian Air Force (first flight May 19, 1972). The Royal Austrailan Navy has ordered ten Sea King Mk.50s for ASW duties, with 1,590shp Gnome H.1400-1 engines, AQS-13B sonar and higher gross weight.

Westland Wasp/Scout   *Great Britain*

Anti-submarine (Wasp) and light liaison (Scout) helicopter, in service.
Data and silhouette: Wasp. Photograph: Scout.

Powered by: One 710shp (derated) Rolls-Royce Bristol Nimbus 503 turboshaft.
Rotor diameter: 32ft 3in (9.83m).
Fuselage length: 30ft 4in (9.24m).
Empty weight: 3,452lb (1,566kg).
Gross weight: 5,500lb (2,495kg).
Max. speed: 120mph (193km/h) at sea level.
Range: 270 miles (435km) at 110mph (177km/h).
Accommodation: Crew of two; provision for three passengers, or for stretcher across rear of cabin.
Armament: Two Mk.44 homing torpedoes or other external stores.

The Wasp and Scout are variants of the same design, which had its origin in the Saunders-Roe P.531 private-venture helicopter (first flight July 20, 1958). Two P.531 prototypes were built, each with a 325shp Turmo engine. Evaluation of three similar aircraft (including one of the prototypes) by the Royal Navy led to an order for development and production of the Wasp HAS. Mk.1, with Nimbus engine, folding tail-boom and four individual undercarriage legs with castoring wheels. A prototype P.531 with Nimbus engine first flew on August 9, 1959, followed by the first Wasp on October 28, 1962. Wasps operate in the anti-submarine role from "Tribal" and "Leander" class frigates, each of which carries one Wasp and two pilots. Seventeen Wasps have been ordered for operation from South African Navy frigates, three for New Zealand, twelve for the Royal Netherlands Navy and three for Brazil. The Scout AH.1 differs from the Wasp in having a 685shp Nimbus 101 or 102 engine, skid undercarriage and fixed tail. The first of a pre-production batch of Scouts ordered for the Army Air Corps flew on August 4, 1960, and the first of a large production series flew on March 6, 1961. Two are operated by the Royal Australian Navy for survey duties, and two by the Uganda Police Air Wing. The Scout has a gross weight of 5,300lb (2,404kg) and max. speed of 131mph (211km/h).

Westland Wessex

Great Britain

Anti-submarine and transport helicopter, in service.
Data and photograph: Wessex HU.Mk. 5.
Silhouette: Wessex Mk.1.

Power plant: One Rolls-Royce Gnome 112 and one Gnome 113 shaft-turbines coupled to give output of 1,550shp.
Rotor diameter: 56ft 0in (17.07m).
Fuselage length: 48ft 4½in (14.74m).
Empty weight: 8,657lb (3,927kg).
Gross weight: 13,500lb (6,120kg).
Max. speed: 132mph (212km/h) at sea level.
Range: 478 miles (770km).
Accommodation: Crew of 1–3; 16 troops, seven litters or 4,000lb (1,814kg) of freight.
Armament: Provision for carrying machine-guns, rocket launchers, torpedoes and SS.11 air-to-surface missiles.

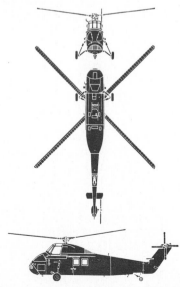

Development of the Wessex began when Westland purchased a licence to build the Sikorsky S-58 (see page 119) in 1956. The deal included an example of the HSS-1 and when this arrived in Britain a 1,100shp Gazelle N.Ga.11 shaft-turbine was substituted for the original piston-engine. The re-engined aircraft flew on May 17, 1957, and a production version, designated Wessex HAS.Mk.1, was ordered by the Royal Navy for anti-submarine duties in the combined hunter-killer role. The first of two pre-production models flew on June 20, 1958. Deliveries of production Wessex 1s, with crew of four, 1,450shp Gazelle 161 engine, dipping sonar and strike weapons, began in 1960. The first operational anti-submarine squadron with the Wessex HAS.Mk.1 was commissioned in July 1961. During 1962, an assault transport version of the Mk.1, carrying 16 troops, entered squadron service on the Commando assault carrier HMS *Albion*. For service with the RAF, the Wessex HC.Mk.2 has a coupled Gnome installation. A test-bed Wessex 1 flew with this power plant on January 18, 1962, followed by the first production Mk.2 on October 5. A similar variant for RN Commando assault duties is the HU.Mk.5 (first flown on May 31, 1963); while the HAS.Mk.3 is similar to the Mk.1 but with a 1,600shp Gazelle 165 and large dorsal radome. Two HCC.Mk.4s (converted from Mk.2) are used by The Queen's Flight. Export models in service are the Wessex HAS.Mk.31B (27, Royal Australian Navy with 1,540shp Gazelle 162), Wessex 52 (9, Iraqi Air Force, as Mk.2) and Wessex 53 (2, Ghana Air Force, as Mk.2).

Yakovlev Yak-25, Yak-26 and Yak-27 (NATO code-names: Flashlight and Mangrove)

U.S.S.R.

Two-seat all-weather fighter, tactical reconnaissance aircraft and trainer, in service.
Data, photograph and silhouette: *Mangrove.*

Powered by: Two 8,820lb (4,000kg) st Klimov RD-9 turbojets, with afterburning.
Span: 38ft 6in (11.75m).
Length: 62ft 0in (18.90m).
Empty weight: 17,000lb (7,710kg).
Gross weight: 25,000lb (11,350kg).
Max. speed: Mach 0.95 (627mph; 1,010km/h) at 36,000ft (11,000m).
Armament: One 30mm cannon in front fuselage.

The original Yak-25 (*Flashlight-A*) entered service as the Soviet Union's standard two-seat all-weather fighter in 1955 and remains operational. It is of fairly conventional sweptwing (45°) all-metal construction, the most unusual feature being its tandem main undercarriage. This consists of a single nose-wheel, with twin main wheels under the fuselage aft of the wing and small outrigger wheels which retract into wing-tip fairings. Power plant comprised originally two AM-5 turbojets, changed to 6,175lb (2,800kg) st Klimov RD-9s in the Yak-25F in 1957.

In the 1956 Aviation Day fly-past over Moscow, prototypes of two Yak-25 variants appeared, with extended wing-root chord and longer engine nacelles. The Yak-25R (*Flashlight-B*) had a single-seat cockpit and a glazed nose for a navigator/bomb aimer for ground attack duties. The Yak-27 (*Flashlight-C*) was an all-weather fighter with pointed nose radome. The Yak-27 does not seem to have entered service in appreciable numbers; but a developed version of the Yak-25R, with wingtips extended beyond the now-pointed balancer wheel fairings and armament reduced to one cannon, entered service as the Yak-26 for tactical reconnaissance, and was given the code-name *Mangrove*. The further developed *Firebar/Brewer* series is described separately on page 144.

Yakovlev Yak-28, Yak-28P and Yak-28U (NATO code-names: Brewer, Firebar and Maestro)
U.S.S.R.

Two-seat all-weather fighter, multi-purpose tactical aircraft and trainer, in service.
Photograph and silhouette: Yak-28P.
Data apply to Yak-28 and are estimated.

Powered by: Two 13,120lb (5,950kg) st Tumansky TDR Mk.R37F turbojets with afterburning on current aircraft.
Span: 42ft 6in (12.95m).
Length: 71ft 0½in (21.65m).
Gross weight: 35,000lb (15,875kg).
Max. speed: Mach 1.1 (733mph; 1,180km/h) at 36,000ft (11,000m).
Range: 1,200–1,600 miles (1,930–2,575km) at 570mph (920km/h).
Armament: One 30mm cannon on each side of fuselage or on starboard side only. Bombs in internal weapon bay; other stores under wings.

These successors to the Yak-25/27 were first seen in public at the 1961 Tushino air display and can be identified by their shoulder-mounted wing, compared with the mid-wing of the Yak-25/27 series. They have extended wingtips and pointed balancer wheel fairings, as on the Yak-26 (*Mangrove*) (see page 143) but the entire wing leading-edge inboard of the nacelle on each side is extended forward. Another major innovation is that the undercarriage has two twin-wheeled units in tandem, with the rear unit much further aft than on the earlier designs. The engine nacelles have intake centre-bodies.

The Yak-28P (*Firebar*) is a tandem two-seat all-weather fighter, with pointed radome and underwing armament of two *Anab* air-to-air guided missiles. The original nose shape is shown in the silhouette. A new and longer radome is being fitted retrospectively as shown in the photograph.

The basic Yak-28 (*Brewer*) is a multi-purpose tactical aircraft, with glazed nose, and can be regarded as a "third generation" counterpart of *Mangrove*. It has one or two 30mm cannon submerged in the sides of the fuselage, an internal weapon-bay and, usually, an under-fuselage radar fairing. *Firebar* superseded *Flashlight-A* and *Brewer* replaced the Il-28. A third variant, the Yak-28U (*Maestro*), is a dual-control training version of *Firebar*, with an additional blister canopy forward of, and lower than the rear canopy and a much larger nose-probe.

Underwing Sparrow missiles distinguish
the Lockheed F-104S Starfighters built by
Aeritalia for the Italian Air Force

Above: As a follow-up to the 'double-delta' Draken, Saab's imaginative designers have produced for the Swedish Air Force the canard AJ 37 Viggen, combining Mach 2 speed with short take-off capability

Top right: Trio of US Marine Corps combat aircraft comprises a Phantom II fighter and Skyhawk attack aircraft, manufactured by McDonnell Douglas, and a VISTOL Harrier in which this same company has US licence rights

Right: In contrast, the F-15A Eagle is the latest air superiority fighter ordered for the USAF. Designed by McDonnell Douglas, it features the twin-fin type of tail unit pioneered by Russia's MiG-25

Above: For allied air forces which require a potent but easy-to-fly supersonic tactical fighter, the USAF has backed development and production of the Northrop F-5E Tiger II. The nose-boom identifies this as the prototype

Top right: Major expansion of the Libyan Air Force was foreshadowed by its massive order for combat, reconnaissance and training versions of the Dassault Mirage. This is a Mirage 5-DE tandem two-seat trainer in Libyan markings

Right: Built by Agusta of Italy for No 1 Squadron of the Swedish Navy, this Bell 206A JetRanger (HKP 6) has under-fuselage armament and emergency floats in a stowed position on its skid undercarriage

Right: Although designed to hunt and destroy submarines, this RAF Nimrod is shown in a more humane role, circling a Soviet submarine which was in trouble in high seas/*Ministry of Defence*

Top: Norway's ten Sea Kings, built in the UK by Westland, are equipped and painted for search and rescue missions

Above: One of a dozen BAC Strikemasters bought by Kuwait, this aggressive-looking ground attack/trainer is finished in typical Middle Eastern light brown top camouflage

Well-worn camouflage, and a heavy load of 'iron bombs' under the wings and in the bomb-bays, identify this Boeing B-52 as one of those which played such a major part in the air war in Vietnam. It was photographed whilst refuelling in flight from a KC-135 tanker

Eager to be seen, rather than made invisible by camouflage, the Hawker Siddeley Gnat T.Mk 1s of the RAF's Red Arrows aerobatic demonstration team are among the most famous military aircraft in the world. This one was photographed during the team's visit to Washington, USA, in 1972
/*Gordon S. Williams*

Aeritalia/Aermacchi AM.3C   *Italy*

The three-seat all-metal AM.3 was developed as a replacement for the L-19s and other observation aircraft currently in service with the Italian Army. It is a joint product of the Aermacchi and Aeritalia companies and utilises the basic wing of the Aermacchi-Lockheed AL.60. The prototype flew for the first time on May 12, 1967, powered by a 340hp Continental GTSIO-520-C engine, and was followed by a second on August 22, 1968; both were subsequently re-engined with the Piaggio-Lycoming GSO-480-B1B6. A hard-point under each wing, immediately outboard of the bracing strut pick-up point, enables the AM.3 to be used for light tactical support duties, carrying a wide variety of armament, including two AS.11 or AS.12 wire-guided missiles, two 250lb bombs, twelve 2.75in rockets, two Minigun pods and 3,000 rounds of ammunition or two pods each containing a pair of 7.62mm machine-guns and 2,000 rounds. Production models are designated AM.3C and the first of 40 for South Africa was rolled out in May 1972. Second customer was expected to be the Italian Army. **Data:** Span 41ft 5½in (12.64m). Length 29ft 5½in (8.98m). Gross weight 3,860lb (1,750kg). Max. speed 173mph (278km/h). Range 615 miles (990km).

Aermacchi-Lockheed AL.60C5 and LASA-60   *Italy/Mexico*

This all-metal utility aircraft was designed and built in prototype form (first flight September 15, 1959) by Lockheed-Georgia. Production was then entrusted to two Lockheed associates—Lockheed-Azcarate S.A. in Mexico and Aermacchi in Italy. The version built in Mexico was a six-seater with nose-wheel undercarriage, powered by a 250hp Continental IO-470-R engine. Only 18 were delivered, for use by No. 209 Search and Rescue Squadron of the Mexican Air Force. The air force of the Central African Federation has ten AL.60C5 Conestogas, built by Aermacchi, with tail-wheel undercarriage and 400hp Lycoming IO-720-A1A engine, and a similar variant is used by the Rhodesian Air Force as the Trojan. **Data** (AL.60C5): Span 39ft 4in (11.99m). Length 28ft 10½in (8.80m). Gross weight 4,500lb (2,041kg). Max. speed 156mph (251km/h). Range 645 miles (1,037km).

Aero 3   *Yugoslavia*

This is a development of the Aero 2 two-seat primary trainer, retaining much of the all-wood structure of the earlier machine, but with a more powerful (185hp) Lycoming O-435-A engine, giving an all-round improvement in performance. Production began in 1957 and the Aero 3 largely replaced the Aero 2 in service with the Yugoslav Air Force. Main external feature that distinguishes the Aero 3 from the 2, apart from the engine cowling, is the one-piece blown plastic canopy which replaced the former "glasshouse". Full dual controls are fitted and the front seat can be covered with a hood for blind flying tuition. **Data:** Span 34ft 5in (10.5m). Length 28ft 1in (8.58m). Gross weight 2,646lb (1,198kg). Max. speed 143mph (230km/h).

Aero L-29 Delfin (NATO code-name: Maya)   *Czechoslovakia*

The prototype of this tandem two-seat basic trainer flew for the first time on April 5, 1959, with a Bristol Siddeley Viper turbojet, but production machines have a locally designed M-701 engine of 1,920 or 1,960lb (870 or 890kg) st. The L-29 was designed to replace piston-engined trainers in service with the Czech Air Force and, after evaluation in competition with jet trainers built in other countries, was also chosen as the standard basic trainer of the Soviet Air Force. Other nations which have L-29s are reported to include Bulgaria, East Germany, Egypt, Hungary, Indonesia, Romania, Syria and Uganda, and about 2,500 had been delivered by the end of 1970. Two underwing attachments can be used to carry external fuel tanks, 100kg bombs, 7.62mm machine-gun pods or up to eight rockets. The L-29A Akrobat single-seater for specialised aerobatics is not yet in series production. **Data** (L-29): Span 33ft 9in (10.29m). Length 35ft 5½in (10.81m). Gross weight 7,804lb (3,540kg). Max. speed 407mph (655km/h). Range 555 miles (894km).

Aero L-39 Super Delfin   *Czechoslovakia*

Following their success with the L-29 Delfin basic jet trainer (page 154), the Aero factory at Vodochodv, near Prague, developed the L-39 basic and advanced trainer. Powered by a 3,306lb (1,500kg) st Walter Titan engine (based on the Russian Ivchenko AI-25W), the L-39 is a subsonic trainer with capability for development in the light strike role, carrying external weapons. The first flight was made on November 4, 1968 and four more prototypes had joined the flight test programme by mid-1970. An initial production batch of 10 was put in hand in 1971 and full production was to begin in 1972. **Data:** Span 29ft 10¾in (9.11m). Length 39ft 8¾in (12.11m). Gross weight 8,380lb (3,800kg). Max. speed 454mph (730km/h). Range 680 miles (1,100km) clean; 930 miles (1,500km) with tiptanks.

Aero Commander Shrike Commander   *U.S.A.*

First major foreign customer for the twin-engined Shrike Commander for military use was the Argentinian Air Force, which placed an order for 14 of these aircraft in March 1968, with an option on four more. The Shrike Commander (known originally as the Model 500U) is used for liaison, training and general transport duties, carrying six people. The engines are 290hp Lycoming IO-540-E1A5s. During 1972, three similar Turbo Commanders, with Garrett AiResearch TPE 331 turboprops, were acquired by the Imperial Iranian Air Force. **Data** (Shrike Commander): Span 49ft 0½in (14.95m). Length 36ft 7in (11.15m). Gross weight 6,750lb (3,062kg). Max. speed 215 mph (346km/h) at 10,000ft (3,050m).

Aérospatiale N 262 *France*

The original N262 was developed by Nord-Aviation as a 26/29-seat transport powered by two Turboméca Bastan turboprops. Layout is conventional, with a pressurised cabin and fairings to house the main undercarriage when it is retracted. Many N262s were sold for commercial operation, and in June 1967 the French Navy ordered 15 of the Srs. A version (photograph), with 1,065eshp Bastan VIC engines, for use as aircrew trainers and light transports. It subse-quently acquired six more, including five previously operated by the French Air Force. The latter had six Srs. A transports and 18 Srs. Ds, with 1,130eshp Bastan VIIAs, for training and liaison duties, taking delivery of the first of these in November 1968. **Data** (Srs. D): Span 71ft 10in (21.90m). Length 63ft 3in (19.28m). Gross weight 23,370lb (10,600kg). Max. speed 260mph (418km/h). Range 1,135 miles (1,825km) at 247mph (397km/h).

Aérospatiale SE 313B Alouette II Artouste, SA 315 Lama and SA 318C Alouette II Astazou *France*

The five-seat SE313B, with 360hp Turbo-méca Artouste IIC turboshaft, first flew on March 12, 1955. Of the total of 923 built, 363 were for the French Services and others for military and civilian customers in 33 different countries, including 267 for the West German Services and 17 for the British Army (as Alouette AH.Mk.2). The French Army also has SA318C Alouette IIs with 360hp (derated) Turboméca Astazou IIA turboshaft, giving higher per-formance. The SA315 Lama combines the airframe of the Alouette II with an 870 shp Artouste IIIB and dynamic components of the Alouette III. Argentina has ordered six and India 40, to be followed by others manufactured in India by HAL with the local name of Cheetah. The first HAL-built SA 315 was delivered in November 1972. **Data** (SA 318C): Rotor diameter 33ft 5½in (10.20m). Length 31ft 11¾in (9.75m). Gross weight 3,630lb (1,650kg). Max. speed 127mph (205km/h). Range 447 miles (720km).

Aérospatiale/Westland SA 341 Gazelle
France/Great Britain

The five-seat SA341 was conceived as a modernised development of the Alouette II, utilising the same transmission system and a 600shp Astazou IIIN engine. The semi-rigid three-blade rotor has glass-fibre blades and the tail rotor is faired inside the tail-fin. The prototype (SA340-01), fitted initially with an Alouette II tail rotor, flew for the first time on April 7, 1967. The second prototype was followed by four pre-production SA341s, of which the third (XW276) was equipped to British Army standards. British variants, assembled at Yeovil, are the Gazelle AH.Mk.1 (99 for the Army and Marines), HT.Mk.2 (30 for the Navy), and HT.Mk.3 and HCC.Mk.4 (13 for the RAF). SA341s will also be licence-built in Yugoslavia. **Data:** Rotor diameter 34ft 5½in (10.5m). Length 31ft 2¾in (9.52m). Gross weight 3,750lb (1,700kg). Max. cruising speed 160mph (257km/h). Range 416 miles (670km).

Aerotec T-23 Uirapuru
Brazil

The prototype of this side-by-side two-seat all-metal light aircraft flew on June 2, 1965, powered by a 108hp Lycoming O-235-C1 engine. A second Uirapuru followed, this time with a 150hp Lycoming O-320-A engine, and was offered to the Brazilian Air Force as a replacement for its locally-built Fokker S.11 and S.12 Instructor basic trainers. Seventy Uirapurus were ordered for this purpose in 1968–69, under the military designation T-23; 20 have been ordered for the Paraguayan Air Force. They have a 160hp Lycoming O-320-B2B and differ from the civilian model in having fully-adjustable seats, stick-type controls and a modified cockpit canopy. **Data:** Span 27ft 10¾in (8.50m). Length 21ft 8in (6.60m). Gross weight 1,825lb (840kg). Max. speed 140mph (225km/h).

AESL Airtrainer CT/4

New Zealand

This primary trainer, of which 25 have been ordered for the Royal Thai Air Force and 37 for the Royal Australian Air Force, was designed 20 years ago in its basic form, and won a design competition for two-seat light aircraft organised by the Royal Aero Club of Great Britain. Its designer was an Australian, Henry Millicer, and it eventually went into production as the Airtourer, first by Victa Ltd in Australia and then by AESL in New Zealand. Four Airtourer T6/24s were delivered to the RNZAF in 1970. The Air-

trainer, first flown on February 21, 1971, is derived from the Airtourer by way of the four-seat Aircruiser. It is aerodynamically similar, but with completely new structure, and is powered by a 210hp Continental IO-360-D engine. Provision is made for bombs, or rocket pods or gun pods beneath the wings. **Data:** Span 26ft (7.92m). Length 23ft 2in (7.06m). Gross weight 2,350lb (1,066kg). Max. speed 188mph (303km/h). Endurance about 5hr.

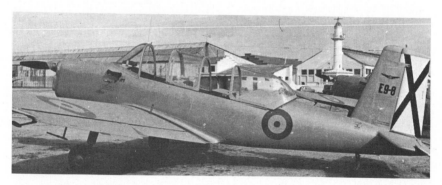

A.I.S.A. I-115

Spain

First flown on July 16, 1952, the I-115 was put into production in 1954 as the standard two-seat primary trainer of the Spanish Air Force, under the designation E-9, to replace the veteran Jungmann biplanes then in service. Altogether 450 were delivered, each powered by a 150hp ENMA Tigre G-IV-B engine. Construction is all-wooden.

Full dual controls and instrumentation are fitted. Many I-115s have been handed over to flying clubs: most of those remaining in military service are used for liaison duties. **Data:** Span 31ft 3in (9.54m). Length 24ft 1in (7.35m). Normal loaded weight 1,980lb (900kg). Max. speed 149mph (240 km/h). Endurance 5hr at 126mph (204km/h).

Alpha Jet

France/Germany

The project to develop a new basic trainer to meet the joint requirements of France and Germany was initiated in July 1969. After evaluation of competitive designs submitted by teams comprising Dassault/Dornier and Nord (Aérospatiale)/Messerschmitt (MBB), the former was selected for development. Basis of this design was a Dornier project, with tandem seating and two SNECMA-Turboméca Larzac 04 turbofan engines, each of 2,960lb (1,345kg) st. First of four prototypes (two each in Germany and France) is scheduled for completion at the end of 1973, with deliveries starting in 1976. France plans to purchase about 200 Alpha Jet trainers, and the Luftwaffe is expected to buy about 100 of a light strike version carrying weapons on underwing pylons. **Data:** Span 30ft 0½in (9.16m). Length 38ft 5in (11.71m). Gross weight 10,542lb (4,782kg). Max. speed about 650mph (1,046km/h).

Antonov An-2 (NATO code-name: Colt)
U.S.S.R.

First flown in 1947, the An-2 was designed as a rugged and versatile replacement for aircraft like the little Po-2, particularly for agricultural work in "outback" areas. Its ability to operate from short strips, thanks to its large wing area, and to carry a payload of around 1¼ tons, made it an ideal utility transport for the Soviet Air Force and many thousands have been built. Many have been supplied for military use in countries such as Afghanistan, Bulgaria, Cuba, Czechoslovakia, East Germany, Hungary, North Korea, Poland and Romania, and the An-2 has been built under licence in Poland and China. Powered by a 1,000hp ASh-62-IR engine, it carries 14 troops, six stretchers or freight, and can operate on wheels, skis or floats. **Data:** Span 59ft 8½in (18.18m). Length 40ft 8¼in (12.40m). Gross weight 12,125lb (5,500kg). Max. speed 157mph (253km/h). Range 562 miles (900km) at 124mph (200km/h).

Antonov An-14 (NATO code-name: Clod)
U.S.S.R.

First flown on March 15, 1958, the An-14 underwent a lengthy period of flight development, during which major changes were made to the wing and tail design and more powerful engines were introduced. Production aircraft have 300hp Ivchenko AI-14RF engines and normally seat 6 passengers in the cabin. Since 1967, examples of the An-14 have been seen in service with the Soviet Air Force and some Communist bloc countries including East Germany. A turboprop derivative, the 15-passenger An-14M, appeared in 1972 and may also be used for military duties in due course. **Data:** Span 72ft 2in (21.99m). Length 37ft 1½in (11.32m). Gross weight 7,935lb (3,600kg). Max. cruising speed 118mph (190km/h). Range 290 miles (470km) with 1,590lb (720kg) payload.

Antonov An-24 (NATO code-name: Coke) and An-26 (NATO code-name: Curl)
U.S.S.R.

First flown in 1960, the Antonov An-24 twin-turboprop short-haul transport has been widely produced for airline service in the USSR and for export, but little military use of the type seems to have taken place. In 1969, a more specifically military derivative, the An-26, made its appearance. This differs from the An-24 primarily in having a redesigned rear fuselage, with a "beavertail" incorporating ramps and loading doors so that vehicles can be accommodated. The door arrangement also appears to permit paradropping of troops or supplies, putting the An-26 in the same category as the Andover. The starboard nacelle contains a 1,985lb (900kg) st RV 19-300 turbojet to boost performance; main engines are 2,820ehp AI-24T turboprops. **Data** (An-26): Span 95ft 9½in (29.20m). Length 77ft 2½in (23.53m). Gross weight 52,911lb (24,000kg). Cruising speed 280mph (450km/h). Range 800 miles (1,300km).

Armstrong Whitworth Sea Hawk

Great Britain

Of 555 Sea Hawks produced by Armstrong Whitworth and Hawker, only about 30 remain in front-line service. These equip the fighter squadron which serves, together with Breguet Alizés, aboard the Indian Navy aircraft carrier *Vikrant*. India purchased 24 Sea Hawk FGA Mk.6s, to the same production standard as the final version for the Royal Navy, which acquired a total of 434 in six marks. Other export orders were from Germany (64 Mk.100 and Mk.101) and the Netherlands (36 Mk.50). India later acquired 22 more Sea Hawks ex-Royal Navy and 28 from Germany. All versions were powered by a Rolls-Royce Nene turbojet, with the 5,400lb (2,450kg) st Nene 103 in the Sea Hawk F. (GA) Mk.6. **Data:** Span 39ft 0in (11.89m). Length 39ft 8in (12.09m). Gross weight 16,200lb (7,348kg). Max. cruising speed 590mph (950km/h) at sea level.

Auster A.O.P. 9 and D-Series

Great Britain

A few examples of the Blackburn Bombardier-engined Auster AOP.9 are still flying on communications duties. Thirty-five were supplied to the Indian Air Force, which continues to use a few survivors. In addition, 15 examples of the Lycoming-engined Auster D5/160 were supplied to the Portuguese Air Force and a further quantity went to this Air Force from a total batch of 150 D4s and D5s built under licence by OGMA in Portugal. **Data** (D5/160): Span 36ft (10.97m). Length 22ft 2in (6.77m). Gross weight 2,400lb (1,088kg). Max. speed 125mph (201km/h). Range 580 miles (933km).

BAC One-Eleven

Great Britain

First military Service to purchase BAC's twin-turbofan short/medium-range airliner for VIP transport duties was the Royal Australian Air Force, which took delivery of two. They replaced piston-engined Convair 440s in No. 34 (VIP) Squadron, which operates from Fairbairn, Canberra, on transport and liaison work for the Australian government. Basically Series 200 aircraft, they are each powered by two 10,410lb (4,722kg) st Rolls-Royce Spey-2 Mk.506 engines. Two others have been acquired as VIP and Presidential transports for operation by the Brazilian Air Force and one operates in British military markings at the RAE Bedford. **Data:** Span 88ft 6in (26.97m). Length 93ft 6in (28.50m). Gross weight 78,500lb (35,610kg). Max. speed 541mph (871km/h). Typical range 1,155 miles (1,860km).

Beagle Basset C.C. Mk. 1

Great Britain

The Basset CC.Mk.1 is a five/eight-seat light transport, of which 20 were built for communications and ferrying duties with the RAF, as Anson replacements. The first one flew on December 24, 1964. It was a member of the Beagle B.206 family, development of which began with the B.206X (first flight August 15, 1961), powered by two 260hp Continental IO-470-A engines. A second prototype, the B.206Y, flew on August 12, 1962, followed by two B.206Z pre-production machines. Each of these three aircraft was fitted with 310hp Rolls-Royce/Continental GIO-470-A engines, which are standard on the commercial and military versions of the B.206 Series I, including the Basset. RAF Communications Squadrons which fly the Basset are Nos. 21, 26, 32 and 207. **Data:** Span 45ft 9½in (13.96m). Length 33ft 9in (10.26m). Gross weight 7,500lb (3,402kg). Max. speed 220mph (354km/h). Range 1,645 miles (2,650km).

Beech C-45 Expeditor

U.S.A.

A total of 5,204 Beechcraft twin-engined military transports/trainers were delivered in World War II. Many remain in service with the US Navy and with over 20 other air forces. US Navy versions are the RC-45J and TC-45J, equipped for photographic and training duties respectively. Most numerous of the other versions are the C-45G and C-45H six-seat utility transports, produced for the USAF post-war by conversion of T-7 and T-11 Kansan trainers; some T-11s also remain in service, particularly in South America. Canada took delivery of 388 Expeditors and still uses more than 100 for training and communications, with the designations Mk.3T, Mk.3N, Mk.3TM, Mk.3NM and Mk.3NMT. **Data** (C-45G): Two 450hp P. & W. R-985-AN-3 piston-engines. Span 47ft 7in (14.50m). Length 33ft 11½in (10.34m). Gross weight 9,000lb (4,082kg). Max. speed 225mph (362km/h). Range 1,200 miles (1,931km).

Beechcraft Musketeer

U.S.A.

Smallest aircraft in the Beechcraft range, the Musketeer has been in production since 1962 and over 2,000 are in service throughout the world. The majority were delivered for private or club use, in two- or four-seat variants. During January 1970, the *Fuerza Aérea Mexicana* took delivery of 20 two-seat Musketeer Sport models to be used as instrument trainers, each with a 150hp Lycoming O-320-E2C engine and fixed tricycle undercarriage. During 1971, the Canadian Armed Forces took delivery of 25 Musketeers to replace Chipmunk primary trainers. **Data:** Span 32ft 9in (9.98m). Length 25ft 0in (7.62m). Gross weight 2,250lb (1,020kg). Max. speed 140mph (225km/h). Range 880 miles (1,420km).

Beech T-34 Mentor

U.S.A.

Derived from the civil Bonanza lightplane, the Beech Mentor first flew on December 2, 1948, as a private venture. Three YT-34s were ordered by the USAF for evaluation in 1950. Subsequently, 350 T-34As were built for the USAF, and the US Navy took delivery of 423 T-34Bs before production ended in October 1957. The Mentor was also built by Canadian Car and Foundry for the USAF (100) and RCAF (25); by Fuji Industries in Japan (140 for JASDF, 36 for Philippine Air Force) and at Cordoba in the Argentine (75). Mentors were supplied by America to Chile, Colombia, Mexico, El Salvador, Saudi Arabia, Spain and Venezuela; and 24 ex-RCAF T-34s were transferred to Turkey. **Data:** One 225hp Continental O-470-13 engine. Span 32ft 10in (10.0m). Length 25ft 11¼in (7.90m). Gross weight 2,950lb (1,338kg). Max. speed 189mph (304km/h). Range 735 miles (1,183 km).

Beech T-42A Cochise

U.S.A.

In February 1965, the USAF chose the Beech B55 Baron to meet its requirement for a twin-engined instrument trainer, following a design competition limited to "off-the-shelf" types. Subsequently, Beech received contracts for 65 aircraft, to be designated T-42A. In 1971, five new T-42As were sold to Turkey, and in 1972 the Spanish Air Force ordered seven B55 Barons. Peru is also expected to acquire T-42As to replace its C-45s. The basic B55 is a four/six-seat light transport, powered by two 260hp Continental IO-470-L engines. **Data:** Span 37ft 10in (11.53m). Length 27ft 0in (8.23m). Gross weight 5,100lb (2,313kg). Max. speed 236mph (380km/h). Range 1,225 miles (1,971km).

Beech U-8 Seminole

U.S.A.

Final version of the Seminole supplied to the US Army was the U-8F, with an enlarged fuselage seating up to six passengers, and 340hp Lycoming IGSO-480 engines. Three pre-production and 68 production U-8Fs were delivered. The commercial Queen Air 65 is used by the Japan Maritime Self-Defence Force as a transport and navigation trainer, and others are used by the air forces of Venezuela and Uruguay. Earlier Seminoles in US Army service include the U-8D, with 340hp GSO-480 engines, and the U-8E, with 295hp GO-480 engines, similar to the commercial Model F50 and D50 Twin Bonanzas respectively; some of these earlier models have been modified to U-8Gs. **Data** (U-8F): Span 45ft 10½in (13.98m). Length 35ft 6in (10.82m). Gross weight 7,700lb (3,493kg). Max. speed 239mph (384km/h). Range 1,220 miles (1,963km). Photograph U-8D.

Beech U-21 (and VC-6A)

U.S.A.

During 1963, Beech converted a Queen Air airframe to have Pratt & Whitney PT6A-6 turboprops, and this aircraft was evaluated by the US Army as the NU-8F. In production guise, with the designation U-21A, the same basic airframe has a double freight-loading door, extensive avionics and an interior layout for 10 troops, 6–8 command personnel or 3 stretchers. Delivery of the U-21As began in May 1967 and subsequent contracts brought the total by late 1970 to 167. These include U-21A, RU-21A and RU-21D variants with 550hp PT6A-20 engines and RU-21B, RU-21C and RU-21E variants with 620hp PT6A-29s and 10,900lb (4,994kg) gross weight. Many of these aircraft have extensive aerial arrays for electronic reconnaissance duties. A single example of the pressurised King Air C90, similar to the U-21A in appearance, serves with the USAF's VIP squadron at Andrews AFB as the VC-6A, and five U-21Fs acquired by the US Army in 1971 are similar to the commercial, pressurised King Air A100. **Data** (U-21F): Span 45ft 10½in (13.98m). Length 39ft 11½in (12.17m). Gross weight 11,500lb (5,216kg). Max. cruising speed 285mph (459km/h). Range 1,395 miles (2,245km).

Beech U-22 Bonanza

U.S.A.

The first major military order for the Bonanza lightplane, in production in various forms since 1947, was announced in 1972 when the Iranian Imperial Air Force contracted for 18. These will be used for training and liaison duties. The USAF has also purchased a number of aircraft based on the Model A36 Bonanza for special duties in SE Asia. Employed in a programme codenamed Pave Eagle, these aircraft are designated QU-22B in their operational form (the prototypes were YQU-22A) and are equipped for electronic surveillance missions. Powered by a 375hp Continental GTSIO-520 engine driving a slow-turning quiet propeller, the QU-22B normally operates under remote control, but carries a pilot/observer to monitor the electronic equipment on board. Armed versions of the Bonanza have also been test-flown by Beech. **Data** (Model A36): Span 33ft 5½in (10.2m). Length 26ft 8in (8.13m). Gross weight 3,600lb (1,633kg). Max. speed 204mph (323km/h). Range 890 miles (1,432km).

Beechcraft 99

U.S.A.

The first purchase of Beechcraft 99As for military use was announced early in 1970, when the Chilean Air Force ordered nine to replace Beech C-45s. Deliveries were completed in August 1970, since when a 99A has been supplied to the Royal Thai Army. Powered by two 680shp Pratt & Whitney PT6A-27 engines, the Beechcraft 99A is basically a 15-seat third-level airliner, about 150 examples of which are in service. The prototype first flew in July 1966, and deliveries of the refined production version began in May 1968. **Data:** Span 45ft 10½in (14.00m). Length 44ft 6¾in (13.58m). Gross weight 10,400lb (4,717kg). Max. cruising speed 284mph (457km/h) at 12,000ft (3,650m). Range up to 1,000 miles (1,610km).

Bell H-13 Sioux

U.S.A.

At least 30 air forces use the Bell 47 helicopter in different versions.

The US Army's OH-13G and US Navy's TH-13M are based on the civil 47G, with 200 hp Franklin 6V4-200-C32 engine. The OH-13H is based on the 47G-2 with 240hp Lycoming VO-435 engine. Late production models include the three-seat OH-13S, a standard 47G-3B with 260hp TVO-435-25 engine, and the TH-13T two-seat instrument trainer version of the 47G-3B-1, with 270hp TVO-435-25, of which 415 were supplied to the US Army; and the 47J-3, with four/five-seat cabin and covered tail boom, which was built by Agusta for anti-submarine duties with the Italian Navy and for other customers. The British Army Sioux AH.Mk.1 and RAF HT.Mk.2 are basically 47G-3B-1s built by Westland. **Data** (47G-3B-1): Rotor diameter 37ft 1½in (11.32m). Fuselage length 31ft 7in (9.63m). Gross weight 2,950lb (1,338kg). Max. speed 105 mph (169km/h). Range 315 miles (507km).

Bell TH-57 SeaRanger and OH-58 Kiowa

U.S.A.

When the US Army re-opened its LOH competition in 1967, the winner this time was Bell, with its Model 206A JetRanger. An initial order was placed for 300, as OH-58As, with 2,200 to be delivered by 1973. The Canadian Armed Forces ordered 74 (as COH-58A); Brazil has 7; the Australian Army and Navy ordered 75 and 9 respectively; Ceylon has nine; and AB-206As were ordered from Agusta by Sweden (22), Iran (70), Austria, Saudi Arabia, Spain, Turkey (50) and the Italian Air Force (60). A version with a larger rotor, the AB-206A-1, is being built for the Italian Army. In January 1968, the US Navy adopted the TH-57A SeaRanger primary light turbine training version, taking delivery of 40. The standard power plant is a 317hp Allison 250-C18 engine. **Data:** Rotor diameter 33ft 4in (10.16m) Length 31ft 2in (9.50m). Gross weight 3,000lb (1,360kg). Max. speed 150mph (241km/h) at sea level.

167

Beriev Be-6 (NATO code-name: Madge)

U.S.S.R.

Standard maritime reconnaissance and anti-submarine flying-boat of the Soviet Naval Air Arm for many years, the Be-6 is powered by two 2,000hp Shvetsov ASh-73 radial piston-engines. It carries a crew of eight, including air-gunners for its defensive armament of 20mm cannon in nose and remotely-controlled dorsal positions. The racks for its warload of torpedoes, depth charges or mines are under the wings immediately outboard of the engines. There is a retractable radome under the rear of the hull and an MAD "tail-sting" is fitted on some aircraft. The Be-6 has been replaced to a large extent by the turboprop-engined Be-12 (see page 19). **Data:** Span 108ft 3in (33m). Length (approx.) 84ft (25.6m). Gross weight 51,500lb (2,336kg). Max. speed 258mph (415km/h). Range 3,000 miles (4,830km).

Boeing E-4A

U.S.A.

The well-known Boeing "Jumbo-Jet" is expected to enter USAF service as a Presidential transport and airborne command post in 1974—as a result of funding included in the FY 1973 budget for three examples. They will replace specially-equipped Boeing 707s (EC-135s) used at present in this role and will probably be followed by additional military models, some possibly to serve as flight refuelling tankers.

The USAF is funding the installation of General Electric CF6 turbofan engines in the Boeing 747, and it is expected that the command post version will have this engine, with the designation F103-GE-100, in place of the less-powerful JT9Ds used in commercial Boeing 747s. **Data** (provisional): Span 195ft 8in (59.64m). Length 231ft 4in (70.51m). Gross weight 775,000lb (351,540kg).

Boeing EC-137D and E-3A   *U.S.A.*

Following evaluation of proposals by McDonnell Douglas and Boeing, the USAF selected the latter company as prime contractor for a new Airborne Warning and Control System (AWACS) aircraft on July 8, 1970. The Boeing proposal was based on the airframe of the commercial Model 707-320B, with the addition of an extensive range of equipment for the airborne early-warning command-and-control role, including a downward-looking radar in a large rotating dorsal radome. Two prototypes were ordered, and the first of these flew on February 9, 1972. Designated EC-137D, they were used for competitive evaluation of Hughes and Westinghouse radars, the latter being selected later in 1972. Subject to funds being available, Boeing is expected to produce four pre-production AWACS aircraft and 42 production models, which will each have four Pratt & Whitney TF33 turbofan engines and will be designated E-3A. Data for the production model are not available: the EC-137D has a span of 145ft 9in (44.42m) and length of 152ft 11in (46.61m).

Boeing T-43A   *U.S.A.*

Choice of the Boeing 737 as a new navigation trainer to replace the Convair T-29 was announced by the USAF in May 1971. This type, powered by two Pratt & Whitney JT8D turbofans, had been produced previously only in commercial versions, but five of the latter had been acquired from the German airline Lufthansa by the Luftwaffe to replace Convair 440 staff transports. The initial USAF order for T-43As is for 19, with deliveries to Mather AFB to start during 1973. Each will have positions in the cabin for 12 students, four advanced students and three instructors. **Data:** Span 93ft 0in (28.35m). Length 94ft 0in (28.65m). Gross weight 115,500lb (52,390kg). Max. speed 586mph (943km/h). Range over 2,000 miles (3,200km).

Boeing VC-137 and Model 707 U.S.A.

Air Force One, the VC-137C used by the President of the United States and operated by the 89th Military Airlift Wing, is basically a Boeing 707-320B with VIP interior. A second, similar aircraft was ordered in 1972; three smaller 707-120s used by the USAF for VIP duties are known as VC-137Bs. Four aircraft operated by the *Luftwaffe* as personnel and freight carriers are standard 707-320Cs, as are two acquired by the Portuguese Air Force. The Canadian Armed Forces also acquired during 1970 five CC-137s (707-320Cs), two of which have special provision to allow them to operate as refuelling tankers for CF-5s and F-101s. The Iranian Imperial Air Force has ordered six similar 707-320C tankers. A Model 720 has been converted by Boeing as a prototype ASW aircraft. **Data:** Span 145ft 9in (44.42m). Length 152ft 11in (46.61m). Gross weight 333,600lb (151,315kg). Max. cruising speed 600 mph (966km/h). Range 4,300 miles (6,920km).

Britten-Norman BN-2A Islander and Defender Great Britain

Among the first military customers for the basic Islander was the Abu Dhabi Defence Force, which has two for communications duties. Several others are now in use with various overseas Services. Intended for more specific military roles, including search and rescue, border patrol and reconnaissance, the Defender appeared in 1971. It has nose-mounted Bendix or RCA radar. Various armament schemes have been proposed, including fixed sideways-firing guns, and gun or rocket pods on four pylons under the wings. The basic BN-2A is powered by 260hp Lycoming O-540-E4C5 engines and was first flown on June 13, 1965; the BN-2A-2 version has 300hp Lycoming IO-540-K engines and first flew on April 30, 1970. **Data:** Span 49ft 0in (14.94m). Length 35ft 8in (10.86m). Gross weight 6,300lb (2,857kg). Cruising speed 160mph (257km/h) at 7,000ft (2,135m). Range up to 1,040 miles (1,673km) with optional wing-tip tanks.

CASA 1.131E

Spain

This is a licence-built version of the Bücker Bü 131 Jungmann two-seat training biplane, which first flew in prototype form in Germany on April 27, 1934. Production by CASA, in Spain, began in 1939 and eventually totalled 550 aircraft, the last of which was delivered to the Spanish Air Force in 1963. The final version, as illustrated, has a 125hp ENMA Tigre G-IV engine and is designated E-3-B. Those still serving with the Spanish Air Force in 1972 were earmarked for early replacement by a newer primary trainer. **Data:** Span 24ft 3in (7.39m). Length 22ft 1in (6.73m). Gross weight 1,587lb (720kg). Max. speed 124mph (200 km/h). Range 310 miles (500km).

CASA 207 Azor

Spain

Largest aircraft of Spanish design yet produced in quantity, the Azor flew for the first time on September 28, 1955. It was produced subsequently for the Spanish Air Force in two versions, under the designation T.7. The first series of ten aircraft are CASA C.207-As (T.7As), equipped to carry a crew of four and 30–40 passengers in an air-conditioned cabin. The second series of ten, known as CASA C.207-Cs (T.7Bs) are freighters with a large cargo-door. All are powered by 2,040hp Bristol Hercules 730 engines. **Data:** Span 91ft 2½in (27.80m). Length 68ft 5in (20.85m). Gross weight 36,375lb (16,500kg). Max. speed 283mph (455km/h). Range 1,620 miles (2,610km).

CASA C.212 Aviocar   *Spain*

Design of the C.212 was undertaken to provide a locally-produced replacement for the Ju 52/3m, Douglas DC-3 and CASA Azor transport aircraft serving with the Spanish Air Force. After evaluation of the design, the Spanish Air Ministry ordered two prototypes of the C.212 in September 1968 and these flew, respectively, on March 26 and October 23, 1971, powered by 755hp AiResearch TPE 331 turboprops. A production batch of 12 was then laid down, as the first step towards meeting Spanish Air Force requirements for about 50, and deliveries were to begin in 1973. The military designation is T.12. **Data:** Span 62ft 4in (19.00m). Length 49ft 10½in (15.20m). Gross weight 13,889lb (6,300kg). Max. speed 249mph (400km/h). Range 400–1,200 miles (640–2,000km).

Cessna O-1 Bird Dog   *U.S.A.*

One of the first light liaison and reconnaissance aircraft developed for the US Army Field Forces after the end of World War II, the O-1 (formerly L-19) Bird Dog won a design competition in April 1950. By March 1964, a total of 3,431 had been delivered to the Army under the designations O-1A and O-1E and to the Marine Corps as O-1B (60 built). The Marines also received 25 O-1Cs, a similar but more powerful type with square-cut fin. The USAF used the modified O-1F and O-1G for forward air control duties in Vietnam. The O-1 was also supplied to France (90), Canada, Cambodia, Austria, Brazil, Chile, Italy, South Korea, Laos, Lebanon, Norway, Pakistan, Thailand and South Vietnam, and was built in Japan by Fuji. Using a combination of airframe spares and locally-produced parts, the Pakistan Army was turning out new Bird Dogs in 1972. **Data** (O-1E): One 213hp Continental O-470-11. Span 36ft 0in (10.9m). Length 25ft 10in (7.89m). Gross weight 2,430lb (1,103kg). Max. speed 115mph (184km/h). Range 530 miles (848km).

Cessna O-2 *U.S.A.*

The USAF adopted this version of the "push and pull" Cessna 337 Super Skymaster late in 1966, to replace the Cessna O-1 in FAC (forward air controller) missions, for which purpose a number of modifications were introduced including four underwing pylons for gun pods, rockets, flares, etc. Powered by two 210hp Continental IO-360-C/D engines, the O-2 has dual control and four removable passenger seats. The USAF had ordered 299 O-2As by 1970, and 12 had been purchased by the I. Iranian AF.

In addition, the USAF acquired 31 O-2Bs in 1967, equipped for psychological warfare duties with high-power air-to-ground broadcast systems, and further contracts have been placed subsequently. A STOL military variant of the Cessna 337 proposed by Reims Aviation, which builds this type in France, is called the Milirole. **Data:** Span 38ft 2in (11.63m). Length 29ft 9in (9.07m). Gross weight 4,630lb (2,100kg). Max. speed 199mph (320km/h).

Cessna T-41 Mescalero *U.S.A.*

In 1964 the USAF ordered 170 standard Cessna 172 light aircraft as basic trainers, under the designation T-41A. These were delivered with civil registrations, as this phase of USAF flying training is done by commercial schools; a further 34 followed in 1967. Eight T-41As were delivered to Ecuador and Singapore has eight Model 172s. The US Army bought 255 similar T-41Bs, with a 210hp Continental IO-360-D engine. Also similar are the T-41C, of which Cessna delivered 45 to the USAF Academy, and the T-41D, of which the

Colombian Air Force purchased 30. Other Cessna high-wing lightplanes in military service include the Model 180, with tailwheel undercarriage and 230hp Continental O-470-R engine, used by the Argentine, Australia, Guatemala, Honduras and Mexico, and the Model 182 (O-470-R and nose-wheel undercarriage) sold to Canada as L-19L. **Data** (T-41A): One 145hp Continental O-300-C engine. Span 35ft 10in (10.92m). Length 26ft 11in (8.20m). Gross weight 2,300lb (1,043kg). Max. speed 138mph (222km/h). Range 720 miles (116km).

Cessna U-3　　　　　　　　　　　　　　_U.S.A._

The U-3A (originally known as the L-27A) is the commercial Cessna 310A (first flown on January 3, 1953) as modified for a USAF design competition for a light twin-engined administrative liaison and cargo aircraft. This competition it won, and an initial contract for 80 was subsequently doubled. The U-3A seats five in a roomy cabin, and can be identified by its unswept fin. It was followed by 35 "all-weather" U-3Bs, based on the commercial 310E with swept fin. In both cases, the primary fuel is carried in tanks mounted on the wing-tips. The French Air Force has 12 somewhat similar six/eight-seat Cessna 411s, with 340hp GTSIO-520 turbosupercharged engines, and ten Cessna 310s which serve in the communications role at the CEV bases at Bretigny and Istres. **Data** (U-3A): Two 240hp Continental O-470-M piston-engines. Span 36ft (10.97m). Length 27ft 1in (8.25m). Gross weight 4,700lb (2,131kg). Max. speed 232mph (373km/h). Range 850 miles (1,368km).

Cessna U-17　　　　　　　　　　　　　_U.S.A._

The Cessna 185 Skywagon has been adopted for military duties by several nations and has also been built in quantity under USAF contract for delivery to foreign nations under MAP arrangements. Although not used by US forces, the Skywagon carries the designation U-17, and since 1963 a total of 169 U-17As and 136 U-17Bs have been ordered. Among the nations which have received U-17s are Costa Rica, South Vietnam and Laos. Skywagons, powered by the 300hp Continental IO-520-D engine, have also been purchased direct from Cessna by the South African Air Force and Peru. The larger Model 207 Turbo-Skywagon has been purchased by the Indonesian Air Force. **Data:** Span 35ft 10in (10.92m). Length 25ft 9in (7.85m). Gross weight 3,300lb (1,500kg). Max. speed 178mph (286km/h). Range 1,075 miles (1,730km).

Convair C-131 Samaritan and T-29 *U.S.A.*

First military Convair-Liner was the T-29A unpressurised navigation, bombardment and radar trainer (first flight September 22, 1949) of which 48 were built for the USAF. The T-29B is pressurised; 105 were built. The T-29C has 2,500hp -99W engines in place of 2,400hp -77 or -99; 119 were built, some later becoming ET-29C. The T-29D advanced navigation/bombardment trainer has no astrodomes; 93 were built. The C-131A Samaritans (26 built) are air evacuation transports based on the Convair 240. The C-131B 48-seat transport/electronic test-bed (36 built) and C-131D transport (33 built) were based on the Model 340. Ten C-131Es were built as ECM trainers, but six were converted into RC-131F photo-survey and charting aircraft. The Navy received 36 C-131F cargo, personnel and evacuation transports, two C-131G (Model 440) transport/research aircraft, and about ten T-29Bs transferred from the USAF. Four VC-131Hs were re-engined with Allison 501D-13 turboprops for VIP use and the Canadian Armed Forces have eight similarly-engined CC-109 Cosmopolitans. Convair 440s are used by the Luftwaffe and the Bolivian Air Force. **Data** (C-131B): Span 105ft 4in (32.10m). Length 79ft 2in (24.13m). Gross weight 47,000lb (21,320kg). Max. speed 293mph (471km/h). Range 450 miles (724km).

Convair PBY Catalina *U.S.A.*

The Catalina amphibian still serves with a few air forces and naval air arms, including those of the Argentine, Brazil, Chile, Nationalist China, Dominica, Ecuador, Indonesia, Mexico and Peru. The series began with the PBY-5 flying-boat, of which 1,196 were built in the United States and Canada. Some of these were supplied to the wartime RAF as the Catalina, and a version was built in Russia as the GST (NATO code-name *Mop*). The PBY-5A was an amphibious development, known as the Canso in Canada, and production of this and the improved PBY-6A totalled 944. Most of those still in service are used for transport and air/sea rescue duties. The engines are 1,200hp P. & W. R-1830s. **Data:** Span 104ft 10in (19.45m). Gross weight 34,000lb (15,422kg). Max. speed 196mph (315km/h). Range 2,520 miles (4,055km).

Curtiss-Wright C-46 Commando   *U.S.A.*

First flown on March 26, 1940, as a 36-passenger airliner, the Commando became one of the most widely used USAAF transports in World War II and a total of 3,180 was built. Although less well remembered than the C-47 Dakotas, they put in good service, especially over "the Hump" to China. Examples were operated by the USAF in the early stages of the Vietnam campaign and some remain in service in foreign air forces, including those of Brazil, Nationalist China, Dominica, Honduras, Japan, South Korea, Peru and Uruguay, mostly of the C-46A, C-46D and C-46F variants. Payload is 50 troops or 16,000lb (7,255kg) of cargo. **Data:** Two 2,000hp P. & W. R-2800-51 or -75 engines. Span 108ft 1in (32.92m). Length 76ft 4in (23.27m). Gross weight 45,000lb (20,410kg). Max. speed 241mph (388km/h). Range 1,800 miles (2,900km).

Dassault Falcon 20   *France*

Several air forces use this small, high-speed aircraft for VIP transport duties, including the RAAF, which has three operated by No. 34 Squadron at Fairbairn, Canadian Armed Forces with seven and the Belgian Air Force with three. Powered by two General Electric CF700 turbofans, each of 4,200 or 4,250lb (1,905 or 1,928kg) st, the Falcon 20 normally carries a crew of two and eight passengers, but is able to take up to 14 seats in its main cabin in less luxurious versions. The French Air Force has a Falcon fitted with the same radar and navigation systems as those carried by a Mirage III fighter, and uses it to train combat pilots in the use of this equipment. The French Air Force has also ordered two of the smaller but similar Falcon 10s. **Data:** Span 53ft 6in (16.30m). Length 56ft 3in (17.15m). Gross weight 28,660lb (13,000kg). Max. speed 534mph (860km/h). Range 2,220 miles (3,570km) at 466mph (750 km/h).

Dassault MD-315 Flamant   *France*

The MD-315 Flamant entered service originally as a light transport, powered by two 580hp SNECMA-Renault 12S-02-201 engines and with accommodation for a crew of two and ten passengers or freight. A total of 137 were built. Another passenger-carrying version is the MD-312 six-seat communications aircraft, of which 142 were built. Flamants remain active with the French Air Force, some now fitted with a glazed nose (as illustrated) for navigation training; and the French Navy has some MD-312s. Other Flamants serve in the air forces of Cambodia and Tunisia. All can be adapted for freighting or ambulance duties and are developments of the original MD-303 prototype, which first flew on February 10, 1947. **Data** (MD-315): Span 67ft 10in (20.68m). Length 41ft (12.50m). Gross weight 12,760lb (5,800kg). Max. speed 236mph (380km/h). Range 755 miles (1,215 km).

Dassault MD-450 Ouragan   *France*

Predecessor of the Mystère series of sweptwing jet fighters, the Ouragan single-seat fighter-bomber flew for the first time on February 28, 1949; a total of 12 pre-production and 350 production machines were built subsequently for the French Air Force. A few are still used in France for test purposes. Of the others, 104 were sold to the Indian Air Force and 75 to the Israel Defence Force. The Indian aircraft (known as Toofani) have been phased out, but Ouragans still equip one second-line squadron in Israel. Power plant is the 5,070lb st Hispano-Suiza (Rolls-Royce) Nene 104B turbojet. Armament consists of four 20mm cannon and 16 rockets or 1,000kg of bombs. **Data:** Span over tip-tanks 43ft 2in (13.16m). Length 35ft 2½in (10.72m). Gross weight 14,990lb (6,800kg). Max. speed 584mph (940km/h).

De Havilland DHC-1 Chipmunk
Canada/Great Britain

First original design by de Havilland Canada, the Chipmunk was built in quantity on both sides of the Atlantic. The parent company produced a total of 218. Another 1,014 were built by de Havilland at Chester in the UK, including the military T.Mk.10 and 20 and civil Mk.21. About 20 are still used at the Army Air Corps Training School in Britain, but those operated by the RAF at University Air Training Squadrons and the Helicopter Training School are being withdrawn during 1973. Chipmunks have been supplied to about a dozen overseas air forces. **Data** (T.Mk.10): One 145hp Gipsy Major 8 piston-engine. Span 34ft 4in (10.46m). Length 25ft 5in (7.48m). Gross weight 2,014lb (915kg). Max. speed 138mph (222km/h). Range 280 miles (450km).

De Havilland DHC-2 Mk.1 Beaver and U-6
Canada

The Beaver first flew on August 16, 1947, and was the second original design of the Canadian de Havilland company. A high proportion of the total of 1,657 built were supplied to 20 military air forces, including 968 delivered to the USAF and US Army under the designation U-6A (formerly L-20A). Others form the standard fixed-wing equipment of the British Army Air Corps. Beavers can operate on wheels, floats or skis or as amphibians, and with the US Forces have operated in the Arctic and in many other parts of the world. **Data:** One 450hp P. & W. R-985-AN-1 or -3 piston-engine. Span 48ft (14.64m). Length 30ft 4in (9.24m). Gross weight 5,100lb (2,313kg). Max. speed 140mph (225km/h). Range 778 miles (1,252km).

De Havilland DHC-3 Otter and U-1 *Canada*

First flown on December 12, 1951, the 11-seat Otter is "big brother" to the Beaver, which it closely resembles in general layout. A total of 460 were built for military and commercial use and some nine air forces fly the type. The 69 Canadian Armed Forces Otters were supplied primarily for Arctic search and rescue, paratroop dropping and photographic duties. About 25 were still active in 1972. The US Army purchased a trial batch of six YU-1s in 1955 and followed this order with another for 84 U-1As which were used as supply aircraft in forward areas, and now serve in the utility and communications role. All Otters can operate on wheels, floats or skis. **Data:** One 600 hp R-1340 piston-engine. Span 58ft (17.69m). Length 41ft 10in (12.80m). Gross weight 8,000lb (3,629kg). Max. speed 160mph 257km/h). Range 945 miles (1,520km).

De Havilland DHC-6 Twin Otter *Canada*

The original 19-passenger DHC-6 Series 100 Twin Otter and the Series 200 differ only in that the 200 has a longer nose to provide increased baggage space. Both have 579 eshp Pratt & Whitney PT6A-20 turboprops, while the Series 300 has 652eshp PT6A-27 engines, increased gross weight and higher performance. Over 300 Twin Otters have been delivered to date, mostly for service with airlines and as business aircraft. Military orders have come from the Argentine Air Force (5), Army (3) and Navy (1); Canadian Armed Forces (8, designated CC-138); Chilean Air Force (7); Jamaica Defence Force (1); Peruvian Air Force (11); Royal Norwegian Air Force (4); Uganda Police Air Wing (1); Paraguayan Air Force (1) and Panamanian Air Force (1). **Data:** Span 65ft 0in (19.81m). Length 51ft 9in (15.77m). Gross weight 12,500lb (5,670kg). Max. speed 210mph (338km/h). Range 794 miles (1,277km).

De Havilland (Hawker Siddeley) D.H.104 Dove, Devon and Sea Devon   *Great Britain*

The Dove was adopted for service with the RAF in 1948, as the Devon C.Mk.1. A change of designation to C.Mk.2 indicated replacement of the original 380hp Gipsy Queen 70-4 or -71 engines with Gipsy Queen 175s; introduction of an enlarged Heron-type canopy was indicated by the designation C.Mk.2/2. The Devon's primary role is that of staff transport, most of the 30 or so examples acquired having been allocated for the personal use of officers commanding

Groups and Commands. A few serve with Communications Squadrons, Nos. 21, 32, 60 and 207. Thirteen similar aircraft were acquired by the Royal Navy for communications duties, as Sea Devon C.Mk.20s. About a dozen other air forces have used Doves in the communications and training role. **Data:** Span 57ft (17.40m). Length 39ft 3in (11.96m). Gross weight 8,950lb (4,060kg). Max. speed 230mph (370km/h). Range 880 miles (1,415km).

De Havilland (Hawker Siddeley) D.H.114 Heron   *Great Britain*

Developed as a four-engined partner to the Dove, the Heron flew for the first time on May 10, 1950 in its original Series 1 form, with fixed undercarriage. The Heron 2 with retractable undercarriage followed in 1952 and a total of more than 140 of the two versions were eventually built. They remain in service in small numbers with a few air forces. In the UK, No. 781 Squadron of the

Fleet Air Arm has four Herons on its strength, and uses them to provide communications links between Naval establishments in the UK. All have four 250hp Gipsy Queen 30 Mk.2 piston-engines. **Data:** Span 71ft 6in (21.8m). Length 48ft 6in (14.8m). Gross weight 13,500lb (6,124kg). Cruising speed 183mph (295km/h).

De Havilland Vampire   *Great Britain*

Having flown for the first time on September 20, 1943, the Vampire is one of the oldest jet fighters still in service. The FB.5/9 fighter-bombers and their "overseas" counterpart, the FB.50, remain operational with a few air forces such as those of Rhodesia, New Zealand, Venezuela, Switzerland and Dominica, mostly as advanced trainers. Also in service is the two-seat training variant of the Vampire, first flown in private-venture prototype form on November 15, 1950. The prototype was followed by two examples for evaluation by the Royal Navy, and then by production deliveries for the RAF, under the

designation T.Mk.11. A total of 804 Vampire Trainers was eventually built, including 73 Sea Vampire T.Mk.22s for the Fleet Air Arm; Australian licence production accounted for another 109 as Mks.33, 34 and 35. Trainers were exported to about 20 countries and are still used by several, including Australia, Rhodesia, New Zealand, India, and Middle East and South American states. **Data:** Span 38ft 0in (11.58m). Length 30ft 9in (9.37m). Gross weight 12,390lb (5,620kg). Max. speed 548mph (882km/h). Range 1,220 miles (1,963km).

Dornier Do 27   *Germany*

Until aircraft manufacture was permitted again in Germany, many German designers worked abroad. Thus, the prototype of this design, designated Do 25 and powered by a 150hp ENMA Tigre G-IVB engine, was built in Spain to meet a Spanish Air Force requirement. It flew on June 25, 1954, and was followed by the prototype Do 27 with 275hp Lycoming GO-480 engine on June 27, 1955. Production of the latter was transferred to Germany, where the first of 428 Do 27As ordered for the German Air Force and Army flew on October 17, 1956.

Others have been supplied to the Belgian, Congolese, Nigerian, Portuguese, Swedish, Swiss, South African and Turkish air forces, and 50 were built in Spain as CASA 127s. The basic Do 27A is a five-seater, convertible for freighting and casualty evacuation. The Do 27H has a 340hp GSO-480 engine. **Data** (Do 27A): Span 39ft 4½in (12.0m). Length 31ft 6in (9.6m). Gross weight 4,070lb (1,850kg). Max. speed 141mph (227km/h). Range 685 miles (1,100km).

Dornier Do 28D Skyservant　　　*Germany*

The 14/15-seat Skyservant is a successor to the STOL Do 28, of which 120 were built. A few of these serve in military guise for communications duties. The Do 28D represented a completely new design, with much increased capacity, and the prototype flew on February 23, 1966. After seven Do 28Ds had been built, production switched to the Do 28D-1/2 with a small increase in wing span and higher gross weight. The largest single order for the Do 28D-2 is from the German Armed Forces, for 121. Of these, 20 are for the Navy and the remainder for the *Luftwaffe* and Army. Another four were acquired by the *Luftwaffe's* VIP transport unit and two by the Turkish Army for its Flying Training School. The Skyservant is powered by two 380hp Lycoming IGSO-540 engines. **Data:** Span 51ft 0¼in (15.55m). Length 37ft 5¼in (11.41m). Gross weight 8,470lb (3,842kg). Max. cruising speed 170mph (273km/h). Range 1,255 miles (2,020km).

Douglas B-26 Invader　　　*U.S.A.*

This bomber was designed to a 1940 specification as a successor to the A-20 and 2,451 were built, including prototypes. Some served the USAF as staff transports (VB-26B), trainers (TB-26C) and drone carriers (DB-26J). Foreign air forces recently using B-26s included those of Chile, Colombia, Dominica, Guatemala, and Peru. In 1963, On Mark Engineering produced the YB-26K for evaluation in the counter-insurgency role, with a completely re-manufactured airframe, 2,500hp R-2800-103W engines, strengthened wings for a maximum of 8,000lb (3,628kg) of external stores in addition to the internal bomb-load, and many other changes. Some B-26Ks entered service with the USAF in Vietnam, being subsequently redesignated A-26A in the "attack" category; others were supplied to allied nations under MAP. During 1967, 18 B-26s of the Brazilian Air Force were modified to B-26K standard, apart from the engines. **Data:** Span 70ft 0in (21.33m). Length 50ft 0in (15.24m). Gross weight 38,500lb (17,463kg). Max. speed 355mph (571km/h). Range 1,400 miles (2,253km).

Douglas C-47 and C-117 Skytrain and Dakota

U.S.A.

Many standard 28-seat C-47s remain in service with the USAF and US Navy. Hundreds more are in service with over 50 air forces throughout the world, often under the British name Dakota. The C-47 Skytrain was the basic production model for the USAF, supplemented by the externally-similar C-117A, B and C staff transports. The C-117D was an improved model for the US Navy with new wings and tail and 1,535hp Wright R-1820 engines. Heavily-armed gunship versions of the type,

designated AC-47D "Spooky", operated in Vietnam with great effectiveness in suppressing small arms fire; others were used for special reconnaissance duties with the designations EC-47N, EC-47P and EC-47Q. **Data** (C-47): Two 1,200hp Pratt & Whitney R-1830-90C piston-engines. Span 95ft (28.95m). Length 64ft 5½in (19.64m). Gross weight 26,000lb (11,793kg). Max. speed 229mph (369km/h). Range 1,500 miles (2,414km).

Douglas C-54 Skymaster

U.S.A.

In production as a new commercial transport when America entered the war in 1941, the Douglas DC-4 was immediately taken over as a military transport, and more than 1,000 were built for the USAF and US Navy. Numerous sub-variants were produced and in small numbers the Skymaster continues to serve with about a dozen air

forces. Standard payload is 50 troops or 32,000lb (14,515kg) of cargo. **Data:** Four 1,450hp Pratt & Whitney R-2000 piston-engines. Span 117ft 6in (35.8m). Length 93ft 11in (28.63m). Gross weight 73,000lb (33,112kg). Max. speed 274mph (441km/h). Range (normal) 1,500 miles (2,410km).

Douglas C-118 Liftmaster and DC-6/DC-7 variants

U.S.A.

The USAF acquired a total of 101 DC-6Cs for service with MATS, under the designation C-118A, following development under military contracts of the prototype DC-6. Designated XC-112A, this prototype first flew on February 15, 1946, and was a development of the C-54. A further 65 similar aircraft were purchased by the US Navy and contributed to MATS operations—61 as R6D-1s and four as R6D-1Zs with executive interiors. These were subsequently redesignated C-118B and VC-118B respectively, and were assigned to Reserve units (to replace C-54s). Commercial DC-6/DC-7 variants have passed into military service elsewhere e.g. two DC-6Bs purchased by the Luftwaffe, a DC-6A used as the Royal aircraft by the Royal Belgian Air Force, 10 DC-6As used for long-range logistic support by the Portuguese Air Force, and a few used by Brazil and Chile. Illustrated is a DC-7C converted in France for ECM duties. **Data:** (C-118): Span 117ft 6in (35.81m). Length 105ft 7in (32.18m). Gross weight 112,000lb (46,266kg). Max. speed 360mph (579km/h). Range 3,860 miles (6,212km).

EKW C-3605

Switzerland

This is the latest variant in a family of general-purpose monoplanes originated by the Swiss factory of Eidgenössisches Konstruktionswerkstätte (EKW) in 1939, when the C-3601 was flown for the first time. The Swiss Air Force took delivery, between 1942 and 1945, of 150 C-3603s and ten C-3604s as reconnaissance bombers. After they had been replaced by newer types, 35 C-3603s remained in service as target tugs and two as trainers, powered by the Hispano HS 12Y-51 engine. On August 19, 1968, EKW flew the C-3605, a converted C-3603 with a 1,150shp Avco Lycoming T5307A turboprop engine. The Swiss Air Force ordered conversion of 23 of the surviving C-3603s to this standard for continued use as target tugs and these began to enter service in 1972. **Data:** Span 45ft 1in (13.74m) Length 39ft 5¾in (12.03m). Gross weight 8,185lb (3,710kg). Max. speed 268mph (432km/h). Range 610 miles (970km).

Embraer EMB-110 Bandeirante (C-95)

Brazil

The prototype of this twin-turboprop light transport was evolved by the aircraft department (PAR) of the official Aeronautical Technical Centre (CTA) under the leadership of the French designer Max Holste. Designated YC-95, it first flew on October 26, 1968, and was followed by the slightly modified second prototype on October 19, 1969. These aircraft accommodate 7–10 passengers and are powered by 550shp Pratt & Whitney PT6A-20 engines. The production version (identified by more rectangular cabin windows) has 680shp PT6A-27 engines and can carry 12 passengers. The first of a batch of 80 which the Brazilian Air Force will use to replace its Beechcraft C-45s flew on August 15, 1972. A projected pressurized version is designated EMB-120. **Data :** Span 50ft 3in (15.32m). Length 46ft 8¼in (14.23m). Gross weight 11,243lb (5,100kg). Max. cruising speed 260mph (418km/h). Max. range 1,150 miles (1,850km).

Fairchild A-10A

U.S.A.

This was one of the two winning designs in the USAF competition for a new "AX" close air support aircraft, the other being Northrop's A-9A. Two prototypes of each design were ordered to permit a "fly-off", leading to selection of one type for production. Powered by two 9,275lb (4,207kg) st General Electric TF34-GE-2 turbofans, the A-10A carries an in-built armament of one 20mm or 30mm cannon and up to 18,500lb (8,392kg) of ordnance on 11 external pylons beneath the wings and fuselage. The first two flew in 1972 and won the 'fly-off', leading to an initial order for ten pre-production A-10As. **Data :** Span 55ft 0in (16.76m). Length 52ft 7in (16.03m). Gross weight 45,825lb (20,786kg). Max. speed 460mph (740km/h).

Fairchild AU-23A Peacemaker (and Pilatus PC-6 Porter and PC-6/A/B/C Turbo-Porter)
U.S.A./Switzerland

This family of aircraft stemmed from the basic Swiss Pilatus PC-6 Porter 8/10-seat STOL utility transport, which has either a 340hp Lycoming GSO-480-B1A6 or 350hp IGO-540-A1A piston-engine. Turbo-Porters, similar except for having a Turboméca Astazou (PC-6/A series), Pratt & Whitney PT6A (PC-6/B series) or AiResearch TPE 331 (PC-6/C series) turboprop, are manufactured also by Fairchild in the USA. From them has been evolved the AU-23A Peacemaker (illustrated) of which 15 have been acquired by the USAF for evaluation with the Helio AU-24A (page 195) under its "Credible Chase" programme. Powered by a 665shp TPE 331-1-101F, the AU-23A carries a side-firing 20mm cannon and has five racks under its fuselage and wings for gun or rocket pods, bombs, broadcasting equipment, or camera and flare packs. Military customers for Porters and Turbo-Porters include the Australian Army, Colombia, Ecuador, Israel, Peru and Sudan. **Data** (PC-6/B2): Span 49ft 8in (15.13m). Length 36ft 1in (11.00m). Gross weight 4,850lb (2,200kg). Max. cruising speed 161mph (259km/h). Max. range 1,006 miles (1,620km).

Fairchild FH-1100
U.S.A.

This five-seat utility helicopter had its origin in the Hiller OH-5A, designed for evaluation in the US Army's competition for a light observation helicopter (LOH). The prototype OH-5A flew on January 26, 1963. When the Hughes OH-6A was chosen for production, Fairchild (which had taken over Hiller) continued development and manufacture of the OH-5A as a private venture for both commercial and military use. The developed version was redesignated FH-1100 and the first production model was completed on June 3, 1966. The Philippine Air Force placed the first military contract for eight. Others have since gone into service with the Argentine Army, Brazilian Navy, and in Ecuador and El Salvador. Power plant is a 317shp Allison 250-C18 turboshaft. **Data:** Rotor diameter 35ft 4¾in (10.79m). Fuselage length 29ft 9½in (9.08m). Gross weight 2,750lb (1,247kg). Max. cruising speed 127mph (204km/h). Range 348 miles (560km).

FMA I.A.35 Huanquero   *Argentina*

The I.A.35 Huanquero (first flown September 21, 1953) is a multi-role military aircraft of which 47 were built in four versions for the Argentine Air Force. The first production machine flew on March 29, 1957. The I.A.35 Type IA is an advanced instrument flying and navigation trainer, carrying two pilots, radio operator, instructor and four pupils. Type III is an ambulance version with accommodation for a crew of three, four patients and attendant. Type IV is a photographic version. Each of these three models is powered by two 620hp I.A.19R El Indio engines. Fourth version is the Type IB for weapon training, powered by 750hp I.A.19R engines and armed with two 0.50in machine-guns, plus underwing racks for 440lb of bombs or rockets. **Data** (Type IA): Span 64ft 3in (19.60m). Length 45ft 10in (13.98m). Gross weight 12,540lb (5,700kg). Max. speed 225mph (362km/h). Range 975 miles (1,570km).

FMA I.A.50 G.II   *Argentina*

In its original Mk.I form, this design utilised many components of the Huanquero, including the twin-fin tail unit. The I.A.50 G.II introduced many changes, including a single swept fin and rudder, de-icing equipment, a shorter rear fuselage and more powerful (930hp) Turboméca Bastan VI-A turboprops. The first of two prototypes flew on April 23, 1963, followed by one pre-production model and an initial series of 18 production aircraft. These comprised 14 troop transports, a VIP transport and two survey aircraft for the Argentine Air Force and one Navy staff transport, and have been followed by a further 20 transports. **Data:** Span 64ft 3¼in (19.59m). Length 50ft 2½in (15.30m). Gross weight 16,200lb (7,350kg). Max. speed 310mph (500km/h). Max. range 1,600 miles (2,575km).

Fokker S.11 Instructor

Netherlands

First flown in 1947, the Instructor is a simple two-seat primary trainer, powered by a 190hp Lycoming O-435-A engine. The first series of 40 was built by Fokker for the Royal Netherlands Air Force and the parent company also supplied 41 to the Israel Defence Force. Macchi acquired the licence to build the Instructor in Italy, under the designation M.416, and delivered 150 to the Italian Air Force. In 1954, Fokker established an associate company in Brazil, which manufactured 100 S.11s and 70 S.12s (similar except for tricycle undercarriage) and these are still used by the Brazilian Air Force. **Data:** Span 36ft 1in (10.99m). Length 26ft 8in (8.13m). Gross weight 2,426lb (1,100kg). Max. speed 130mph (209km/h). Range 400 miles (644km).

Fokker-VFW F.28

Netherlands

First military order for an F.28, announced in 1970, came from the Argentine Air Force, for use as a Presidential aircraft. Another has been acquired by the Dutch Royal Flight to replace an F.27 used in this role; one has been delivered for the President of Colombia and another has been acquired for VIP use by the Government of Nigeria. The F.28 prototype made its first flight on May 9, 1967 and deliveries for commercial use began on February 24, 1969. Initial production aircraft were to Mk.1000 standard with accommodation for up to 65 passengers; the Mk.2000 has a lengthened fuselage for up to 79 passengers. Both variants are powered by Rolls-Royce RB. 183-2 Spey Mk.555-15 engines. **Data:** Span 77ft 4¼in (23.58m). Length 89ft 10¾in (27.40m). Gross weight 65,000lb (29,485kg). Max. cruising speed 528mph (849km/h) at 21,000ft (6,400m). Range 956 miles (1,538km).

Fuji LM-1/LM-2 Nikko and KM-2   *Japan*

The LM-1 Nikko is a liaison aircraft, developed from the Beech T-34 Mentor by Fuji, who built the latter under licence in Japan. It retains the standard 225hp Continental O-470-13A engine of the trainer, and differs only in the centre-fuselage structure which seats four persons in pairs, with side doors and a removable hatch for loading bulky freight. The first Nikko flew on June 6, 1955, and 27 were delivered subsequently to the Japanese Ground Self-Defence Force. Some have been converted to LM-2 standard, with more powerful engine and optional fifth seat. Generally similar in appearance are 28 KM-2 two/four-seat primary trainers of the Maritime Self-Defence Force; but these have a 340hp Lycoming IGSO-480-A1C6 engine. **Data** (KM-2): Span 32ft 10in (10.0m). Length 26ft 0¾in (7.94m). Gross weight 3,860lb (1,750kg). Max. speed 230mph (370km/h). Range 570 miles (915km).

Fuji T1   *Japan*

Designed to replace the T-6 piston-engined trainers of the JASDF, the prototype of this tandem two-seat intermediate jet trainer was ordered in 1956 and flew on January 19, 1958. The first 40 production machines each had a 4,000lb (1,814kg) st Bristol Siddeley Orpheus 805 turbojet and bear the company designation T1F2 (JASDF designation T1A). They were followed by 22 T1F1s (T1B) with 2,645lb (1,200kg) st Ishikawajima-Harima J3-IHI-3, the prototype of which flew on May 17, 1960. A prototype T1F3 (T1C) with 3,085lb (1,400kg) st J3-IHI-7, flew in April 1965, but a proposal to convert all T1F1s to this standard was abandoned. All versions have provision for one 0.50in machine-gun and 1,500lb (680kg) of underwing bombs, rockets or missiles instead of drop tanks. **Data** (T1A): Span 34ft 5in (10.50m). Length 39ft 9in (12.12m). Gross weight 11,000lb (5,000kg). Max. speed 575mph (925km/h). Range 1,210 miles (1,950km).

Grumman HU-16 Albatross　　　　　　*U.S.A.*

The XJR2F-1 Albatross prototype, built for the US Navy as a utility transport amphibian, first flew on October 24, 1947. The USAF ordered a total of 305, as SA-16As, for search and rescue. Most of these were converted to SA-16B with increased span and higher weights. Designations were changed to HU-16A and HU-16B respectively in 1962. The US Navy purchased aircraft similar to the SA-16A as UF-1s, and put in hand a similar conversion programme, to produce UF-2s; these are now HU-16C and HU-16D respectively, while the Coast Guard version is HU-16E. Foreign nations using the type include Canada (10, designated CSR-110), Argentina, Brazil, Chile, Indonesia, Italy, Nationalist China, the Philippines, Portugal, Spain and Japan. A special model for anti-submarine duties was produced in 1961, with a large nose radome, retractable MAD in the rear fuselage, an ECM radome on the wing, an underwing searchlight and provision for carrying depth charges. Sixteen were supplied to Norway and seven to Spain; during 1969, most of the Norwegian aircraft were transferred to Greece. The Albatross has two 1,425hp Wright R-1820-76A engines. **Data:** Span 96ft 8in (29.46m). Length 62ft 10in (19.18m). Gross weight 37,500lb (17,010kg). Max. speed 236mph (379km/h) at sea level.

Grumman TC-4C　　　　　　*U.S.A.*

Two examples of the Grumman Gulfstream executive transport were purchased for use by the US Coast Guard in 1963 with the designation VC-4A. They serve as VIP transports. Plans to buy a training variant for use by the USN as TC-4B were shelved, but in December 1966 the Navy ordered nine TC-4Cs as flying classrooms for training bombardier/navigators for service in the A-6 Intruder. For this purpose a large radome was incorporated in the nose and the cabin was modified to house a complete A-6 avionics system. Powered by two 2,185ehp Rolls-Royce Dart 529-8X turboprops, the TC-4C made its first flight on June 14, 1967. **Data:** Span 78ft 6in (23.92m). Length 67ft 11in (20.70m). Gross weight 36,000lb (16,330kg). Max. cruising speed 348mph (560km/h).

Grumman TF-9J Cougar

U.S.A.

The Cougar was evolved as a sweptwing derivative of the straight-wing Panther, the first jet fighter built for the US Navy by Grumman. Cougar single-seat fighters were designated originally F9F-6 to -8 (later F-9), but none remain in service. The TF-9J tandem two-seat operational training version (first flown April 4, 1956) was used for combat missions in Vietnam, and equips a number of training units in the US. A handful also still serve with the Argentine Navy as advanced trainers. Each has an 8,500lb (3,855kg) st Pratt & Whitney J48-P-8A turbojet and provision for two 20mm cannon and 2,000lb (907kg) of underwing stores. A total of 399 TF-9Js was built. **Data:** Span 34ft 6in (10.51m). Length 48ft 6in (14.78m). Gross weight 20,600lb (9,344kg). Max. speed 705mph (1,135km/h). Range 1,000 miles (1,610km).

Handley Page Hastings

Great Britain

Design of the Hastings heavy freighter and troop transport began during World War II, and the prototype first flew on May 7, 1946. An initial batch of 100 was built, designated C.Mk.1, and these entered service with Transport Command in time to play their part in the Berlin Air Lift of 1948/49. They were followed by 42 C.Mk.2 and four C.Mk.4 aircraft with more powerful engines and other changes. The few Hastings still in service are C.Mk.1As and T.Mk.5s at the Strike Command Bombing School. Eight T.Mk.5s were produced in 1959, by converting C.Mk.1s to have radar bomb-sights and equipment to train V-bomber crews. Powered by four 1,640hp Bristol Hercules engines, they can be recognised by the large radome under the fuselage. **Data:** Span 113ft 0in (34.44m). Length 82ft 1in (25.01m). Gross weight 80,000lb (36,287kg). Max. speed 354mph (570km/h). Range 3,260 miles (5,246km) at 276mph (444km/h).

Handley Page Herald

Great Britain

The Series 400 Herald is a military transport development of the standard airliner versions of the Dart-engined Herald, the prototype of which flew for the first time on March 11, 1958. It has a specially-strengthened cabin floor, for carrying heavy freight, and the door at the rear of the cabin is designed to open in flight for supply dropping and parachuting. When roller conveyors are fitted to the floor, thirty-two 300lb (136kg) supply packs can be dropped by parachute in under ten seconds, with the aircraft flying at just over 100mph (160km/h). The Royal Malaysian Air Force has eight Herald 401s in service with No. 4 Squadron, based at Kuala Lumpur. Each is powered by two 2,105ehp R-R Dart 527 turboprops. **Data:** Span 94ft 9in (28.88m). Length 75ft 6in (23.01m). Gross weight 43,000lb (19,100 kg). Max. cruising speed 275mph (443km/h) at 15,000ft (4,575m). Range 1,760 miles (2,830km) with max. fuel.

Hawker Siddeley 748

Great Britain

The Hawker Siddeley Group began the design of this twin-Dart transport in January 1959, and the first prototype flew on June 24, 1960. In addition to the RAF's specially-developed Andover C.Mk.1 (page 66), standard HS.748s are in service with RAF Strike Command (4) and the Queen's Flight (2) as Andover CC.Mk.2s. Similar aircraft have been delivered to the Brazilian Air Force (6), the Royal Australian Air Force (eight T.Mk.2 and two C.Mk.2), the RAN (two), the Ecuadorian Air Force (three) and several Royal or Presidential Flights overseas. The Indian Air Force is getting 45 from HAL licence production, the first four being Srs 1 and the others Srs 2. They will be followed by more than 50 specialised freighters, with large loading door. The standard power plant comprises two 2,105ehp Rolls-Royce Dart 531 turboprops. Up to 62 passengers can be carried. **Data:** Span 98ft 6in (30.02m). Length 67ft 0in (20.42m). Gross weight 44,500lb (20,184 kg). Max. cruising speed 278mph (448km/h). Range 530 miles (852km).

Hawker Siddeley Argosy   *Great Britain*

Developed for the RAF from the civil AW 650 (which in turn was a private-venture development of a design intended to meet a specification for a Valetta replacement) the Argosy C.Mk.1 served as a tactical transport from 1962 to 1971, primarily with No. 114 Squadron. It has been replaced in the UK by the Lockheed Hercules, but some still served in 1972 with No. 70 Squadron based at Akrotiri, Cyprus. A few have been converted to Argosy E.Mk.1 for operation on radio and radar calibration duties by No. 59 Squadron at Wyton. **Data:** Span 115ft (35.05m). Length 89ft 2in (27.18m). Gross weight 105,000lb (47,627kg). Cruising speed 269mph (433km/h) at 20,000ft (6,100m). Range 1,070 miles (1,722km).

Hawker Siddeley (D.H.) Comet *Great Britain*

Ten Comet 2s modified for the RAF, after their use had been abandoned by BOAC, were used to equip No. 216 Squadron. They were retired from Transport Command in 1967, but three structurally unmodified Comet 2Rs with Avon 118 turbojets are used by No. 51 Squadron at RAF Wyton, while other Comets are flown by the Ministry of Technology on various research tasks, in RAF markings. Strike Command's No. 216 Squadron at RAF Brize Norton still has five Comet C.Mk.4s (first one flew November 15, 1961). These are equivalent to the civil Comet 4C, with a longer fuselage and external fuel tanks on the wings, and are powered by four 10,500lb (4,762kg) st Avon 350 engines. **Data:** Span 114ft 10in (35.0m). Length 118ft 0in (35.96m). Gross weight 162,000lb (73,482kg). Max. cruising speed 542mph (872km/h). Range 2,590 miles (4,168km).

Hawker Siddeley H.S.125, and Dominie T. Mk. 1
Great Britain

The Hawker Siddeley 125 Srs.2 was ordered for the RAF in September 1962, as a navigational trainer, under the name Dominie T.Mk.1. The first of 20 production models flew on December 30, 1964, and deliveries to No. 1 Air Navigation School at Stradishall, Suffolk, began in the Autumn of 1965. The Dominie T.1 is similar to the commercial twin-jet executive versions of the HS.125, with 3,000lb (1,360kg) st Bristol Siddeley Viper 520 turbojets; but is equipped to carry a pilot, pilot assister, two students and an instructor. The RAF also has five HS.125 CC.Mk.1 transports and two lengthened CC.Mk.2s (Srs. 600). Other air forces using the HS.125 include those of Malaysia (1), Brazil (10) and South Africa (4, named Mercurius). **Data** (Srs. 600): Span 47ft 0in (14.32m). Length 50ft 5¾in (15.37m). Gross weight 25,000lb (11,340kg). Max. speed 359 mph (578km/h). Range 1,876 miles (3,020km).

Hawker Siddeley HS.1182
Great Britain

This design was selected by the RAF during 1972 as its new basic trainer to replace the Gnat, the Hunter and eventually the Jet Provost for pilot training. Powered by a Rolls-Royce/Turboméca RT.172-06 Adour turbofan, without reheat, the HS.1182 seats two in tandem and has a secondary ground-attack role, for which purpose it can carry a 30mm Aden gun pod beneath the fuselage and some 5,000lb (2,268kg) of weapons on four underwing pylons. First flight of a prototype is expected to be made in the Spring of 1974, and deliveries of a production batch of 175 should begin during 1976. **Data:** Span 30ft 10in (9.4m). Length 33ft 11in (11.96m). Gross weight 10,250lb (4,650kg). Max. speed approx. 650mph (1,046km/h).

Helio AU-24A   *U.S.A.*

Fifteen of these armed versions of the Helio Stallion have been acquired by the USAF, under its "Credible Chase" programme, for evaluation in competition with a similar number of Fairchild AU-23A Peacemakers (page 186). The basic Stallion is an eight/eleven-seat utility monoplane, embodying the STOL design features of the Courier/U-10 series but powered by a 680shp Pratt & Whitney PT6A-27 turboprop engine. Modifications to convert it to AU-24A military standard were designed and incorporated by Kaman. They make possible operation at a much-increased gross weight, including a 20mm gun firing through a side door and up to 500lb (227kg) of external stores on an under-fuselage attachment, 600lb (272kg) on an inboard underwing rack each side and 300lb (136kg) on outboard underwing racks. **Data:** Span 41ft 0in (12.50m). Length 39ft 7in (12.07m). Gross weight 6,300lb (2,857kg). Max. speed 216 mph (348km/h). Max. range (civil Stallion) 1,090 miles (1,755km).

Helio U-10   *U.S.A.*

Service interest in the Helio Courier STOL aircraft was first shown in 1952 when the US Army acquired a single aircraft for evaluation under the original designation YL-24. Six years later, the USAF bought three of the more powerful five-seat Super Couriers, with 295hp Lycoming GO-480-G1D6 engine, under the designation L-28A (now U-10A), to evaluate operational techniques of STOL aircraft. Full-span leading-edge slats, large flaps, one-piece horizontal tail surfaces and a slow-turning oversize propeller enable this version to take off in 114 yards (104m) and land in 70 yards (64m) with a full load, and to remain controllable at speeds down to 30mph (48km/h). Large numbers entered USAF service for counter-insurgency duties in Vietnam, South America and elsewhere, including U-10Bs with paradrop door and extra fuel giving an endurance of 10 hours. A later production version, designated U-10D, has a gross weight of 3,600lb (1,633kg). **Data:** Span 39ft (11.89m). Length 31ft (9.45m). Gross weight 3,400lb (1,542kg). Max. speed 167mph (269km/h). Range up to 1,380 miles (2,220km).

Hiller H-23 Raven *U.S.A.*

Production of the Hiller UH-12 series totalled over 2,000, of which the majority were built for the US Army and the armed forces of a dozen other countries. Of the many versions still in use, the most important are the OH-23D (250hp Lycoming VO-435 engine) and OH-23G (305hp Lycoming VO-540). The Royal Navy acquired 21 similar aircraft as trainers, known by the designation Hiller HT.Mk.2. These versions carry three persons side-by-side. Also in service is the four-seat Hiller E4, used by the US Army under the designation OH-23F, mainly for utility transport support of survey parties. **Data** (OH-23G): Rotor diameter 35ft 5in (10.80m). Length 28ft 6in (8.69m). Gross weight 3,100lb (1,405kg). Max. speed 96mph (154km/h). Range 500 miles (805km).

Hindustan HAOP-27 Krishak Mk.2 *India*

This two/three-seat air observation post aircraft was developed by Hindustan from its popular two-seat Pushpak light aircraft and utilises the same basic fabric-covered metal wing. The first of two prototypes flew in November 1959, with a 190hp Continental engine. The 68 production Krishaks supplied to the Indian Army have 225hp Continental O-470-J engines. Dual controls are standard and the cabin can be adapted to carry a stretcher for air ambulance duties. **Data:** Span 37ft 6in (11.43m). Length 27ft 7in (8.41m). Gross weight 2,800lb (1,270kg). Max. speed 130mph (209km/h). Max. range 500 miles (805km).

Hindustan HJT-16 Mk.1 Kiran   *India*

This side-by-side two-seat jet basic trainer was designed to replace the Indian Air Force's Vampires. Detailed design work began in 1961, under the leadership of Dr. V. M. Ghatage, but the need to give priority to the HF-24 fighter delayed the first flight of the prototype Kiran until September 4, 1964. A second prototype followed and deliveries of the initial series of 24 pre-production aircraft began in March 1968. Production Kirans are following at the rate of two or three a month, and eventual deli-very of about 150 is envisaged. Standard power plant at present is the 2,500lb (1,135kg) st Rolls-Royce Bristol Viper 11 turbojet, but Hindustan have under development for the Kiran a 2,500lb st turbojet of their own design, designated HJE-2500, for potential use later. The crew have ejection seats in a pressurized cockpit. **Data:** Span 35ft 1¼in (10.70m). Length 34ft 9in (10.60m). Gross weight 9,259lb (4,200kg). Max. speed 432 mph (695km/h). Endurance 1hr 45min on internal fuel.

Hindustan HT-2   *India*

India's first domestically-designed aero-plane, the HT-2 was a product of the Hindu-stan Aeronautics factory at Bangalore. The first HT-2, a conventional tandem-seat basic trainer, flew on August 13, 1951, with a de Havilland Gipsy Major 10 engine. The second prototype, flown on February 19, 1952, had a 155hp Blackburn Cirrus Major III engine and production HT-2s for the Indian Air Force and Navy are to this standard. **Data:** Span 35ft 2in (10.72m). Length 24ft 8½in (7.53m). Gross weight 2,240lb (1,016kg). Max. speed 130mph (209km/h). Range 350 miles (563km).

Hispano HA-200 Saeta and HA-220 Super Saeta

Spain

The HA-200 serves with the Spanish Air Force as the E-14 two-seat advanced flying and armament trainer. The first prototype flew on August 12, 1955, followed by five pre-production models and 30 HA-200As (first flight October 11, 1962) with 880lb (400kg) st Turboméca Marboré IIA turbojets and armament of two 7.7mm machine-guns and underwing rockets. The HA-200B, developed for the Egyptian Air Force and produced at Helwan as the Al-Kahira, has a single 20mm cannon and different equipment. Ten supplied by Hispano have been followed by 90 built in Egypt. The 55 HA-200Ds have modernised systems; and 40 of them have the heavier armament specified, with 1,058lb (480kg) st Marboré VI turbojets, for the HA-200E. The "E" did not enter production, but from it was developed the single-seat HA-220 ground-attack aircraft, of which 25 were built for the Spanish Air Force. **Data** (HA-220): Span 34ft 2in (10.42m). Length 29ft 5in (8.97m). Gross weight 8,157lb (3,700kg). Max. speed 413 mph (665km/h). Range 1,055 miles (1,700km). Photograph: HA-220.

Hughes OH-6A Cayuse

U.S.A.

The OH-6A was chosen for production in May 1965. Deliveries began in 1966 against contracts which eventually totalled 1,434. The OH-6A is powered by a 252.5hp Allison T63-A-5A turboshaft and carries a crew of two, plus two passengers or four soldiers sitting on the floor, or equivalent freight. There is provision for carrying two twin machine-gun packs or grenade launchers on the sides of the cabin. The similar Hughes 500M has been delivered to several foreign armed forces and is built by Kawasaki in Japan (as OH-6J for JGSDF) and Nardi in Italy. **Data:** Rotor diameter 26ft 4in (8.03m). Length 23ft 0in (7.01m). Gross weight 2,700lb (1,225kg). Max. speed 150 mph (241km/h). Range 380 miles (611km).

Hughes TH-55A Osage U.S.A.

Hughes Tool Company entered the light helicopter field in 1955, when it began design and development of the two-seat Model 269. The prototype flew in October 1956. The design was then simplified for production and the US Army purchased five of the resulting Model 269A for evaluation, under the designation YHO-2HU. Commercial sales began in 1961 and 1,671 of all versions had been delivered by March 1971. Those now in production have two or three seats and a 180hp Lycoming HIO-360 engine. In mid-1964, the US Army ordered 20 Model 269A-1s, under the designation TH-55A, and follow-up orders brought the total of TH-55As to 792, to meet the Army's needs for a standard light helicopter primary trainer. Small numbers have been bought for military use by other countries, including Algeria, Brazil, Colombia, Ghana, Kenya and Nicaragua. **Data:** Rotor diameter 25ft 3½in (7.71m). Length 21ft 11¾in (6.80m). Gross weight 1,670lb (757kg). Max. speed 86mph (138km/h). Range 204 miles (328km).

Hunting Pembroke and Sea Prince Great Britain

First to order military versions of the Prince feeder-liner was the Royal Navy, which acquired three standard Sea Prince C.Mk.1s (first flown March 24, 1950) and four C.Mk.2s, with lengthened noses, for communications duties, together with eight Sea Prince T.Mk.1s (first flown June 28, 1951) equipped as flying classrooms for radar and navigation training, and easily recognised by their "thimble" nose radome. All versions have two 550hp Alvis Leonides 125 engines. The Pembroke C.Mk.1 staff transport and light freighter has an 8ft 6in (2.59m) increase in span. The RAF acquired 46 as staff transports, each furnished to carry a crew of two and eight passengers, and during 1969 began a modernization programme to prolong their life. Pembrokes serve also with the air forces of Belgium, the Congo (Zaire), Federal Germany, the Sudan, Sweden and Zambia. **Data** (Pembroke): Span 64ft 6in (19.66m). Length 46ft (14.02m). Gross weight 13,500lb (6,125kg). Max. speed 224mph (360km/h). Range 1,150 miles (1,850km). Photograph: Pembroke.

Hunting Provost

Great Britain

Last piston-engined basic trainer used by the RAF, the Provost has long been replaced in the UK by its turbine-powered development, the Jet Provost. However, the export model Provost T.Mks. 51, 52 and 53 remain in service with the air forces of Burma, Eire (illustrated), Malaysia, Rhodesia and Sudan. All versions are side-by-side two-seaters with a 550hp Alvis Leonides 126 engine. The Mks. 52 and 53 are suitable also for light attack duties, carrying two 0.303in machine-guns and underwing attachments for 500lb (227kg) of bombs or eight 60lb rockets. The prototype Provost flew (with an A.S. Cheetah engine) on February 23, 1950 and a total of 461 was built. **Data:** Span 35ft 2in (10.72m). Length 28ft 8in (8.73m). Gross weight 4,400lb (1,995kg). Max. speed 200mph (322km/h).

IAI-201 Arava

Israel

Israel Aircraft Industries began development of this twin-turboprop STOL light transport in 1966 and first flew the IAI-101 civil prototype on November 27, 1969. Because of the immediate prospect of orders, effort was switched entirely to the military IAI-201, of which a prototype (4X-IAB) has been flying since late 1971. This is powered by two 783shp Pratt & Whitney PT6A-34 engines and has accommodation for a crew of two and 23 fully-equipped troops, 16 paratroops and two despatchers, eight stretchers and three seated casualties or medical attendants, or 2½ tons of freight. The rear of the fuselage pod swings open for loading bulky items. Optional armament includes an 0.50in gun pack on each side of the fuselage above a pylon-mounted pack containing six 82mm rockets, and an aft-firing machine-gun. **Data:** Span 69ft 6in (20.88m). Length 42ft 7½in (12.99m). Gross weight 15,000lb (6,803kg). Max. speed 203mph (326km/h). Max. range 806 miles (1,297km).

Ilyushin Il-12 and Il-14 (NATO code-names: Coach and Crate respectively)

U.S.S.R.

The Il-12 first flew in 1944 as a general-purpose military transport to succeed the Li-2, the Russian-built Dakota. It could carry only 27 passengers because of its high structure weight, but was put into service by the Soviet Air Force, with 1,775hp Shvetsov ASh-82FNV two-row radials.

The Il-14 appeared in 1953, with reduced structure weight and 1,900hp ASh-82T engines. In the Il-14P, gross weight was reduced to 36,380lb (16,500kg), leading to improved take-off and climb performance while carrying 18–26 passengers. In the Il-14M, which appeared in 1956, the fuselage was stretched by 3.3ft (1.0m) and the gross weight restored to 38,000lb (17,235kg) with 32 passengers.

Air forces of the Warsaw Pact nations, and their allies, continue to fly the Il-14. A few Il-12s also remain in service. **Data** (Il-14M): Span 103ft 11in (31.67m). Length 73ft 3½in (22.34m). Gross weight 38,000lb (17,235kg). Max speed 258mph (415km/h). Range 937 miles (1,508km). Photograph: Il-14.

Kaman H-43 Huskie

U.S.A.

Development of this helicopter began in 1950, when the US Navy ordered the five-seat OH-43D (originally HOK-1) piston-engined version. There followed large USAF orders for the HH-43B, with 825hp Lycoming T53-L-1B turboshaft, and HH-43F with 1,150hp T53-L-11A, derated to 825hp to give a big power reserve for operations at high altitudes and/or in hot climates. The USAF versions are used mainly for crash rescue duties at airfields, carrying a pilot, two fire-fighters and a 1,000lb (450kg) pack of fire-fighting and rescue gear. The HH-43B and F have also been supplied to Burma, Colombia, Morocco, Iran, Pakistan and Thailand. A special drone version of the HH-43F was developed for the US Navy as the QH-43G. **Data** (HH-43F): Rotor diameter 47ft (14.33m). Length 25ft 2in (7.67m). Gross weight 9,150lb (4,150kg). Max. speed 120mph (193km/h). Range 504 miles (811km). Photograph: HH-43B.

Kamov Ka-15 (NATO code-name: Hen)
U.S.S.R.

The Ka-15 was the first really practical helicopter designed by Nikolai Kamov, following his earlier work on single-seat ultra-light types. It flew for the first time in 1952 and was subsequently put into large-scale production for the Soviet Navy and, as the Ka-15M, for civil crop-spraying, ambulance, postal and other duties. The naval version is operated from platforms on ships and is a side-by-side two-seater powered by a 255hp. Ivchenko AI-14V radial piston-engine. Like all of Kamov's helicopters, it has two three-blade contra-rotating co-axial rotors. **Data:** Rotor diameter 32ft 8½in (9.97m). Length 19ft 6in (5.94m). Gross weight 2,500lb (1,135kg). Max speed 93 mph (150km/h). Range 290 miles (465km).

Lockheed C-121 Constellation
U.S.A.

Military versions of the Super Constellation airliner have served primarily with the USAF and USN for airborne early warning and with MAC in the transport role (72 troops). With large radomes above and below the fuselage, ten RC-121Cs (later EC-121Cs) went into service with Air Defense Command in 1953. Seventy RC-121Ds (some later modified to EC-121H with new equipment) had 3,250hp Wright R-3350-91 engines and were distinguished by wing-tip tanks. The last examples of the C-121 series in service included some EC-121D/H aircraft with Aerospace Defense Command, mainly in a fighter control role with crew of 27; C-121Gs with Air National Guard squadrons; and some remanufactured C-121Js (known as Blue Eagles) used by the US Navy as airborne TV and radio transmitters and studios in Vietnam. The Indian Air Force took over nine L-1049Gs from Air-India. Eight of these are used in the maritime search role and one for transport duties. **Data** (EC-121D): Span 126ft 2in (38.45m). Length 116ft 2in (35.40m). Gross weight 143,600lb (65,135kg). Max. speed 321mph (516km/h). Range 4,600 miles (7,400km).

Lockheed C-140 JetStar U.S.A.

Sixteen JetStars were delivered to the USAF. Five, designated C-140A, are used by the Air Force Communications Service which is responsible for checking worldwide military navigation aids. The others, designated VC-140B, are 11/16-seat transports operated by the Special Air Missions Wing of Military Airlift Command. Three JetStars were acquired by the Federal German Air Force for VIP transport duties; others are operated by the air forces of Indonesia (1), Libya (1), Mexico (1) and Saudi Arabia (2). The prototype JetStar flew on September 4, 1957, powered by two Bristol Siddeley Orpheus turbojets. Production models have four 3,000lb (1,360kg) st Pratt & Whitney JT12A-6A or 3,300lb (1,497kg) st JT12A-8 engines, mounted in pairs on each side of the rear fuselage. **Data:** Span 54ft 5in (16.60m). Length 60ft 5in (18.42m). Gross weight 42,000lb (19,051 kg). Max. speed 566mph (911km/h). Range 2,235 miles (3,595km). Photograph: VC-140B.

Lockheed F-80C Shooting Star and T-33A U.S.A.

America's first operational jet-fighter, the Shooting Star still serves with the air forces of Ecuador and Uruguay in its F-80C version. First flown on March 1, 1948, the F-80C is a single-seater with a 5,400lb (2,450kg) st Allison J33-A-35 turbojet and armament of six 0.50in machine-guns and two 1,000lb bombs or ten rockets. The T-33A advanced trainer is similar, except for having two seats in tandem, and is used by some 35 air forces throughout the world, often in AT-33 armed trainer/attack form. A total of 5,691 T-33As, and T-33Bs for the US Navy, were built by Lockheed. A further 210 were produced under licence by Kawasaki in Japan. Canadair built 656 as CL-30 Silver Stars with the 5,100lb (2,313kg) st Rolls-Royce Nene 10. Also in service in Iran, Pakistan, Thailand and Yugoslavia is the RT-33A single-seat photo-reconnaissance aircraft with camera-carrying nose. **Data** (T-33A): Span 38ft 10½in (11.85m). Length 37ft 9in (11.51m). Gross weight 14,440lb (6,550kg). Max. speed 600mph (965km/h). Range 1,345 miles (2,165km). Photograph: T-33A.

Lockheed PV-2 Harpoon   *U.S.A.*

Developed from the wartime Ventura series, the Harpoon entered service with the US Navy in 1944 as a patrol bomber; 535 were built, with two 2,000hp Pratt & Whitney R-2800-31 engines. Typical armament comprised five 0.50in guns in the nose, a two-gun dorsal turret, bombs in internal weapons-bay and underwing bombs and rockets. Four still serve with the Peruvian Air Force on coastal patrol and ASW duties. Others are operated in Angola by the Portuguese Air Force for bombing and air support missions. **Data:** Span 74ft 11¾in (22.85m). Length 52ft 1½in (15.89m). Gross weight 36,000lb (16,330kg). Max. speed 282mph (454km/h). Range 1,790 miles (2,880km).

Lockheed U-2   *U.S.A.*

Designation of this Lockheed design in the USAF's Utility category was a deliberate attempt to mislead, since the specific role of the aircraft when first produced in 1954 was strategic reconnaissance over Soviet and other territory. A number of U-2s operated in this role until 1960, when one was destroyed over Russia and its pilot captured. Subsequently, a number were modified to WU-2 configuration for high-altitude weather flights. Some were supplied to the Chinese Nationalist Air Force for reconnaissance flights over mainland China, but were withdrawn after several had been shot down. Production of the type is believed to have totalled 53 in several versions, including five two-seat U-2Ds. The first U-2As had 11,200lb (5,080kg) st J57-P-37A turbojets. The U-2B has the more powerful J75 engine and several continue in service for special high-altitude reconnaissance and weather flights. **Data:** Span 80ft (24.38m). Length 49ft 7in (15.11m). Gross weight about 20,000lb (9,075kg). Max. speed 520mph (837km/h) above 36,000ft (11,000m).

McDonnell Douglas C-9 Nightingale   *U.S.A.*

The USAF selected the C-9A Nightingale version of the commercial DC-9 Series 30 during 1967 to meet a requirement for a new aeromedical transport. The initial order was for eight, to be operated by the 375th Aeromedical Airlift Wing in place of C-131 Samaritans within the US. Thirteen more were ordered subsequently. The C-9A can carry up to 40 patients on stretchers or more than 40 in standard seats and contains a special-care compartment. Powered by

14,500lb (6,575kg) st Pratt & Whitney JT8D-9 turbofans, the first C-9A was delivered to Scott AFB on August 10, 1968. Also based on the DC-9 Series 30, the US Navy's C-9B is a fleet logistic support transport of which five were ordered in April 1972. **Data** (C-9A): Span 93ft 5in (28.47m). Length 119ft 3½in (36.37m). Gross weight 98,000lb (44,450kg). Max. cruising speed 565mph (909km/h) at 25,000ft (7,620m).

Max Holste M.H.1521 Broussard   *France*

The M.H.1521 Broussard is a six-seat utility transport suitable for service in regions where airfields are few and maintenance facilities scanty. It is powered by a 450hp Pratt & Whitney R-985 engine and has large slotted flaps which enable it to take off in under 220 yards (200m). With two seats removed, there is room for two stretchers; all passenger seats are removable for cargo-carrying operations. The prototype flew for the first time on November 17, 1952, and was followed by a second prototype and 27

pre-production aircraft. Initial orders for 180 production Broussards for the French Army and Air Force were stepped up to a total of 335 in 1957. Small numbers were passed on to many former French colonies, to help form the nucleus of an air force; others serve in Morocco and Portugal. **Data:** Span 45ft 1in (13.75m). Length 28ft 4½in (8.65m). Gross weight 5,953lb (2,700kg). Max. speed 161mph (260km/h). Range 745 miles (1,200km).

Messerschmitt-Bölkow-Blohm HFB 320 Hansa
Germany

The unique sweptforward wings of the Hansa were adopted to permit the wing centre-section structure to pass through the fuselage without impairing the space available in the main cabin, and to give passengers an exceptional downward view. Standard versions carry seven or twelve passengers. The prototype flew for the first time on April 21, 1964, and deliveries began in September 1967. Current Hansas have 3,100lb (1,406kg) st General Electric CJ610-9 turbojets in rear-mounted pods. Eight were delivered to the *Luftwaffe* for VIP transport and military flight test duties. Six more are being equipped for ECM missions, and 10 will be used for flight checks and avionics calibration. **Data:** Span 47ft 6in (14.49m). Length 54ft 6in (16.61m). Gross weight 20,280lb (9,200kg). Max. speed 513mph (825km/h). Range 1,472 miles (2,370km) at 420mph (675km/h).

Mikoyan/Gurevich MiG-15 (NATO code-names: Fagot and Midget)
U.S.S.R.

The MiG-15 first flew on December 30, 1947, and was produced in very large numbers, in Czechoslovakia and Poland as well as in Russia. The basic version (S-102 in Czechoslovakia, LiM-1 in Poland) had an RD-45 turbojet, which was a copy of the Rolls-Royce Nene with a rating of around 5,450lb (2,470kg) st. This engine was replaced by a developed 5,950lb (2,700kg) st Klimov VK-1 turbojet in the MiG-15*bis* (S-103 in Czechoslovakia, LiM-2 in Poland). Armament comprised one 37mm N-37 and two 23mm NR-23 cannon.

In addition to the basic fighter version, the tandem two-seat MiG-15UTI (NATO code-name *Midget*) operational trainer was built in quantity, with an RD-45 turbojet (CS-102 in Czechoslovakia).

The MiG-15*bis* continues in service, especially in the Middle East and Africa, where many nations have received Soviet aid. The MiG-15UTI is a standard trainer in more than 20 countries, including the Soviet Union. **Data** (MiG-15*bis*): Span 33ft 1¼in (10.09m). Length 36ft 4in (11.07m). Gross weight 14,238lb (6,460kg). Max. speed 668mph (1,075km/h). Photograph: MiG-15UTI

MIL Mi-1 and Mi-3 (NATO code-name: Hare)

U.S.S.R.

The Mi-1 was the first helicopter produced in quantity in Russia. The prototype was completed in September 1948 and production began in 1950, initially for the Soviet Air Force and later for the civil airline Aeroflot. Basic versions are the four-seat Mi-1, three-seat Mi-1T and multi-purpose Mi-1NKh which can carry on the fuselage sides two stretcher containers or 33-gallon (150 litre) fuel tanks.

All versions of the Mi-1 have a 575hp AI-26V engine. Mi-1s were built in Poland under the designation SM-1. Also in service with the Polish Air Force is the SM-2, with modified front fuselage housing five persons. **Data** (SM-1): Rotor diameter 47ft 1in (14.35m). Fuselage length 39ft 9in (12.12m). Gross weight 5,425lb (2,460kg). Max. speed 106mph (170km/h). Range 370 miles (595km). Photograph: SM-1.

MIL Mi-2 (NATO code-name: Hoplite)

Poland

By utilising two small and lightweight turbo-shaft engines, mounted above the cabin, Mil produced a helicopter that will carry $2\frac{1}{2}$ times the payload of the piston-engined Mi-1 without any significant change in overall dimensions. Known in Russia as the V-2, the Mi-2 was announced in the Autumn of 1961 and has since been in large-scale production at the WSK-Swidnik in Poland, for both military and civil use. The basic version carries a pilot and up to eight passengers and is powered by 437shp

Isotov GTD-350 turboshaft engines. The ambulance version carries four stretchers and an attendant: cargo can be carried either internally or slung underneath from a hook. Air forces using the Mi-2 include those of Bulgaria, Hungary, Poland, Romania and the Soviet Union. **Data:** Rotor diameter 47ft $6\frac{3}{4}$in (14.50m). Length 37ft $4\frac{3}{4}$in (11.40m). Normal gross weight 7,826lb (3,550kg). Max. speed 130mph (210km/h). Max. range 360 miles (580km) at 118 mph (190km/h).

Mitsubishi MU-2   *Japan*

The first prototype of this 6/14-seat STOL utility transport flew on September 14, 1963, powered by two 562hp Turboméca Astazou turboprop engines. The production MU-2 has more powerful AiResearch TPE 331 turboprops and a 3ft 3½in (1.0m) greater wing span than the prototypes. Military versions are the MU-2C, of which four had been delivered to the Japanese Ground Self-Defence Force by the Spring of 1972, with reconnaissance cameras and provision for two nose machine-guns, bombs, rockets, etc.; and the MU-2E search

and rescue model, of which 16 have gone to the Japanese Air Self-Defence Force, with nose radome, extra fuel, bulged observation windows and sliding door for lifeboat dropping. Military designations are LR-1 and MU-2S respectively. **Data** (commercial MU-2D with 605shp TPE 331-25 engines): Span 39ft 2in (11.95m). Length 33ft 3in (10.13m). Gross weight 9,350lb (4,240kg). Max. cruising speed 310mph (500km/h). Range 1,300 miles (2,100km). Photograph: LR-1.

Mitsubishi T-2 and FS-X   *Japan*

This tandem two-seat supersonic trainer and light attack aircraft has been under development for the Japanese Air Self-Defence Force since September 1967, when Mitsubishi was named as prime contractor. The first of two XT-2 prototypes flew for the first time on July 20, 1971. It is expected that contracts will be placed initially for 59 T-2 trainers, for service from 1974, and 68 FS-X ground-support models to replace the JASDF's F-86F fighters. The T-2 is

Japan's first home-designed supersonic aircraft, powered by two licence-built Rolls-Royce/Turboméca Adour turbofans, each rated at 7,143lb (3,240kg) st with afterburning. It has provision for a cannon in the front fuselage and underwing stores. **Data:** Span 25ft 11in (7.90m). Length 58ft 4¾in (17.80m). Gross weight 20,833lb (9,450kg). Max. speed 1,060mph (1,700km/h) at 36,000ft (11,000m). Ferry range 1,610 miles (2,600km).

Morane-Saulnier M.S. 760 Paris   *France*

The first of two prototypes of this four-seat liaison or two-seat training aircraft flew on July 29, 1954. The first production M.S.760A Paris I, with two 880lb (400kg) st Turboméca Marboré II turbojets, followed on February 27, 1958. This version is in service with the French Air Force for liaison duties; the French Navy has a few M.S.760B Paris IIs with 1,058lb (480kg) st Marboré VI engines. A total of 165 Paris I and II aircraft were built in France for military and civil use, including many for the armed services of Brazil and the Argentine. These countries also assembled the Paris under licence, but only the Argentine still uses the type, in both training and light attack versions, the latter with guns in fuselage and up to 900lb (410kg) of underwing bombs or rockets. The Paraguayan Air Force has a single Paris for light jet training. **Data** (Paris I): Span 33ft 3in (10.13m). Length 33ft 7in (10.24m). Gross weight 7,650lb (3,470kg). Max. speed 405mph (652km/h). Range 930 miles (1,500km).

NAMC YS-11   *Japan*

First flown in prototype form on August 30, 1962, the basic YS-11-100 is a 52/60-passenger short-range transport powered by two 3,060ehp Rolls-Royce Dart Mk.542-10K turboprop engines. It entered commercial service in the Spring of 1965. Military versions include the YS-11-103/105 32/48-seat VIP transport (4 for JASDF), YS-11-112 cargo transport (1 for JMSDF), YS-11A-218 transport (1 for JASDF), YS-11A-206 anti-submarine trainer (4 for JMSDF), YS-11A-305 passenger/cargo transport (1 for JASDF), and YS-11A-402 cargo transport (7 for JASDF). The JMSDF has also ordered two 400 series cargo transports, and three 600 series with gross weight of 55,115lb (25,000kg). **Data** (YS-11-200 series): Span 104ft 11¾in (32.00m). Length 86ft 3½in (26.30m). Gross weight 54,010lb (24,500kg). Max. cruising speed 291mph (469km/h). Max. range 2,000 miles (3,215km).

Neiva C-42 and L-42 Regente   *Brazil*

The Regente is of all-metal construction. It flew for the first time on September 7, 1961 and was ordered for the Brazilian Air Force in two versions. These comprised 80 C-42 four-seat utility models and 40 air observation post L-42s, with stepped-down rear fuselage for improved all-round visibility. The prototype Regente had a 145hp Continental O-300 engine, but the production models are powered by a 210hp Continental IO-360-D. **Data:** Span 29ft 11½in (9.13m). Length 23ft 8in (7.21m). Gross weight 2,293lb (1,040kg). Max. speed 153mph (246km/h). Range 590 miles (950km). Photograph: L-42.

Neiva IPD-6201 Universal (T-25)   *Brazil*

This two/three-seat basic trainer was ordered into production in 1968 to meet a Brazilian Air Force requirement for a replacement for its T-6 Texans. The prototype had flown for the first time on April 29, 1966, and had completed extensive flight testing and evaluation by the time the official contract for 150 aircraft was signed. The power plant is a 300hp Lycoming IO-540-K1D5 piston-engine and construction is all-metal. The pilot and instructor sit side-by-side, with space for a third person to the rear. The Brazilian Air Force designation is T-25. **Data:** Span 36ft 1in (11.00m). Length 28ft 2½in (8.60m). Gross weight 3,748lb (1,700kg). Max. speed 195mph (315km/h). Max. range 975 miles (1,570km).

Nord 3202 and 3212   *France*

One hundred of these two-seat primary trainers were acquired to replace the Stampe SV-4 biplanes that had been used for basic, aerobatic, and blind-flying instruction at French Army training schools. The original version was the Nord 3200 (first flown September 10, 1954) with a 260hp Salmson 8.AS.04 engine. Then came the Nord 3201 (first flown June 22, 1954) which was similar except for its 170hp SNECMA-Régnier engine. A fur-

ther engine change led to the production-type Nord 3202 (first flown April 17, 1957), with a 240hp Potez 4D.32 engine in the first 50 machines and a 260hp Potez 4D.34 in the last 50. When fitted with a radio-compass for instrument flying training, the designation is changed to Nord 3212. **Data** (4D.32 engine): Span 31ft 2in (9.50m). Length 26ft 8in (8.12m). Gross weight 2,690lb (1,220kg). Max. speed 161mph (260km/h). Range 620 miles (1,000km).

North American (and Cavalier) F-51D Mustang   *U.S.A.*

About 60 North American F-51D Mustang fighters of World War II vintage remain in first-line service in Bolivia, Dominica, El Salvador, Guatemala, Haiti and Indonesia. Each is powered by a 1,695hp Packard V-1650-7 (Rolls-Royce Merlin) piston-engine and is armed with six 0.50in wing-mounted machine-guns, plus two 1,000lb bombs and 5in rockets on eight underwing attachments. The aircraft in Bolivia and El Salvador were acquired from Cavalier Aircraft Corporation, which received a USAF contract in 1967 to build a small batch of Mustangs for counter-insurgency duties with certain air forces

which received MAP assistance. The basic Cavalier F-51D is a tandem two-seat fighter assembled from component parts, some manufactured as new. The height of the fin is increased, and armament and avionics are updated to 1968 standards. The Cavalier TF-51D trainer, also delivered in small numbers, has four guns, dual controls and a larger canopy. **Data** (Cavalier F-51D): Span 37ft 0½in (11.29m). Length 32ft 2½in (9.81m). Gross weight 12,500lb (5,670kg). Max. speed 457mph (735km/h). Max. range 1,980 miles (3,185km) at 290mph (466km/h).

North American T-6 Texan

U.S.A.

Remembered in Britain as the Harvard, this veteran two-seat basic trainer remained in production in the United States and, later, Canada, from 1938 until 1954 and more than 10,000 were built. In 1949–50, a total of 2,068 early models were modernised as T-6G Texans, and these are still in service with more than 30 air forces throughout the world. The Texan has a 550hp Pratt & Whitney R-1340-AN-1 engine and can carry underwing rockets and light bombs for weapon training and close support duties. **Data:** Span 42ft (12.80m). Length 29ft 6in (8.99m). Gross weight 5,617lb (2,548kg). Max. speed 212mph (341km/h). Range 870 miles (1,400km).

North American Rockwell T-2 Buckeye

U.S.A.

No prototype of the Buckeye was built and the first of the original series of 217 T-2A production models flew on January 31, 1958. This version is a tandem two-seater with a 3,400lb (1,540kg) st Westinghouse J34-WE-48 turbojet, and is suitable for the complete syllabus of naval training. On August 30, 1962 North American flew the first of two prototypes (converted from T-2As) of the T-2B, built to evaluate the potential of the airframe when fitted with two 3,000lb (1,360kg) st Pratt & Whitney J60-P-6 turbojets. Production orders for a total of 97 T-2Bs were placed in 1964–67 and the first of these aircraft flew on May 21, 1965. During 1968, a prototype T-2C was produced by installing 2,950lb (1,339kg) st General Electric J85-GE-4 engines in a T-2B; after which a total of 183 T-2Cs were ordered with these engines, the first 84 as an amendment of the T-2B contract. Twelve T-2Ds for Venezuela differ from the T-2C only in avionics and deletion of carrier landing capability. **Data** (T-2C): Span 38ft 1½in (11.62m). Length 38ft 3½in (11.67m). Gross weight 13,179lb (5,977kg). Max. speed 522mph (840km/h). Range 1,047 miles (1,635km).

North American Rockwell T-39 Sabreliner

U.S.A.

The Sabreliner prototype flew for the first time on September 16, 1958, with two General Electric J85 turbojets; but production models for military use have 3,000lb (1,360kg) st Pratt & Whitney J60 (JT12) engines. The T-39A (143 delivered) is a basic utility trainer in service with the USAF. The six T-39Bs have Doppler radar and NASARR all-weather search and ranging radar and are used to train aircrew destined for F-105 Thunderchief squadrons. The US Navy's 42 T-39Ds have a Magnavox radar system for maritime radar training. Nine CT-39Es acquired by the USN are similar to the commercial Sabreliner 40. A further variant is the T-39F, equipped to train ECM operators for the F-105G aircraft. **Data** (T-39A/D): Span 44ft 5in (13.54m). Length 43ft 9in (13.34m). Gross weight 17,760lb (8,055kg). Max. cruising speed 502mph (808km/h). Range 1,950 miles (3,138km).

North American Rockwell XFV-12A   *U.S.A.*

As the result of a design competition initiated in November 1971, the NR 356 project entered by the Columbus Division of North American Rockwell is being developed for US Navy evaluation. Two prototypes were ordered on October 18, 1972. By utilising some major components of existing aircraft, it is hoped to achieve a first flight with conventional take-off by mid-1974, and the first hovering flight by the end of the same year. For vertical take-off and landing, exhaust gases from the 30,000lb (13,610kg) st Pratt & Whitney F401-PW-400 series afterburning turbofan will be ducted to ejector flaps pivoted spanwise in both the mainplanes and the canard foreplanes. Bu sucking in outside air to supplement the exhaust, such a system is claimed to give one-third more vertical thrust than pure jet-lift. The main-wheel units retract into fairings at the base of the tail-fins. The wingtips outboard of these fairings fold down in flight to form ventral fins. Armament is envisaged as one 20mm M61 cannon, four Sparrows and Sidewinders for interception missions. Attack missions would also be operated from the Navy's projected new Sea Control Ships. **Data** (approx.): Span (wingtips folded) 30ft (9.14m). Length 42ft (12.80m). Gross weight (STOL) 20,000lb (9,070kg). Max speed Mach 2.2 to 2.4. Combat radius at least 575 miles (925km).

Northrop T-38A Talon *U.S.A.*

Structurally, the T-38A two-seat supersonic basic trainer is almost identical with the F-5 tactical fighter (see page 109). It lacks the fighter's wing leading-edge flaps and is powered by two 3,850lb (1,746kg) st General Electric J85-GE-5A afterburning turbojets. The first prototype ordered by the USAF flew on April 10, 1959, powered by YJ85-GE-1 engines without afterburners. The second aircraft was similar and was followed by four YT-38 trials aircraft with 3,600lb

(1,633kg) st YJ85-GE-5 afterburning engines. The first production T-38As became operational in March 1961 and a total of 1,187 were eventually built. Forty-six were purchased by the *Luftwaffe* for training German pilots in the USA; the US Navy has five. **Data:** Span 25ft 3in (7.70m). Length 46ft 4½in (14.12m). Gross weight 11,820lb (5,360kg). Max. speed Mach 1.3 (860mph; 1,385km/h). Range 1,140 miles (1,835km).

Pazmany/CAF PL-1B Chienshou *Taiwan*

In 1968 the Chinese Nationalist Air Force was looking for a small primary trainer which could be built in Taiwan as the first stage in creating an aircraft industry. The type selected was the PL-1, of which construction plans are marketed by the designer, Ladislao Pazmany of San Diego, California. The slightly modified prototype, designated PL-1A and powered by a 125 hp Lycoming O-290-D engine, was built in 100 days at the Aeronautical Research Laboratory, Taichung, and flew for the first time on October 26, 1968. It was followed by

two more PL-1A prototypes, and then by the first of 50 production PL-1Bs (10 for the Chinese Army) with wider cockpit, larger rudder and more powerful (150hp) Lycoming O-320-E2A engine. The PL-1B is a side-by-side two-seater, of all-metal construction. A very similar PL-2 has been built by the Vietnam Air Force. Others are under construction by the air forces of Thailand and South Korea. **Data:** Span 28ft (8.53m). Length 19ft 8in (5.99m). Gross weight 1,440lb (653kg). Max. speed 150mph (241km/h). Max. range 405 miles (650km).

Piaggio P.148

Italy

In 1951 the Italian Air Force chose the P.148 as standard equipment for its primary training schools. The first prototype flew on February 12, 1951, and 100 production P.148s were delivered subsequently. A few were passed on to the Somali Air Corps in 1962, and 12 were supplied to the Congolese Air Force (Zaire). The P.148 ceased to be used for primary training in the Italian Air Force when an all-through jet syllabus was adopted, based on the Aermacchi MB326. However, it was re-introduced in 1970 when, as in other air forces, the value of some initial training on piston-engined aircraft was recognised.

The P.148 is basically a side-by-side two-seater, but a third seat can be fitted in the rear of the cabin. It is powered by a 190hp Lycoming O-435-A. **Data:** Span 36ft 6in (11.12m). Length 27ft 8½in (8.45m). Gross weight 2,646lb (1,200kg). Max. speed 146 mph (235km/h). Range 570 miles (920km).

Piaggio P.149D

Italy

The P.149 started out as a four-seat touring development of the P.148, with a tricycle undercarriage and more powerful engine. It was flown in prototype form (with 260hp Lycoming GO-435) on June 19, 1953, but did not enter large-scale production until West Germany chose it as the standard basic trainer/liaison aircraft for the *Luftwaffe*. The first of 72 Piaggio-built P.149Ds (with 270hp GO-480) was delivered to Germany in May 1957, and was followed six months later by the first of 190 which were licence-built by Focke-Wulf. About 70 of these continue in service and P.149Ds are used also by the air forces of Nigeria, Tanzania and Uganda. Up to five persons can be carried in the liaison role. **Data:** Span 36ft 6in (11.12m). Length 28ft 9½in (8.78m). Gross weight 3,704lb (1,680kg). Max. speed 192 mph (310km/h). Range 680 miles (1,095km).

Piaggio P.166M (and Albatross) *Italy*

Piaggio developed the P.166 light transport from its P.136 twin-engined amphibian, with a normal fuselage instead of a flying-boat hull, but with similar basic outline. More than 100 have been built, including 51 P.166Ms for training, ambulance and communications duties with the Italian Air Force. Powered by two 340hp Lycoming GSO-480-B1C6 engines, driving pusher propellers, the P.166M can carry up to ten people or items of freight as large as an Orpheus turbojet. Nine are used by the South African Air Force for coastal patrol, and have the local name Albatross. Latest production version is the P.166S, of which 20 are being delivered for search and surveillance duties. Under development are ASW, para-dropping and armed military versions of the new P.166-BL2, with increased fuel and weight. **Data (P.166M):** Span 46ft 9in (14.25m). Length 38ft 1in (11.60m). Gross weight 8,115lb (3,680kg). Max. speed 222mph (357km/h). Range 1,200 miles (1,930km).

Piaggio PD-808 *Italy*

The El Segundo Division of Douglas Aircraft Company was responsible for the basic design of this 6/10-seat twin-jet utility transport; detail design and manufacture were entrusted to Piaggio. The Italian Government paid for two prototypes, and the first of these flew on August 29, 1964. Of the 25 PD-808s ordered subsequently for the Italian Air Force, 13 had been delivered by early 1972, made up of four six-seat VIP transports, six nine-seat transport/navigation trainers, and three ECM aircraft with a crew of five. Power is provided by two 3,360lb (1,524kg) st Rolls-Royce Bristol Viper 526 turbojets, mounted on the sides of the rear fuselage. **Data:** Span 43ft 3½in (13.20m). Length 42ft 2in (12.85m). Gross weight 18,000lb (8,165kg). Max. speed 529mph (852km/h). Range 1,322 miles (2,128km).

Pilatus P.3   *Switzerland*

The tandem two-seat Pilatus P-3 is used by the Swiss Air Force as an intermediate trainer, following *ab initio* pilot training and before the pupil graduates on to the Vampire jet advanced trainer. The first of two prototypes flew on September 3, 1953, and a total of 72 were acquired by the Swiss Air Force to replace its T-6 Texans. Power plant is a 260hp Lycoming GO-435-C2A piston-engine, and one 7.9mm machine-gun and racks for two rockets or four small bombs can be fitted for weapon training. Six P-3s were supplied to the Brazilian Navy in 1963 and five of these are now in service with an Air Force liaison and observation squadron. **Data:** Span 34ft 1in (10.40m). Length 28ft 8in (8.75m). Gross weight 3,300lb (1,500kg). Max. speed 193mph (310km/h). Range 465 miles (750km).

Piper L-4, L-18 and U-7A   *U.S.A.*

At least two air forces (those of Indonesia and Paraguay) still have in service some original L-4 Piper Cubs, with 65hp Continental O-170-3 engine. Far more numerous, and flown by some 16 air forces, are L-18s and U-7s, based on the post-war Super Cub. The 105 standard Super Cub 95s (90hp Continental C90) purchased as L-18Bs were all supplied to Turkey. They were followed by 838 similar L-18Cs for the US Army and America's allies, including Belgium, Denmark, France, Germany, Iran, Israel, Norway and Thailand. Last version of the Piper Cub to serve with the US forces, the U-7A (formerly L-21A) went into production in 1951 with a 125hp Lycoming O-290-11 engine. Thirty went to the US Army and 120 to the USAF, from which they passed to other operators. They were followed by 582 U-7Bs (originally L-21Bs), with 135hp O-290-D2 engine, of which about 70 were fitted with tandem wheels on each leg for operation from rough ground. All of these Cub variants are tandem two-seaters, for observation and liaison duties. **Data** (U-7A): Span 35ft 3in (10.73m). Length 22ft 7in (6.88m). Gross weight 1,580lb (717kg). Max. speed 123mph (198km/h). Range 770 miles (1,240km).

Piper PA-28-140 Cherokee 140   *U.S.A.*

First country to adopt this two/four-seat sporting and training aircraft for military use is Tanzania, which took delivery of five in the first half of 1972. They are being used as *ab initio* trainers for the Tanzanian People's Defence Force Air Wing, which is expected to receive its first MiG-19 combat aircraft from China in 1973. The Cherokee 140 is powered by a 150hp Lycoming O-320 engine. Two of the "stretched" six/seven-seat Cherokee Six version of the same basic design are operated by the Chilean Air Force. **Data** (Cherokee 140): Span 36ft 2in (11.02m). Length 23ft 3½in (7.10m). Gross weight 2,150lb (975kg). Max. speed 142mph (229km/h). Max. range 839 miles (1,350km).

Piper U-11A Aztec   *U.S.A.*

The PA-23-250 Aztec was introduced by Piper in 1959 as a five-seat development of their Apache four-seat light twin, with more powerful engines and swept fin. The US Navy ordered 20 of this original version, with 250hp Lycoming O-540-A1A engines, "off the shelf" for utility transport duties and these remain in service under the designation U-11A (originally UO-1). The later six-seat Turbo Aztec E, with 250hp TIO-540-C1A engines and longer nose, serves with the Spanish Air Force, which acquired six in 1972, to supplement two standard Aztecs. The French Air Force also has two Aztecs. **Data** (Turbo Aztec E): Span 37ft 2½in (11.34m). Length 31ft 2¾in (9.52m). Gross weight 5,200lb (2,360kg). Max. speed 253mph (407km/h). Range 1,310 miles (2,108km). Photograph: Turbo Aztec E.

Piper PA-31 Turbo Navajo   *U.S.A.*

As part of its re-equipment programme, to replace older types like the Piper L-4 Cub and Apache, the Argentine Army acquired five Turbo Navajo light transports in 1969. These are six/nine-seat light transports, powered by two 310hp Lycoming TIO-540-A engines. The prototype of the basic Navajo was flown on September 30, 1964, as the first of a new Piper family of larger aircraft for business and commuter airline service. It was followed by the turbo-charged Turbo Navajo and then, in 1970, by the PA-31P Pressurised Navajo. The Chilean Air Force has one Turbo Navajo. The Spanish Air Force has one Turbo and one Pressurised Navajo. **Data** (Turbo Navajo): Span 40ft 8in (12.40m). Length 32ft 7½in (9.94m). Gross weight 6,500lb (2,948kg). Max. speed 261mph (420km/h). Max. range 1,730 miles (2,780km).

Potez/Aérospatiale CM 170 Magister, Super Magister and CM 175 Zephyr   *France*

The first of three prototypes of the Magister tandem two-seat jet trainer flew on July 23, 1952. Eleven months later, the French Air Force placed a pre-production order for ten (first flown July 7, 1954) followed by production orders for a total of 387 (first flown February 29, 1956). The original design and manufacturing company, Fouga, became part of the Potez group, which continued production until the Magister was taken over by Sud-Aviation (now Aérospatiale) in 1967. Magisters built by these companies continue to serve in Algeria, Israel, Finland, France, Belgium, Cambodia, Morocco, Brazil, Lebanon and Libya. Others, built under licence by Valmet of Finland and Israel Aircraft Industries, serve in Finland, Israel and Uganda. The standard CM 170 Magister has two 880lb (400kg) st Turboméca Marboré IIA turbojets and can carry two machine-guns, plus underwing racks for two 50kg bombs, four 25kg rockets, up to 36 smaller rockets or two AS.11 guided missiles. The last 130 aircraft for the French Air Force and those for Brazil are Super Magisters with 1,058lb (480kg) st Marboré VI engines. Thirty-two CM 175 Zephyrs for the French Navy (first flown May 30, 1959) are equipped for carrier operation. **Data** (Magister): Span 39ft 10in (12.14m). Length 33ft (10.06m). Gross weight 7,055lb (3,200kg). Max. speed 444mph (714km/h). Range 735 miles (1,200km).

PZL-104 Wilga/Gelatik 32 *Poland/Indonesia*

The original Wilga 1 prototype flew for the first time on April 24, 1962, powered by a 180hp Narkiewicz WN-6B engine. The fuselage and tail unit were then redesigned completely, giving the aircraft its present unique spindly outline. The resulting Wilga 2 flew on August 1, 1963, with a 195 hp WN-6RB engine. Other prototypes followed, equipped for both four-seat liaison and agricultural duties, including one with a Continental O-470 engine. Fifty-six of this version are being built under licence in Indonesia, with the name Gelatik (Rice-bird) and are serving with the Indonesian Air Force. Early aircraft have a 225hp O-470-13A; current Gelatik 32s have a 230hp O-470-L. The Polish Air Force is receiving standard Polish-built Wilgas, with 260hp AI-14R radial engines, to replace its Yak-12s. **Data** (Gelatik): Span 36ft 5in (11.10m). Length 26ft 6¾in (8.10m). Gross weight 2,711lb (1,230kg). Max. speed 127 mph (205km/h). Range 435 miles (700km). Photograph: Wilga.

Republic F-84G Thunderjet *U.S.A.*

The F-84G Thunderjet remains in service in Portugal and Yugoslavia. It is a single-seat fighter-bomber, with a 5,600lb (2,540kg) st Allison J35-A-29 turbojet and armament of six 0.5in machine-guns, plus underwing attachments for four 1,000lb bombs or up to 32 5in rockets. It can be refuelled in flight, the max. unrefuelled range being 2,000 miles (3,220km). The prototype F-84 flew on February 28, 1946, and a total of 4,457 were built in the following seven years. **Data:** Span 36ft 5in (11.10m). Length 38ft 1in (11.61m). Gross weight 23,525lb (10,670 kg). Max. speed 622mph (1,000km/h).

Republic F-84F Thunderstreak and RF-84F Thunderflash

U.S.A.

Combining the basic Thunderjet fuselage with a swept-back wing and tail unit, the prototype YF-84F flew on June 3, 1950. A second prototype had a 7,220lb (3,275kg) st Wright J65-W-3 engine in place of the J35, and this version went into production as the F-84F. Production totalled 2,711, of which about half went to NATO air forces under MDAP, with an armament of six 0.50in machine-guns and underwing attachments for 6,000lb (2,720kg) of stores. Republic also built 718 of a reconnaissance version of the

same design, known as the RF-84F Thunderflash, in which wing-root intakes replace the nose intake, to permit installation of cameras in the nose. Some F-84Fs and RF-84Fs remain in service with NATO air forces, including those of Greece and Turkey. **Data** (F-84F): Span 33ft 7¼in (10.24m). Length 43ft 4¾in (13.23m). Gross weight 28,000lb (12,700kg). Max. speed 695mph (1,118km/h) at sea level. Max. range over 2,000 miles (3,220km). Photograph: RF-84F.

Saab-91 Safir

Sweden

The Saab-91A two/three-seat basic trainer, first flown in prototype form on November 20, 1945, had a 145hp D.H. Gipsy Major 10. The Saab-91B changed to a 190hp Lycoming O-435-A engine and remains a standard basic trainer of the Swedish Air Force (75 delivered as SK50B) and Norwegian (25) and Ethiopian (16) air forces. The Saab-91C differs from the B only in having four seats and was sold to the Swedish Air Force (14 SK50Cs) and Ethiopia (14). Final version was the Saab-91D,

which differs from the C in having a 180hp Lycoming O-360-A1A engine, propeller spinner, more powerful generator and rudder trim. Orders for the D were received from the air forces of Finland (35), Tunisia (15) and Austria (24). **Data** (Saab-91D): Span 34ft 9in (10.60m). Length 26ft 4in (8.03m). Gross weight 2,660lb (1,205kg). Max. speed 165mph (265km/h). Range 660 miles (1,060km). Photograph: Austrian Saab-91D.

Saab-MFI 17   *Sweden*

This aircraft had its origin in the MFI-9/ Bölkow Junior series, designed by Bjorn Andreasson and used as lightweight attack aircraft by the Biafran forces in the Nigerian civil war. When Saab took over the MFI company, they supported development of the two/three-seat Saab-MFI 15 for military training and general-purpose duties. The "17" differs primarily in having six underwing attachments for up to 660lb (300kg) of rocket pods, wire-guided anti-tank missiles, droppable containers or other stores. Power plant is a 200hp Lycoming IO-360-A1B piston-engine. The Saab-MFI 17 entered production in the Autumn of 1972, to meet an order for 20 from an unspecified foreign customer. **Data:** Span 28ft 6½in (8.70m). Length 22ft 11½in (7.00m). Gross weight 2,425lb (1,100kg). Max. speed 160 mph (257km/h). Endurance 4hr 45 min.

SAN/Robin Jodel D.140R Abeille   *France*

Flown for the first time in mid-1965, the Abeille is a specialised glider-towing version of the D.140E Mousquetaire IV, which was itself developed by Société Aéronautique Normande from the basic Jodel family of light aircraft. The French Air Force ordered from SAN a number of Abeilles to equip its gliding clubs. When the company went into liquidation, the balance of this contract was taken over and completed by Avions Pierre Robin at Dijon. The Abeille can carry four persons and is powered by a 180hp Lycoming O-360-A2A engine. **Data:** Span 33ft 8¼in (10.27m). Length 25ft 8in (7.82m). Gross weight 2,645lb (1,200kg). Max. speed 155mph (250km/h). Range 870 miles (1,400km).

Scottish Aviation Bulldog *Great Britain*

This two-seat primary trainer was developed originally by Beagle Aircraft as the B.125 Series 1. Its all-metal airframe was basically similar to that of the civil Pup, with structural and equipment changes to suit it for military use. In particular, the Bulldog has a large rearward-sliding jettisonable canopy over its side-by-side seats and is powered by a 200hp Lycoming IO-360-A1B6 engine. The prototype flew for the first time on May 19, 1969. When Beagle went into liquidation, production was taken over by Scottish Aviation, which flew its Bulldog 100 Series prototype on February 14,

1971. Deliveries began in July 1971, to meet orders from Sweden (58 Model 101 for Swedish Air Force and 20 for Swedish Army, with option on 25 more), Malaysia (15 Model 102) and Kenya (5 Model 103). The 130 Bulldogs ordered in 1972 for the RAF will be of the new 120 Series, with strengthened centre-section and increased aerobatic gross weight. The Sw.AF designation is SK61. **Data:** Span 33ft (10.06m). Length 23ft 3in (7.09m). Gross weight 2,350lb (1,065kg). Max. speed 150mph (240km/h). Range 621 miles (1,000km).

Scottish Aviation Jetstream 201 *Great Britain*

After a chequered history, the Jetstream has been given a new surge of life by its choice as the type to replace RAF Varsity multi-engined pilot training aircraft. The present order is for 26 Jetstream 201s, for delivery in 1973–75. Power plant will comprise two 940shp Turboméca Astazou XVI turboprops, permitting higher operating weights and performance than the Astazou XIIs and XIVs fitted in the prototype (first flown August 18, 1967) and early Mk.1 aircraft built by Handley Page. The design was taken over by Jetstream Aircraft Ltd. after

the Handley Page company ceased operations. In 1972 full responsibility for the programme was taken over by Scottish Aviation, which absorbed Jetstream Aircraft. The RAF trainers are being produced in parallel with standard 12/18-passenger executive and airline transport versions, to which the following data apply. **Data:** Span 52ft 0in (15.85m). Length 47ft 1½in (14.37m). Gross weight 12,500lb (5,670kg). Max. speed 285mph (459km/h). Max. range 1,382 miles (2,224km).

Short Skyvan Series 3M — *Great Britain*

The prototype of this military version of the Short Skyvan Srs. 3 STOL utility transport flew for the first time in early 1970. It is powered by two 715shp AiResearch TPE 331-201 turboprops and can carry 22 equipped troops, 16 paratroops and a despatcher, 12 stretcher cases and two medical attendants or 5,000lb (2,270kg) of freight. Entry to the cabin is via a rear loading ramp. Special equipment includes a Bendix weather radar on the nose, anchor cables for parachute static lines, inward-facing paratroop seats, stretcher mounts and roller conveyors in the cabin floor. Initial deliveries comprised two aircraft for the Austrian Air Force and the first of ten for the Sultan of Oman's Air Force. Others are used by the Argentine Naval Prefectura, Royal Thai Police (3), the Nepalese Army (2), and the Air Arms of Ecuador and Indonesia. The Singapore Air Defence Command ordered six in 1972. **Data:** Span 64ft 11in (19.79m). Length 41ft 4in (12.60m). Gross weight 14,500lb (6,577kg). Max. cruising speed 203mph (327km/h). Max. range 670 miles (1,075km).

SIAI-Marchetti S.208M — *Italy*

The prototype of the S.208 five-seat light aircraft flew for the first time on May 22, 1967. It embodies many components of SIAI-Marchetti's popular S.205 series, but introduced one more seat and a more powerful (260hp) Lycoming O-540-E4A5 engine. In addition to civilian production, the company is building 44 of a version designated S.208M for the Italian Air Force. This differs from the standard model by having a jettisonable cabin door, and is intended for liaison and training duties. **Data:** Span 35ft 7½in (10.86m). Length 26ft 3in (8.00m). Gross weight 3,307lb (1,500kg). Max. speed 199mph (320km/h). Max. range 1,250 miles (2,000km).

SIAI-Marchetti SF.260MX   *Italy*

The prototype of this two/three-seat aircraft, designed by Ing. Stelio Frati, was built by Aviamilano as the F.250 and flew on July 15, 1964. Production was undertaken by SIAI-Marchetti, who exchanged the original 250hp engine for a 260hp Lycoming O-540-E4A5 and redesignated the aircraft SF.260. In addition to manufacturing 150 civil-registered SF.260s, many for use as airline trainers, SIAI-Marchetti received orders for military SF.260MXs for the Air Forces of Belgium (36), the Congo (Zaire, 12), Singapore (16) and Zambia (8). This version has a larger rudder and specialised equipment for military training. A strengthened and armed version, with wing pylons for bombs or rockets, is known as the SF.260W Warrior and first flew in May 1972. **Data:** Span 26ft 11¾in (8.25m). Length 23ft 3½in (7.10m). Gross weight 2,998lb (1,360kg). Max. speed 211mph (340km/h). Max. range 894 miles (1,440km).

SIAI-Marchetti SM.1019   *Italy*

This two-seat light military STOL aircraft is a turboprop development of the Cessna L-19/O-1 Bird Dog which can be produced either as a new airframe or by extensive modification of existing aircraft. The entire airframe is updated to meet current operational requirements, and is fitted with new, angular vertical tail surfaces and a lengthened nose for the 317shp Allison 250-B15G turboprop. Up to 500lb of rockets, bombs or camera packs can be carried on two underwing racks. The first of two prototype SM.1019s flew on May 24, 1969, and production of 100 aircraft for the Italian Army began in 1972. **Data:** Span 36ft (10.97m). Length 27ft 11½in (8.52m). Gross weight 2,800lb (1,270kg). Max. cruising speed 155mph (250km/h).

Sikorsky S-55 and H-19 Chickasaw U.S.A.

The H-19 is the military counterpart of the civil Sikorsky S-55, with accommodation for a crew of two and up to ten troops or six stretchers. The parent company built 1,281, of which most went to the US armed forces. Versions included the USAF's UH-19B, Army UH-19D, Marine CH-19E and Naval UH-19F, all with 800hp Wright R-1300-3 engine, and the Army's UH-19C with 600hp Pratt & Whitney R-1340. Others were manufactured in Japan by Mitsubishi. More than 20 air forces used versions of the S-55 and H-19 for utility transport, search and rescue, casualty evacuation and other duties. **Data** (R-1300 engine): Rotor diameter 53ft (16.15m). Length 42ft 3in (12.88m). Gross weight 7,900lb (3,583kg). Max. speed 112mph (180km/h). Range 360 miles (580km).

Sikorsky S-56 (H-37 Mojave) U.S.A.

To meet a US Marine requirement for a heavy assault aircraft with quick-loading provisions, the S-56 was designed with clam-shell nose-doors, and with a monorail along the cabin ceiling carrying a 2,000lb capacity winch. The prototype, known as the XHR2S-1, first flew on December 18, 1953. Production HR2S-1s were similar, with two 2,100hp Pratt & Whitney R-2800-54 engines; the first flew on October 25, 1955 and about 60 were delivered. Those still in service in 1962 were redesignated CH-37C.

Following evaluation of an HR2S-1 in 1954, the US Army purchased 94 S-56s as H-37A Mojaves for transport duties. Between June 1961 and the end of 1962, Sikorsky modified 90 of these to H-37B (now CH-37B) configuration, with Lear autostabilisation equipment, crash-resistant fuel cells and provision for loading and unloading while the helicopter is hovering. Each carries 36 troops or equivalent freight. **Data:** Rotor dia. 72ft (21.95m). Fuselage length 64ft 10in (19.76m). Gross weight 31,000lb (14,060kg). Max. speed 130mph (209km/h). Range 145 miles (233km).

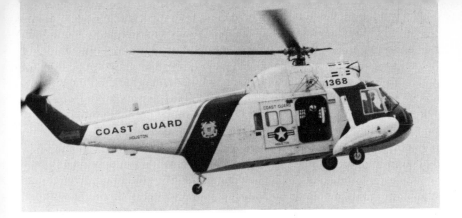

Sikorsky S-62 and HH-52A   *U.S.A.*

The twelve-passenger S-62A utilises many components of the S-55, including main and tail rotor systems. Its 730shp General Electric CT58-110 engine gives 130 more horsepower than the S-55's piston-engine, but is so much lighter in weight that the S-62A can carry a much greater payload. The prototype flew on May 14, 1958.

The S-62B is similar but utilizes an S-58 main rotor system, with reduced rotor diameter. A total of 99 specially-equipped search and rescue models were built for the US Coast Guard, under the designation HH-52A. The S-62C is a commercial and foreign military version of the HH-52A and is in service with the Indian, Japanese and Philippine armed forces and the Thai Police. Some of these were assembled in Japan by Mitsubishi. **Data** (HH-52A): Rotor diameter 53ft (16.15m). Length 44ft 6½in (13.58m). Gross weight 8,300lb (3,765 kg). Max. speed 109mph (175km/h). Max. range 474 miles (763km).

Soko G2-A and G-3 Galeb   *Yugoslavia*

First flown in prototype form in May 1961, the G2-A Galeb tandem two-seat basic trainer is conventional in design and, like many of its counterparts in other countries, is powered by a Rolls-Royce Bristol Viper turbojet. The second prototype embodied improvements and was representative of the production version, of which many are being built for and are in service with the Yugoslav Air Force. The engine in the production G2-A is a Viper 11 Mk.22-6 of 2,500lb (1,134kg) st. For weapon training or light attack duties, it is fitted with two 0.50in machine-guns and underwing racks for bombs and rockets. Under development is the G-3 Galeb-3 with 3,395lb (1,540kg) st Viper engine, the centre and rear fuselage and wings of the J-1 Jastreb (see page 124) and increased weapon load. Two G2-A Galebs have been supplied to Zambia. **Data** (G2-A): Span 38ft 1½in (11.62m). Length 33ft 11in (10.34m). Gross weight 8,440–9,210lb (3,828–4,178kg). Max. speed 505mph (812km/h). Range 770 miles (1,240 km).

TS-11 Iskra   *Poland*

The TS-11 Iskra (Spark) flew for the first time on February 5, 1960. It came second to the Czech L-29 Delfin in the competition to find a new jet trainer for the Warsaw Pact nations; but Poland decided to continue development and production of the Iskra to meet its own requirements and the first formal delivery to the Air Force was made in March 1963. Quantity deliveries began in the following year and were continuing in 1972. Design is conventional, with two seats in tandem and a 2,205lb (1,000kg) st nation-ally-designed SO-1 turbojet (1,760lb; 800kg st HO-10 in early aircraft). A version known as the Iskra 100 (illustrated) has a 23mm gun in its nose and four underwing racks for bombs or rockets. In September 1964, an Iskra set up four international records in Class C-1-d, including a speed of 521.33 mph (839km/h) over a 15/25-km course. **Data:** Span 33ft 0in (10.07m). Length 36ft 10¾in (11.25m). Gross weight 8,377lb (3,800kg). Max. speed 447mph (720km/h). Range 907 miles (1,460km).

Tupolev Tu-124 (NATO code-name: Cookpot)   *U.S.S.R.*

This scaled-down version of the Soviet Union's first jet airliner, the Tu-104, flew in June 1960 as the first Soviet transport aircraft fitted with turbofan engines. It is used widely by Aeroflot; three were delivered to CSA Czech Airlines, one to Interflug, and others serve in small numbers with the air forces of East Germany, Iraq and India. Some are reported in service with the Soviet Air Force. The standard airline version is powered by two 11,905lb (5,400kg) st Soloviev D-20P turbofans and accommodates 56 passengers. The Bulgarian Air Force is reported to operate a Tu-134 (NATO *Crusty*), a 64/80-seat development of the Tu-124 with two rear-mounted D-30 turbofans, each giving 14,990lb (6,800kg) st. **Data** (Tu-124): Span 83ft 9½in (25.55m). Length 100ft 4in (30.58m). Gross weight 83,775lb (38,000kg). Max. speed 603mph (970km/h). Max range 1,305 miles (2,100km).

UTVA-60 and UTVA-66   *Yugoslavia*

The Yugoslav Air Force has a number of these sturdy four-seat utility aircraft built by the Fabrika Aviona UTVA at Pancevo. The UTVA-60, powered by a 270hp Lycoming GO-480-B1A6 engine, was manufactured in utility and ambulance versions. In addition, there was a floatplane version, designated UTVA-60H, with 296hp Lycoming GO-480-G1H6 engine. The UTVA-60H is known to be in military service, as is the new

UTVA-66, which exists in the same versions and has a 270hp GSO-480-B1J6 engine, fixed leading-edge slots, larger tail surfaces, increased fuel capacity and other changes. **Data** (UTVA-66): Span 37ft 5in (11.40m). Length 27ft 6in (8.38m). Gross weight 4,000lb (1,814kg). Max. speed 155mph (250km/h). Max. range 466 miles (750km). Photograph: UTVA-66.

Vickers Varsity T.Mk.1   *Great Britain*

RAF requirements for a general-purpose crew trainer were met conveniently by adapting the Valetta design to have a nose-wheel undercarriage and special features for the training role. The length of the nose and the wing span were both increased, and an under-fuselage pannier was added to accommodate the bomb-aiming station and 600lb (272kg) of practice bombs. The result was an aircraft with provision for training pilots, radio operators, navigators

and bomb-aimers simultaneously. The prototype flew for the first time on July 17, 1949, and a total of 164 was produced during the 4½ years that followed. About 50 continue in service with Training Command. **Data:** Two 1,950hp Bristol Hercules 264 engines. Span 95ft 8in (29.16m). Length 67ft 6in (20.57m). Gross weight 37,500lb (17,010kg). Max. speed 288mph (463km/h). Range 2,650 miles (4,265km).

Westland Whirlwind

Great Britain

The Whirlwind began, in its Series 1 form, as a licence-built Sikorsky S-55, but later underwent considerable development. In the Series 2, the usual Wright or Pratt & Whitney piston-engine was replaced by a 750hp Alvis Leonides Major, giving considerably improved performance. The Series 3, first flown on February 28, 1959, switched to a 1,050hp Rolls-Royce Bristol Gnome H.1000 turboshaft. A total of more than 400 Series 1 and 2 Whirlwinds were built for civil and military use, including many for the RAF, Royal Navy and seven other air forces. A few remain in service as transports for 10 passengers, six stretchers or freight, search and rescue aircraft and for other duties. Many RAF and Royal Navy Whirlwinds were converted to Series 3 standard, under the designations HAR. Mk.10 and Mk.9 respectively, to supplement new production. The Ghana Air Force has three Series 3 Whirlwinds; the Brazilian Navy has five and the Nigerian Air Force one. **Data** (Srs.3): Rotor diameter 53ft (16.15m). Length 44ft 2in (13.46m). Gross weight 8,000lb (3,630kg). Max. speed 106 mph (170km/h). Range 300 miles (482km).

Yakovlev Yak-18 (NATO code-name: Max)

U.S.S.R.

In a variety of forms, this sturdy all-metal aircraft has been the standard primary trainer of the Soviet Air Force and civil flying schools since 1946, and is also in service in a dozen other countries. Numerous versions have appeared since the early tandem two-seat Yak-18 (*Max*) with 160hp M-11FR engine and tail-wheel landing gear. These include the Yak-18U with nose-wheel and longer fuselage; Yak-18A with 300hp AI-14RF engine; Yak-18P single-seat version of the -18A with forward-retracting or inwards-retracting landing gear; Yak-18PM single-seat aerobatic version; Yak-18PS tail-wheel version of the PM; and the four-seat Yak-18T, with enclosed cabin. **Data** (Yak-18A): Span 34ft 9½in (10.60m). Length 27ft 4¾in (8.35m). Gross weight 2,910lb (1,320kg). Max. speed 186mph (300km/h). Range 435 miles (700km). Photograph: Yak-18PS.

Yakovlev Yak-40 (NATO code-name: Codling)

U.S.S.R.

Confirmation that this unique little tri-jet transport is in military, as well as commercial, service came in the Summer of 1971, when two Yak-40s were seen in Yugoslav Air Force markings. By 1973, three had been delivered to this Air Force, with others likely to follow.

The Yak-40 first flew on October 21, 1966, and more than 200 were in service by April 1970, mostly with Aeroflot. Manufacture of 300 more had been authorised at that time, and several thousand short-haul routes inside the Soviet Union will be served eventually by these aircraft. The three 3,300lb (1,500kg) st Ivchenko AI-25 turbofans enable the Yak-40 to take off in 2,625ft (800m) with a full load of 27–40 passengers. It can operate from grass or dirt strips, will take off and climb on any two engines and maintain cruising height on one. **Data:** Span 82ft 0¼in (25.0m). Length 66ft 9½in (20.36m). Gross weight 36,375lb (16,500kg). Max. speed 373mph (600km/h). Max. range 1,210 miles (1,950km).

Photo Credits

Index

A-1 Skyraider, Douglas 43
A-3 Skywarrior, Douglas 44
A-4 Skyhawk, McDonnell Douglas 89
A-6 Intruder, Grumman 57
A-7 Corsair II, Vought 137
A-10A, Fairchild 185
A32A Lansen, Saab 112
A-37, Cessna 30
A.106, Agusta 10
AC-47, Douglas 183
AC-119, Fairchild 49
AC-130, Lockheed 81
AESL Airtrainer CT/4 158
AH-1 HueyCobra/SeaCobra, Bell 17
AISA I-115 158
AJ37 Viggen, Saab 114
AL.60C5, Aermacchi-Lockheed 153
AM.3C, Aeritalia/Aermacchi 153
An-2, "Colt", Antonov 159
An-12, "Cub", Antonov 11
An-14, "Clod", Antonov 160
An-22, "Cock", Antonov 12
An-24, "Coke", Antonov 160
An-26, "Curl", Antonov 160
AOP.9, Auster 161
AT-26 Xavante, Embraer 6
AT-33, Lockheed 203
AU-23 Peacemaker, Fairchild 186
AU-24, Helio 195
AV-8A, Hawker Siddeley 69
Abeille, D.140R, SAN/Robin 222
Aeritalia G91 4
Aeritalia G222 5
Aeritalia/Aermacchi AM.3C 153
Aermacchi MB326 6
Aermacchi-Lockheed AL.60C5 153
Aero 3 154
Aero L-29 Delfin 154
Aero L-39 Super Delfin 155
Aero Commander Shrike Commander 155
Aérospatiale N 262 156
Aérospatiale SA316/319 Alouette III 7
Aérospatiale SA321 Super Frelon 8
Aérospatiale SE313/SA318 Alouette II and SA315 Lama 156
Aérospatiale/Westland SA330 Puma 9
Aérospatiale/Westland SA341 Gazelle 157
Aerotec T-23 Uirapuru 157
Agusta A.106 10
Agusta-Bell 204B/205 18
Airtrainer CT/4, AESL 158
Albatross, HU-16, Grumman 190
Albatross, P.166M, Piaggio 216
Alizé, Br 1050, Breguet 25
Alouette II Artouste, SE313, Aérospatiale 156
Alouette II Astazou, SA318, Aérospatiale 156
Alouette III, SA316/319, Aérospatiale 7
Alpha Jet 159
Andover, Hawker Siddeley 66, 192
Antonov An-2, "Colt" 159
Antonov An-12, "Cub" 11
Antonov An-14, "Clod" 160
Antonov An-22, "Cock" 12
Antonov An-24, "Coke" 160
Antonov An-26, "Curl" 160
Arava, IAI-201 200
Argosy, Hawker Siddeley 193
Argus, CP-107, Canadair 29
Armstrong Whitworth Sea Hawk 161
Atlantic, Br 1150, Breguet 26
Auster D-Series and AOP 9 161
Aviocar, C.212, CASA 172
Avro Shackleton 13
Azor, CASA 171

Aztec, U-11A, Piper 218

B-1A, North American Rockwell 106
B-26 Invader, Douglas 182
B-52 Stratofortress, Boeing 20
B-57 Canberra, Martin & General Dynamics 92
B-66 Destroyer, Douglas 45
BAC 167 Strikemaster 15
BAC Jet Provost 15
BAC Lightning 14
BAC One-Eleven 162
BAC VC10 16
Be-6, "Madge", Beriev 168
Be-12, "Mail", Beriev 19
Br. 1050 Alizé, Breguet 25
Br. 1150 Atlantic, Breguet 26
"Backfire", Tu-?, Tupolev 106
"Badger", Tu-16, Tupolev 132
Bandeirante, EMB-110, Embraer 185
Baron, Beech 164
Basset CC.Mk.1, Beagle 162
Beagle Basset CC.Mk.1 162
"Beagle", Il-28, Ilyushin 74
"Bear", Tu-95, Tupolev 135
Beaver, DHC-2 Mk.1, de Havilland 178
Beech C-45 Expeditor 163
Beech QU-22 166
Beech RU-21 165
Beech T-34 Mentor 164
Beech T-42A Cochise 164
Beech U-8 Seminole 165
Beech U-21 165
Beech U-22 Bonanza 166
Beech VC-6A 165
Beech Baron 164
Beech Musketeer 163
Beechcraft 99 166
Belfast, Short 118
Bell 206 JetRanger 167
Bell 209 HueyCobra/SeaCobra 17
Bell AH-1 HueyCobra/SeaCobra 17
Bell H-13 Sioux 167
Bell OH-58 Kiowa 167
Bell TH-57 SeaRanger 167
Bell UH-1 Iroquois 18
Beriev Be-6, "Madge" 168
Beriev Be-12, "Mail" 19
Bird Dog, O-1, Cessna 172
"Bison", Mya-4, Myasishchev 101
"Blinder", Tu-22, Tupolev 133
Boeing B-52 Stratofortress 20
Boeing C-97 Stratofreighter 21
Boeing C-135 Stratolifter 22
Boeing E-3 169
Boeing E-4 168
Boeing EC-135 22
Boeing EC-137D (AWACS), 169
Boeing KC-97 Stratofreighter 21
Boeing KC-135 Stratotanker 22
Boeing Model 707 170
Boeing Model 737 169
Boeing RC-135 22
Boeing T-43A 169
Boeing VC-97 21
Boeing VC-137 170
Boeing YC-97 21
Boeing Vertol CH-46 Sea Knight 23
Boeing Vertol CH-47 Chinook 24
Boeing Vertol CH-113 Labrador 23
Boeing Vertol CH-113A Voyageur 23
Boeing Vertol HKP-4 23
Boeing Vertol UH-46 Sea Knight 23
Boeing Vertol Model 107-II 23
Bonanza, Beech 166

Breguet Br. 1050 Alizé   25
Breguet Br. 1150 Atlantic   26
"Brewer", Yak-28, Yakovlev   144
Bristol 175 Britannia   27
Britannia, Bristol   27
Britten-Norman BN-2A Islander/Defender   170
Broussard, M.H.1521, Max Holste   205
Bronco, OV-10, North American Rockwell   107
Buccaneer, Hawker Siddeley   67
Buckeye, T-2, North American Rockwell   212
Buffalo, DHC-5, de Havilland (Canada)   41
Bulldog, Scottish Aviation   223

C-1, Kawasaki   78
C-1 Trader, Grumman   63
C-2A Greyhound, Grumman   58
C-5A Galaxy, Lockheed   80
C-7A, de Havilland (Canada)   40
C-8A, de Havilland (Canada)   41
C-9, McDonnell Douglas   205
C-42 Regente, Neiva   210
C-45 Expeditor, Beech   163
C-46 Commando, Curtiss-Wright   176
C-47 Skytrain, Douglas   183
C-54 Skymaster, Douglas   183
C-95, Embraer   185
C-97, Boeing   21
C-117 Skytrain, Douglas   183
C-118 Liftmaster, Douglas   184
C-119 Flying Boxcar, Fairchild   49
C-121 Constellation, Lockheed   202
C-123 Provider, Fairchild   50
C-124 Globemaster II, Douglas   46
C-130 Hercules, Lockheed   81
C-131 Samaritan, Convair   175
C-133 Cargomaster, Douglas   47
C-135 Stratolifter, Boeing   22
C-140 JetStar, Lockheed   203
C-141 StarLifter, Lockheed   82
C-160, Transall   131
C.212 Aviocar, CASA   172
C-3605, EKW   184
CASA 207 Azor   171
CASA 1.131E   171
CASA C.212 Aviocar   172
CC-106 Yukon, Canadair   27
CC-115, de Havilland (Canada)   41
CC-137, Boeing   170
CC-138, de Havilland (Canada)   179
CF-5, Northrop   109
CF-101, McDonnell   88
CH-3, Sikorsky   121
CH-34 Choctaw, Sikorsky   119
CH-37, Sikorsky   226
CH-46 Sea Knight, Boeing Vertol   23
CH-47 Chinook, Boeing Vertol   24
CH-53, Sikorsky   123
CH-54, Sikorsky   122
CH-113 Labrador, Boeing Vertol   23
CH-113A Voyageur, Boeing Vertol   23
CHSS-2, Sikorsky   120
CL-28 Argus, Canadair   29
CL-41 Tutor/Tebuan, Canadair   28
CL-44 Yukon, Canadair   27
CM-170 Magister, Potez/Aérospatiale   219
CM-175 Zephyr, Potez/Aérospatiale   219
COH-58A, Bell   167
CP-107 Argus, Canadair   29
CS2F, Grumman   63
CS-102, MiG-15UTI   206
CT-39E, North American Rockwell   213
CT-114 Tutor, Canadair   28
CUH-1, Bell   18
CV-2 Caribou, de Havilland (Canada)   40
Canadair CC-106 Yukon   27
Canadair CL-28 Argus   29
Canadair CL-41 Tutor/Tebuan   28

Canadair CL-44 Yukon   27
Canadair CP-107 Argus   29
Canadair CT-114 Tutor   28
Canberra, English Electric   48
Canberra, B-57, Martin & General Dynamics   92
Cargomaster, C-133, Douglas   47
Caribou, DHC-4, de Havilland (Canada)   40
Catalina, PBY, Convair   175
Cavalier F-51D Mustang   211
Cavalier TF-51D Mustang   211
Cayuse, OH-6A, Hughes   198
Cessna A-37   30
Cessna O-1 Bird Dog   172
Cessna O-2   173
Cessna T-37   30
Cessna T-41 Mescalero   173
Cessna U-3   174
Cessna U-17   174
Cheetah   156
Cherokee 140, Piper   218
Chickasaw, H-19, Sikorsky   226
Chienshou, PL-1B, Pazmany/CAF   214
Chinook, CH-47, Boeing Vertol   24
Chipmunk, DHC-1, de Havilland   178
Choctaw, CH-34, Sikorsky   119
"Clod", An-14, Antonov   160
"Coach", Il-12, Ilyushin   201
Cochise, T-42A, Beech   164
"Cock", An-22, Antonov   12
"Codling", Yak-40, Yakovlev   231
"Coke", An-24, Antonov   160
"Colt", An-2, Antonov   159
Comet, Hawker Siddeley (de Havilland)   193
Commando, C-46, Curtiss-Wright   176
Constellation, C-121, Lockheed   202
Convair C-131 Samaritan   175
Convair F-102 Delta Dagger   31
Convair F-106 Delta Dart   32
Convair PBY Catalina   175
Convair T-29   175
Convair TF-102 Delta Dagger   31
"Cookpot", Tu-124, Tupolev   228
"Coot", Il-18, Ilyushin   73
Corsair II, A-7, Vought   137
Cougar, TF-9J, Grumman   191
"Crate", Il-14, Ilyushin   201
Crusader, F-8, Vought   138
"Cub", An-12, Antonov   11
"Curl", An-26, Antonov   160
Curtiss-Wright C-46 Commando   176

D-Series, Auster   161
D.140R Abeille, SAN/Robin   222
DC-6 Series, Douglas   184
DH104 Dove, de Havilland (Hawker Siddeley)   180
DH112 Venom, de Havilland   42
DH114 Heron, de Havilland (Hawker Siddeley)   180
DHC-1 Chipmunk, de Havilland   178
DHC-2 Mk.1 Beaver, de Havilland (Canada)   178
DHC-3 Otter, de Havilland (Canada)   179
DHC-4 Caribou, de Havilland (Canada)   40
DHC-5 Buffalo, de Havilland (Canada)   41
DHC-6 Twin Otter, de Havilland (Canada)   179
Do 27, Dornier   181
Do 28D Skyservant, Dornier   182
Dakota, Douglas   183
Dassault MD-315 Flamant   177
Dassault MD-450 Ouragan   177
Dassault MD-452 Mystère IVA   38
Dassault Etendard IV   33
Dassault Falcon   176
Dassault Milan   36
Dassault Mirage III   34
Dassault Mirage IV-A   35

Dassault Mirage 5   36
Dassault Mirage F1   37
Dassault Super Mystère B-2   39
Defender, Britten-Norman   170
de Havilland (Canada) C-8A   41
de Havilland (Canada) CC-115   41
de Havilland (Canada) CV-7A   41
de Havilland (Hawker Siddeley) DH104 Dove   180
de Havilland (Hawker Siddeley) DH114 Heron   180
de Havilland (Canada) DHC-1 Chipmunk   178
de Havilland (Canada) DHC-2 Mk.1 Beaver   178
de Havilland (Canada) DHC-3 Otter   179
de Havilland (Canada) DHC-4 Caribou   40
de Havilland (Canada) DHC-5 Buffalo   41
de Havilland (Canada) DHC-6 Twin Otter   179
de Havilland (Hawker Siddeley) Devon   180
de Havilland (Hawker Siddeley) Sea Devon   180
de Havilland Sea Venom   42
de Havilland Vampire   181
de Havilland Venom   42
Delfin, L-29, Aero   154
Delta Dagger, F-102, Convair   31
Delta Dart, F-106, Convair   32
Destroyer, B-66, Douglas   45
Devon, de Havilland (Hawker Siddeley)   180
Dominie T.Mk.1, Hawker Siddeley   194
Dornier Do 27   181
Dornier Do 28D Skyservant   182
Douglas A-1 Skyraider   43
Douglas A-3 Skywarrior   44
Douglas B-26 Invader   182
Douglas B-66 Destroyer   45
Douglas C-47 Skytrain   183
Douglas C-54 Skymaster   183
Douglas C-117 Skytrain   183
Douglas C-118 Liftmaster   184
Douglas C-124 Globemaster II   46
Douglas C-133 Cargomaster   47
Douglas DC-6 Series   184
Douglas EA-1   43
Douglas EA-3   44
Douglas EB-66   45
Douglas EKA-3   44
Douglas KA-3   44
Douglas R6D-1   184
Douglas RA-3   44
Douglas RB-66   45
Douglas TA-3   44
Douglas VA-3   44
Douglas WB-66   45
Douglas Dakota   183
Dove, de Havilland (Hawker Siddeley)   180
Draken, Saab-35   113

E-1 Tracer, Grumman   63
E-2 Hawkeye, Grumman   59
E-3, Boeing   169
E-4, Boeing   168
EA-1, Douglas   43
EA-3, Douglas   44
EA-6 Prowler, Grumman   60
EB-57, Martin   92
EB-66, Douglas   45
EC-1, Grumman   63
EC-47, Douglas   183
EC-121, Lockheed   202
EC-130, Lockheed   81
EC-135, Boeing   22
EC-137, Boeing   169
EKA-3, Douglas   44
EKW C-3605   184
EMB-110 Bandeirante, Embraer   185
EP-3 Orion, Lockheed   85
Eagle, F-15, McDonnell Douglas   91
Embraer EMB-110 Bandeirante   185

Embraer AT-26 Xavante   6
English Electric Canberra   48
Etendard IV, Dassault   33
Expeditor, C-45, Beech   163

F-4 Phantom II, McDonnell Douglas   90
F-5, Northrop   109
F-6 (MiG-19)   94
F-8 Crusader, Vought   138
F-14 Tomcat, Grumman   61
F-15 Eagle, McDonnell Douglas   91
F.27M Troopship, Fokker-VFW   53
F.28, Fokker-VFW   188
F-51D Mustang, Cavalier   211
F-51D Mustang, North American   211
F-80C Shooting Star, Lockheed   203
F-84F Thunderstreak, Republic   221
F-84G Thunderjet, Republic   220
F-86 Sabre, North American   103
F-100 Super Sabre, North American   104
F-101 Voodoo, McDonnell   88
F-102 Delta Dagger, Convair   31
F-104 Starfighter, Lockheed   83
F-105 Thunderchief, Republic   111
F-106 Delta Dart, Convair   32
F-111, General Dynamics   55
FB-111A, General Dynamics   56
FH-1100, Fairchild   186
FMA I.A.35 Huanquero   187
FMA I.A.50 G-II   187
FMA I.A.58 Pucara   52
FS-X, Mitsubishi   208
"Fagot", MiG-15, Mikoyan/Gurevich   206
Fairchild A-10A   185
Fairchild AC-119   49
Fairchild AU-23A Peacemaker   186
Fairchild C-119 Flying Boxcar   49
Fairchild C-123 Provider   50
Fairchild FH-1100   186
Fairchild Porter   186
Fairey (Westland) Gannet   51
Falcon, Dassault   176
"Farmer", MiG-19, Mikoyan   94
Fennec, Sud-Aviation   105
"Fiddler", Tu-28, Tupolev   134
"Firebar", Yak-28, Yakovlev   144
"Fishbed", MiG-21, Mikoyan   95
"Fishpot", Su-9, Sukhoi   129
"Fitter", Su-7, Sukhoi   127, 128
"Flagon", Su-11, Sukhoi   130
Flamant, MD-315, Dassault   177
"Flashlight", Yak-25/27, Yakovlev   143
"Flogger", MiG-23, Mikoyan   96
Flying Boxcar, C-119, Fairchild   49
Fokker-VFW F.27M Troopship   53
Fokker-VFW F.28   188
Fokker S.11 Instructor   188
"Foxbat", MiG-25, Mikoyan   97
"Fresco", MiG-17, Mikoyan/Gurevich   93
Fuji KM-2   189
Fuji LM-1/LM-2 Nikko   189
Fuji T1   189

G-II, I.A.50, FMA   187
G2-A/G-3 Galeb, Soko   227
G91, Aeritalia   4
G222, Aeritalia   5
GAF Nomad 22   54
Galaxy, C-5A, Lockheed   80
Galeb, G2-A/G-3, Soko   227
Gannet, Fairey (Westland)   51
Gazelle, SA341, Aérospatiale/Westland   157
Gelatik, PZL-104   220
General Dynamics F-111   55
General Dynamics FB-111A   56
General Dynamics RB-57   92
General Dynamics RF-111A   55

Globemaster II, C-124, Douglas   46
Gnat, Hawker Siddeley/HAL   68
Greyhound, C-2A, Grumman   58
Grumman A-6 Intruder   57
Grumman C-1 Trader   63
Grumman C-2A Greyhound   58
Grumman CS2F   63
Grumman E-1 Tracer   63
Grumman E-2 Hawkeye   59
Grumman EA-6 Prowler   60
Grumman EC-1   63
Grumman F-14 Tomcat   61
Grumman HU-16 Albatross   190
Grumman KA-6   57
Grumman OV-1 Mohawk   62
Grumman S-2 Tracker   63
Grumman TC-4C   190
Grumman TF-9J Cougar   191

H-2 Seasprite, Kaman   76
H-3, Sikorsky   120, 121
H-13 Sioux, Bell   167
H-19 Chickasaw, Sikorsky   226
H-23 Raven, Hiller   196
H-37 Mojave, Sikorsky   226
H-43 Huskie, Kaman   201
H-53 Sea Stallion, Sikorsky   123
HA-200 Saeta, Hispano   198
HA-220 Super Saeta, Hispano   198
HAOP-27 Krishak Mk.2, Hindustan   196
HC-130, Lockheed   81
HF-24 Marut, Hindustan   72
HFB 320 Hansa   206
HH-1, Bell   18
HH-2 Seasprite, Kaman   76
HH-3A, Sikorsky   120
HH-3E/F, Sikorsky   121
HH-34, Sikorsky   119
HH-52A, Sikorsky   227
HH-53, Sikorsky   123
HJT-16 Mk.1 Kiran, Hindustan   197
HKP-4, Boeing Vertol   23
H.S.125, Hawker Siddeley   194
H.S.748, Hawker Siddeley   192
H.S.1182, Hawker Siddeley   194
HSS-2, Sikorsky   120
HT-2, Hindustan   197
HU-16 Albatross, Grumman   190
Handley Rage Hastings   191
Handley Page Herald   192
Handley Page Victor   64
Hansa, HFB 320   206
"Hare", Mi-1, Mil   207
"Harke", Mi-10, Mil   99
Harpoon, PV-2, Lockheed   204
Harrier, Hawker Siddeley   69
Hastings, Handley Page   191
Hawker Hunter   65
Hawker Siddeley H.S.125   194
Hawker Siddeley H.S.748   192
Hawker Siddeley H.S.1182   194
Hawker Siddeley Andover   66, 192
Hawker Siddeley Argosy   193
Hawker Siddeley Buccaneer   67
Hawker Siddeley (de Havilland) Comet   193
Hawker Siddeley Dominie T.Mk.1   194
Hawker Siddeley/HAL Gnat   68
Hawker Siddeley Harrier   69
Hawker Siddeley Nimrod   70
Hawker Siddeley Vulcan   71
Hawkeye, E-2, Grumman   59
Helio AU-24A   195
Helio U-10   195
"Hen", Ka-15, Kamov   202
Herald, Handley Page   192
Hercules, C-130, Lockheed   81
Heron, DH114, de Havilland   180

Hiller H-23 Raven   196
Hindustan HAOP-27 Krishak Mk.2   196
Hindustan HF-24 Marut   72
Hindustan HJT-16 Mk.1 Kiran   197
Hindustan HT-2   197
"Hip", Mi-8, Mil   100
Hispano HA-200 Saeta   198
Hispano HA-220 Super Saeta   198
"Hook", Mi-6, Mil   99
"Hoplite", Mi-2, Mil   207
"Hormone", Ka-25, Kamov   77
"Hound", Mi-4, Mil   98
Huanquero, I.A.35, FMA   187
HueyCobra, AH-1G, Bell   17
Hughes OH-6A Cayuse   198
Hughes TH-55A Osage   199
Hunter, Hawker   65
Hunting Pembroke   199
Hunting Provost   200
Hunting Sea Prince   199
Huskie, H-43, Kaman   201

I-115, AISA   158
I.A.35 Huanquero, FMA   187
I.A.50 G-II, FMA   187
I.A.58 Pucara, FMA   52
IAI-201 Arava   200
Il-12, "Coach", Ilyushin   201
Il-14, "Crate", Ilyushin   201
Il-18, "Coot", Ilyushin   73
Il-28, "Beagle", Ilyushin   74
Il-28U, "Mascot", Ilyushin   74
Il-38, "May", Ilyushin   75
IPD-6201 Universal, Neiva   210
Ilyushin Il-12, "Coach"   201
Ilyushin Il-14, "Crate"   201
Ilyushin Il-18, "Coot"   73
Ilyushin Il-28, "Beagle"   74
Ilyushin Il-28U, "Mascot"   74
Ilyushin Il-38, "May"   75
Impala, Atlas   6
Instructor, S.11, Fokker   188
Intruder, A-6, Grumman   57
Invader, B-26, Douglas   182
Iroquois, UH-1, Bell   18
Iskra, TS-11   228
Islander, Britten-Norman   170

J32 Lansen, Saab   112
J35 Draken, Saab   113
JA37 Viggen, Saab   114
JC-130, Lockheed   81
Jaguar, SEPECAT   116
Jastreb, Soko   124
Jet Provost, BAC   15
JetRanger, Bell   167
JetStar, C-140, Lockheed   203
Jetstream 201, Scottish Aviation   223

KA-3, Douglas   44
KA-6, Grumman   57
Ka-15, "Hen", Kamov   202
Ka-25, "Hormone", Kamov   77
KC-97 Stratofreighter, Boeing   21
KC-130, Lockheed   81
KC-135 Stratotanker, Boeing   22
KM-2, Fuji   189
KV-107, Kawasaki   23
Kaman H-2 Seasprite   76
Kaman H-43 Huskie   201
Kamov Ka-15, "Hen"   202
Kamov Ka-25, "Hormone"   77
Kawasaki C-1   78
Kawasaki KV-107   23
Kawasaki P-2J   79
Kiowa, OH-58, Bell   167

Kiran Mk.I, HJT-16, Hindustan 197
Kraguj, P-2, Soko 125
Krishak Mk.2, HAOP-27, Hindustan 196

L-4, Piper 217
L-18, Piper 217
L-29 Delfin, Aero 154
L-39 Super Delfin, Aero 155
L-42 Regente, Neiva 210
LASA-60 153
LC-130, Lockheed 81
LH-34, Sikorsky 119
LiM-2(MiG-15) 206
LiM-5 (MiG-17) 93
LM-1/LM-2 Nikko, Fuji 189
Labrador, CH-113, Boeing Vertol 23
Lama, SA315, Aérospatiale 156
Lansen, Saab-32 112
Liftmaster, C-118, Douglas 184
Lightning, BAC 14
Lockheed AC-130 81
Lockheed C-5A Galaxy 80
Lockheed C-121 Constellation 202
Lockheed C-130 Hercules 81
Lockheed C-140 JetStar 203
Lockheed C-141 StarLifter 82
Lockheed EC-121 202
Lockheed EC-130 81
Lockheed EP-3 Orion 85
Lockheed F-80C Shooting Star 203
Lockheed F-104 Starfighter 83
Lockheed HC-130 81
Lockheed JC-130 81
Lockheed KC-130 81
Lockheed LC-130 81
Lockheed P-2 Neptune 84
Lockheed P-3 Orion 85
Lockheed PV-2 Harpoon 204
Lockheed RC-121 202
Lockheed RC-130 81
Lockheed RP-3 Orion 85
Lockheed S-3A Viking 86
Lockheed SR-71 87
Lockheed T-33A 203
Lockheed TF-104 83
Lockheed U-2 204
Lockheed VC-140 203
Lockheed WC-130 81
Lockheed WP-3 85
Lockheed YF-12A 87
Lynx, Westland 139

MB326, Aermacchi 6
MD-315 Flamant, Dassault 177
MD-450 Ouragan, Dassault 177
MD-452 Mystère IVA, Dassault 38
M.H. 1521 Broussard, Max Holste 205
Mi-1/Mi-3, "Hare", Mil 207
Mi-2, "Hoplite", Mil 207
Mi-4, "Hound", Mil 98
Mi-6, "Hook", Mil 99
Mi-8, "Hip", Mil 100
Mi-10, "Harke", Mil 99
MiG-15, "Fagot", Mikoyan/Gurevich 206
MiG-17, "Fresco", Mikoyan/Gurevich 93
MiG-19, "Farmer", Mikoyan 94
MiG-21, "Fishbed", Mikoyan 95
MiG-23, "Flogger", Mikoyan 96
MiG-25, "Foxbat", Mikoyan 97
MRCA, Panavia 110
M.S. 760 Paris, Morane-Saulnier 209
MU-2, Mitsubishi 208
Mya-4, "Bison", Myasishchev 101
"Madge", Be-6, Beriev 168
"Maestro", Yak-28, Yakovlev 144
Magister, CM-170, Potez/Aérospatiale 219
"Maiden", Su-9, Sukhoi 129

"Mail", Be-12, Beriev 19
"Mangrove", Yak-26, Yakovlev 143
Martin B-57, Canberra 92
Marut, HF-24, Hindustan 72
"Mascot", Il-28U, Ilyushin 74
"Max", Yak-18, Yakovlev 230
Max Holste M.H. 1521 Broussard 205
"May", Il-38, Ilyushin 75
"Maya", L-29 Delfin, Aero 154
McDonnell CF-101 Voodoo 88
McDonnell F-101 Voodoo 88
McDonnell RF-101 Voodoo 88
McDonnell TF-101 Voodoo 88
McDonnell Douglas A-4 Skyhawk 89
McDonnell Dogulas C-9 Nightingale 205
McDonnell Douglas F-4 Phantom II 90
McDonnell Douglas F-15 Eagle 91
McDonnell Douglas RF-4 Phantom II 90
McDonnell Douglas TA-4 Skyhawk 89
Mentor, T-34, Beech 164
Mescalero, T-41, Cessna 173
Messerschmitt-Bölkow-Blohm HFB 320 Hansa 206
"Midget", MiG-15UTI 206
Mikoyan MiG-19, "Farmer" 94
Mikoyan MiG-21, "Fishbed" 95
Mikoyan MiG-23, "Flogger" 96
Mikoyan MiG-25, "Foxbat" 97
Mikoyan/Gurevich MiG-15, "Fagot" 206
Mikoyan/Gurevich MiG-17, "Fresco" 93
Mil Mi-1/Mi-3, "Hare" 207
Mil Mi-2, "Hoplite" 207
Mil Mi-4, "Hound" 98
Mil Mi-6, "Hook" 99
Mil Mi-8, "Hip" 100
Mil Mi-10, "Harke" 99
Milan, Dassault 36
Mirage III, Dassault 34
Mirage IV-A, Dassault 35
Mirage 5, Dassault 36
Mirage F1, Dassault 37
Mitsubishi FS-X 208
Mitsubishi MU-2 208
Mitsubishi T-2 208
Model 107-II, Boeing Vertol 23
Model 204B/205, Agusta-Bell 18
Model 206 JetRanger, Agusta-Bell 167
Model 209 HueyCobra, Bell 17
Mohawk, OV-1, Grumman 62
Mojave, H-37, Sikorsky 226
"Mongol", MiG-21UTI 95
Morane-Saulnier M.S.760 Paris 209
"Moss", Tu-114, Tupolev 136
"Moujik", Su-7, Sukhoi 127
Musketeer, Beech 163
Mustang, F-51D, Cavalier 211
Mustang, F-51D, North American 211
Myasishchev Mya-4, "Bison" 101
Mystère IVA, MD-452, Dassault 38

N 262, Aerospatiale 156
NAMC YS-11 209
NF-5, Northrop 109
Neiva C-42 Regente 210
Neiva IPD-6201 Universal 210
Neiva L-42 Regente 210
Neptune, P-2, Lockheed 84
Nikko, LM-1/LM-2, Fuji 189
Nightingale, C-9, McDonnell Douglas 205
Nimrod, Hawker Siddeley 70
Nomad 22, GAF 54
Noratlas 2501/2504, Nord 102
Nord 2501/2504 Noratlas 102
Nord 3202 211
Nord 3212 211
North American F-51D Mustang 211
North American F-86 Sabre 103

North American F-100 Super Sabre 104
North American T-6 Texan 212
North American T-28 Trojan 105
North American Rockwell B-1A 106
North American Rockwell OV-10 Bronco 107
North American Rockwell RA-5C Vigilante 108
North American Rockwell T-2 Buckeye 212
North American Rockwell T-39 Sabreliner 213
North American Rockwell XFV-12A 213
Northrop CF-5/F-5/NF-5/SF-5 109
Northrop F-5E Tiger II 109
Northrop T-38A Talon 214
Nuri, Sikorsky S-61A-4 120

O-1 Bird Dog, Cessna 172
O-2, Cessna 173
OH-6A Cayuse, Hughes 198
OH-13, Bell 167
OH-23, Hiller 196
OH-58A Kiowa, Bell 167
OV-1 Mohawk, Grumman 62
OV-10 Bronco, North American Rockwell 107
One-Eleven, BAC 162
Orion, P-3, Lockheed 85
Osage, TH-55A, Hughes 199
Otter, DHC-3, de Havilland (Canada) 179
Ouragan, MD-450, Dassault 177

P-2 Kraguj, Soko 125
P-2 Neptune, Lockheed 84
P-2J, Kawasaki 79
P-3 Orion, Lockheed 85
P-3, Pilatus 217
P.148, Piaggio 215
P.149D, Piaggio 215
P.166M/Albatross, Piaggio 216
PA-28-140 Cherokee, Piper 218
PA-31 Turbo Navajo, Piper 219
PBY Catalina, Convair 175
PC-6 Porter, Pilatus 186
PC-6/A/B/C Turbo-Porter, Pilatus 186
PD-808, Piaggio 216
PL-1B Chienshou, Pazmany/CAF 214
PS-1, Shin Meiwa 117
PV-2 Harpoon, Lockheed 204
PZL-104 Wilga/Gelatik 220
Panavia MRCA 110
Paris, M.S.760, Morane-Saulnier 209
Pazmany/CAF PL-1B Chienshou 214
Peacemaker, AU-23, Fairchild 186
Pembroke, Hunting 199
Phantom II, McDonnell Douglas 90
Piaggio P.148 215
Piaggio P.149D 215
Piaggio P.166M/Albatross 216
Piaggio PD-808 216
Pilatus P-3 217
Pilatus PC-6 Porter 186
Pilatus PC-6/A/B/C Turbo-Porter 186
Piper L-4 217
Piper L-18 217
Piper PA-28-140 Cherokee 218
Piper PA-31 Turbo Navajo 219
Piper U-7A 217
Piper U-11A Aztec 218
Porter, PC-6, Pilatus 186
Potez/Aérospatiale CM 170 Magister 219
Potez/Aérospatiale CM 175 Zephyr 219
Potez/Aérospatiale Super Magister 219
Provider, C-123, Fairchild 50
Provost, Hunting 200
Prowler, EA-6, Grumman 60
Pucara, I.A.58, FMA 52
Puma, SA330, Aérospatiale/Westland 9

QU-22, Beech 166

R6D-1, Douglas 184
RA-3B, Douglas 44
RA-5C Vigilante, North American Rockwell 108
RB-57, Martin & General Dynamics 92
RB-66, Douglas 45
RC-121, Lockheed 202
RC-130, Lockheed 81
RC-135, Boeing 22
RF-4, McDonnell Douglas 90
RF-5, Northrop 109
RF-8, Vought 138
RF-84F Thunderflash, Republic 221
RF-101 Voodoo, McDonnell 88
RF-111A, General Dynamics 55
RH-3A, Sikorsky 120
RH-53, Sikorsky 123
RP-3 Orion, Lockheed 85
RT-33A, Lockheed 203
RU-21, Beech 165
Raven, H-23, Hiller 196
Regente, C-42/L-42, Neiva 210
Republic F-84F Thunderstreak 221
Republic F-84G Thunderjet 220
Republic F-105 Thunderchief 111
Republic RF-84F Thunderflash 221

S-2 Tracker, Grumman 63
S-3A Viking, Lockheed 86
S.11 Instructor, Fokker 188
S32C Lansen, Saab 112
S35E Draken, Saab 113
S37 Viggen, Saab 113
S-55, Sikorsky 226
S-56, Sikorsky 226
S-58, Sikorsky 119
S-61B, Sikorsky 120
S-61R, Sikorsky 121
S-62, Sikorsky 227
S-64 Skycrane, Sikorsky 122
S-65, Sikorsky 123
S-102/3 (MiG-15) 206
S-104 (MiG-17) 93
S.208M, SIAI-Marchetti 224
SA315 Lama, Aérospatiale 156
SA316 Alouette III, Aérospatiale 7
SA318C Alouette II Astazou, Aérospatiale 156
SA319 Alouette II, Aérospatiale 7
SA321 Super Frelon, Aérospatiale 8
SA330 Puma, Aérospatiale/Westland 9
SA341 Gazelle, Aérospatiale/Westland 157
SE313 Alouette II Artouste, Aérospatiale 156
SF-5, Northrop 109
SF.260M SIAI-Marchetti 225
SH-2 Seasprite, Kaman 76
SH-3 Sea King, Sikorsky 120
SH-34 Seabat, Sikorsky 119
SK35C Draken, Saab 113
SK37 Viggen, Saab 114
SK50, Saab 221
SK60, Saab 115
SM-1 207
SM-2 207
SM.1019, SIAI-Marchetti 225
S.O.4050 Vautour, Sud-Aviation 126
SR-71, Lockheed 87
Su-7, "Fitter", Sukhoi 127, 128
Su-9, "Fishpot", Sukhoi 129
Su-11, "Flagon", Sukhoi 130
Saab-32 Lansen 112
Saab-35 Draken 113
Saab-37 Viggen 114
Saab-91 Safir 221
Saab-105 115
Saab-MFI 17 222
Sabre, F-86, North American 103
Sabreliner, T-39, North American Rockwell 213

Saeta, HA-200, Hispano   198
Safir, Saab-91   221
Samaritan, C-131, Convair   175
SAN/Robin Jodel D.140R Abeille   222
Scottish Aviation Bulldog   223
Scottish Aviation Jetstream 201   223
Scout, Westland   141
Seabat, SH-34, Sikorsky   119
SeaCobra, AH-1J, Bell   17
Sea Devon, de Havilland (Hawker Siddeley)   180
Sea Hawk, Armstrong Whitworth   161
Seahorse, UH-34, Sikorsky   119
Sea King, SH-3, Sikorsky   120
Sea King, Westland   140
Sea Knight, CH-46, Boeing Vertol   23
Sea Prince, Hunting   199
SeaRanger, TH-57, Bell   167
Seasprite, H-2, Kaman   76
Sea Stallion, H-53, Sikorsky   123
Seminole, U-8, Beech   165
SEPECAT Jaguar   116
Shackleton, Avro   13
Shin Meiwa PS-1   117
Shooting Star, F-80C, Lockheed   203
Short Belfast   118
Short Skyvan   224
Shrike Commander, Aero Commander   155
SIAI-Marchetti S.208M   224
SIAI-Marchetti SF.260MX   225
SIAI-Marchetti SM.1019   225
Sikorsky CH-3   121
Sikorsky CH-34 Choctaw   119
Sikorsky CH-37   226
Sikorsky CH-53 Sea Stallion   123
Sikorsky CH-54 Tarhe   122
Sikorsky H-3 Sea King   120
Sikorsky H-19 Chickasaw   226
Sikorsky H-34   119
Sikorsky H-37 Mojave   226
Sikorsky H-53 Sea Stallion   123
Sikorsky HH-3A   120
Sikorsky HH-3E/F   121
Sikorsky HH-34   119
Sikorsky HH-52A   227
Sikorsky HH-53   123
Sikorsky LH-34   119
Sikorsky RH-3A   120
Sikorsky RH-53   123
Sikorsky S-55   226
Sikorsky S-56   226
Sikorsky S-58   119
Sikorsky S-61A/B   120
Sikorsky S-61R   121
Sikorsky S-62   227
Sikorsky S-64   122
Sikorsky S-65   123
Sikorsky SH-3 Sea King   120
Sikorsky SH-34 Seabat   119
Sikorsky UH-34 Seahorse   119
Sikorsky VH-3A   120
Sikorsky VH-34   119
Sioux, H-13, Bell   167
Skycrane, S-64, Sikorsky   122
Skyhawk, A-4, McDonnell Douglas   89
Skymaster, C-54, Douglas   183
Skyraider, A-1, Douglas   43
Skyservant, Do 28D, Dornier   182
Skytrain, C-47, C-117, Douglas   183
Skyvan, Short   224
Skywarrior, A-3, Douglas   44
Soko G2-A/G-3 Galeb   227
Soko Jastreb   124
Soko P-2 Kraguj   125
Starfighter, F-104, Lockheed   83
StarLifter, C-141, Lockheed   82
Stratofortress, B-52, Boeing   20
Stratofreighter, KC-97, Boeing   21

Stratolifter, C-135, Boeing   22
Stratotanker, KC-135, Boeing   22
Strikemaster, BAC 167   15
Sud-Aviation Fennec   105
Sud-Aviation S.O.4050 Vautour   126
Sukhoi Su-7, "Fitter"/"Moujik"   127, 128
Sukhoi Su-9, "Fishpot"/"Maiden"   129
Sukhoi Su-11, "Flagon"   130
Super Delfin, L-39, Aero   155
Super Frelon, SA321, Aérospatiale   8
Super Magister, Potez/Aérospatiale   219
Super Mystère B-2, Dassault   39
Super Sabre, F-100, North American   104
Super Saeta, HA-220, Hispano   198

T1, Fuji   189
T-2, Mitsubishi   208
T-2 Buckeye, North American Rockwell   212
T-6 Texan, North American   212
T-11, Beech   163
T-23 Uirapuru, Aerotec   157
T-28 Trojan, North American   105
T-29, Convair   175
T-33A, Lockheed   203
T-34 Mentor, Beech   164
T-37, Cessna   30
T-38A Talon, Northrop   214
T-39 Sabreliner, North American Rockwell   213
T-41 Mescalero, Cessna   173
T-42A Cochise, Beech   164
T-43A, Boeing   169
TA-3, Douglas   44
TA-4, McDonnell Douglas   89
TC-4C, Grumman   190
TF-8 Crusader, Vought   138
TF-9J Cougar, Grumman   191
TF-51D, Cavalier   211
TF-101, McDonnell   88
TF-102, Convair   31
TF-104, Lockheed   83
TH-1 Iroquois, Bell   18
TH-13, Bell   167
TH-55A Osage, Hughes   199
TH-57 SeaRanger, Bell   167
TS-11 Iskra   228
Tu-16, "Badger", Tupolev   132
Tu-22, "Blinder", Tupolev   133
Tu-28, "Fiddler", Tupolev   134
Tu-?, "Backfire", Tupolev   106
Tu-95, "Bear", Tupolev   135
Tu-114, "Moss", Tupolev   136
Tu-124, "Cookpot", Tupolev   228
Talon, T-38A, Northrop   214
Tarhe, CH-54, Sikorsky   122
Tebuan, CL-41G, Canadair   28
Texan, T-6, North American   212
Thunderchief, F-105, Republic   111
Thunderflash, RF-84F, Republic   221
Thunderjet, F-84G, Republic   220
Thunderstreak, F-84F, Republic   221
Tiger II, F-5E, Northrop   109
Tomcat, F-14, Grumman   61
Tracer, E-1, Grumman   63
Tracker, S-2, Grumman   63
Trader, C-1, Grumman   63
Transall C-160   131
Trojan (AL.60C5)   153
Trojan, T-28, North American   105
Troopship, F.27M, Fokker-VFW   53
Tupolev Tu-16, "Badger"   132
Tupolev Tu-22, "Blinder"   133
Tupolev Tu-28, "Fiddler"   134
Tupolev Tu-?, "Backfire"   106
Tupolev Tu-95, "Bear"   135
Tupolev Tu-114, "Moss"   136
Tupolev Tu-124, "Cookpot"   228
Turbo Commander, Aero Commander   155

Turbo Navajo, Piper 219
Turbo-Porter, PC-6, Pilatus 186
Tutor, CT-114, Canadair 28
Twin Otter, DHC-6, de Havilland (Canada) 179

U-1 Otter, de Havilland (Canada) 179
U-2, Lockheed 204
U-3, Cessna 174
U-6 Beaver, de Havilland (Canada) 178
U-7A, Piper 217
U-8 Seminole, Beech 165
U-10, Helio 195
U-11A Aztec, Piper 218
U-17, Cessna 174
U-21, Beech 165
UC-123, Fairchild 50
UH-1 Iroquois, Bell 18
UH-2 Seasprite, Kaman 76
UH-34 Seahorse, Sikorsky 119
UH-46, Boeing Vertol 23
Uirapuru, T-23, Aerotec 157
Universal, IPD-6201, Neiva 210
UTVA-60 229
UTVA-66 229

VA-3, Douglas 44
VC-6A, Beech 165
VC10, BAC 16
VC-97, Boeing 21
VC-135, Boeing 22
VC-137, Boeing 170
VC-140, Lockheed 203
VH-3A, Sikorsky 120
VH-34, Sikorsky 119
Vampire, de Havilland 181
Varsity T.Mk.1, Vickers 229
Vautour, S.O.4050, Sud-Aviation 126
Venom, de Havilland 42
Vickers Varsity T.Mk.1 229
Victor, Handley Page 64
Viggen, Saab-37, Saab 114
Vigilante, RA-5C, North American Rockwell 108
Viking, S-3A, Lockheed 86
Voodoo, F-101, McDonnell 88
Vought A-7 Corsair II 137
Vought F-8 Crusader 138
Vought RF-8 Crusader 138
Vought TF-8 Crusader 138
Voyageur, CH-113A, Boeing Vertol 23

Vulcan, Hawker Siddeley 71

WB-66, Douglas 45
WC-130, Lockheed 81
WG.13 Lynx, Westland 139
WP-3 Orion, Lockheed 85
Wasp, Westland 141
Wessex, Westland 142
Westland Gannet 51
Westland Sea King 140
Westland Wasp/Scout 141
Westland Wessex 142
Westland WG.13 Lynx 139
Westland Whirlwind 230
Westland/Aérospatiale SA330 Puma 9
Westland/Aérospatiale SA341 Gazelle 157
Whirlwind, Westland 230
Wilga, PZL-104 220

XC-1, Kawasaki 78
XT-2, Mitsubishi 208
Xavante, Embraer AT-26 6

YA-7H Corsair II-2, Vought 137
YAT-37D, Cessna 30
YC-97, Boeing 21
YCH-47, Boeing Vertol 24
YF-12A, Lockheed 87
YOV-10D Bronco, North American Rockwell 107
YS-11, NAMC 209
Yak-18, "Max", Yakovlev 230
Yak-25, "Flashlight", Yakovlev 143
Yak-26, "Mangrove", Yakovlev 143
Yak-27, "Flashlight", Yakovlev 143
Yak-28, "Brewer", Yakovlev 144
Yak-28, "Firebar", Yakovlev 144
Yak-28, "Maestro", Yakovlev 144
Yak-40, "Codling", Yakovlev 231
Yakovlev Yak-18, "Max" 230
Yakovlev Yak-25, "Flashlight" 143
Yakovlev Yak-26, "Mangrove" 143
Yakovlev Yak-27, "Flashlight" 143
Yakovlev Yak-28, "Brewer" 144
Yakovlev Yak-28, "Firebar" 144
Yakovlev Yak-28, "Maestro" 144
Yakovlev Yak-40, "Codling" 231
Yukon, CC-106, Canadair 27

Zephyr, CM-175, Potez/Aérospatiale 219